Y0-BBX-358

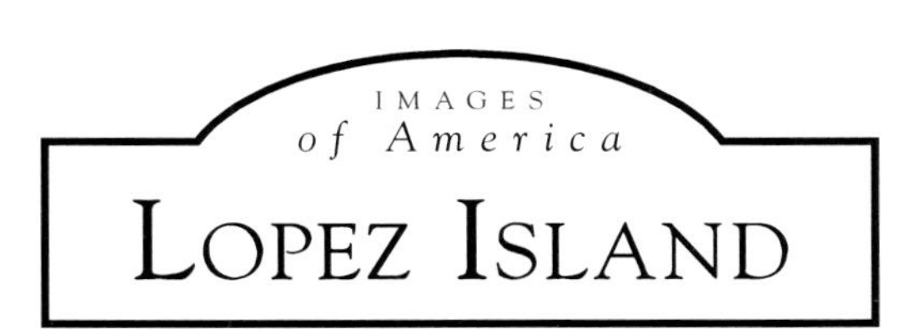
IMAGES
of America
LOPEZ ISLAND

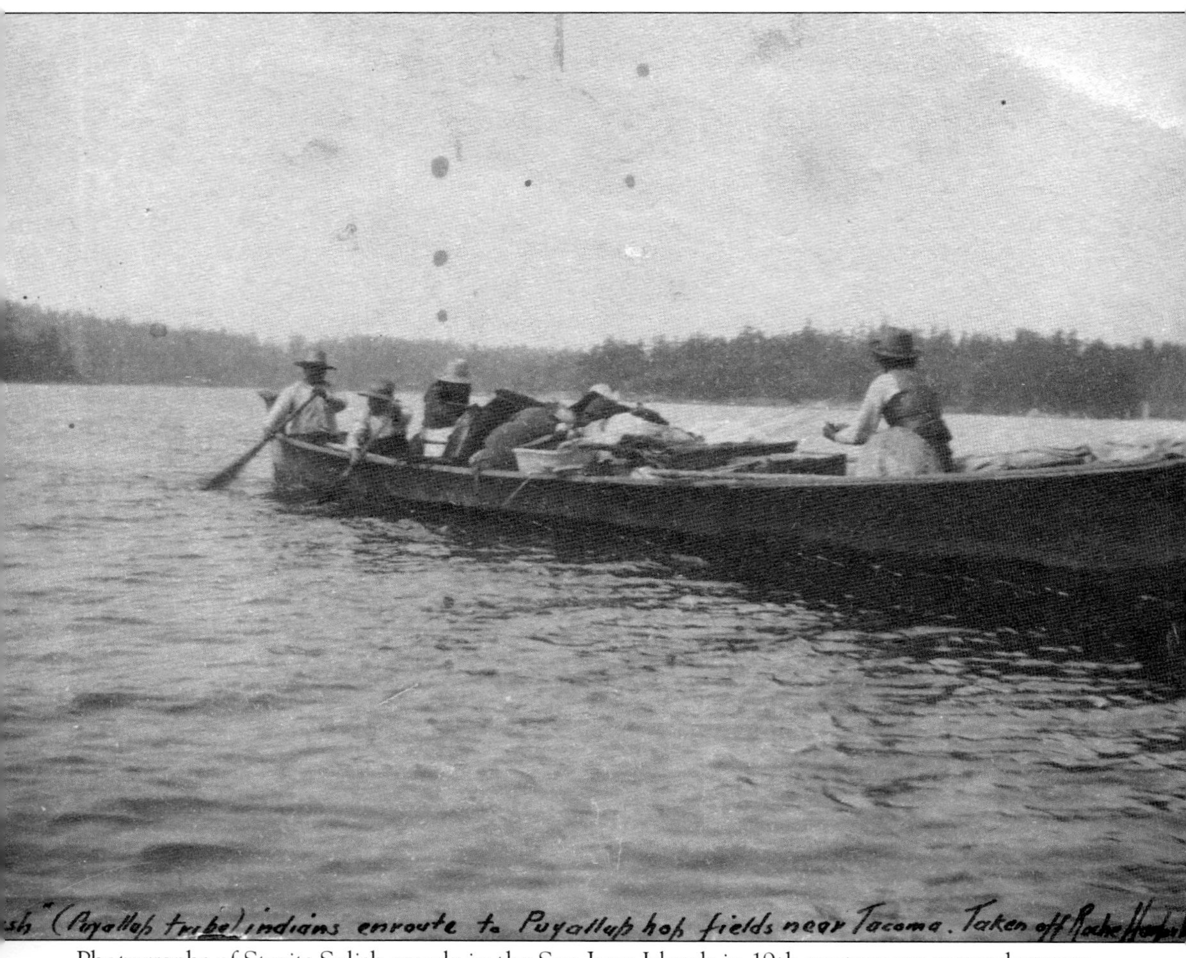

Photographs of Straits Salish people in the San Juan Islands in 19th century are somewhat rare. This one, taken in the waters off Roche Harbor, captures members of the Puyallup Tribe rowing on their way to the hop fields near Tacoma. In 1898, a writer from the American Museum of Natural History described Native American's trench fortifications he found at Hunter Bay, MacKaye Harbor, and Richardson. (Courtesy of Lopez Island Historical Society and Museum.)

On the Cover: In this 1897 photograph, homesteaders, settlers, women in long skirts, babes in arms, and barefooted children stand amid horse-drawn wagons and a dramatically draped flag to celebrate the Fourth of July together at Point Lookout on Lopez Hill. Islanders traditionally celebrated the Fourth of July with gusto, a custom kept to this day. Lopez is famous for one of Washington's most spectacular fireworks shows, attracting thousands to the island each year and more than doubling the island's population. (Courtesy of Lopez Island Historical Society and Museum.)

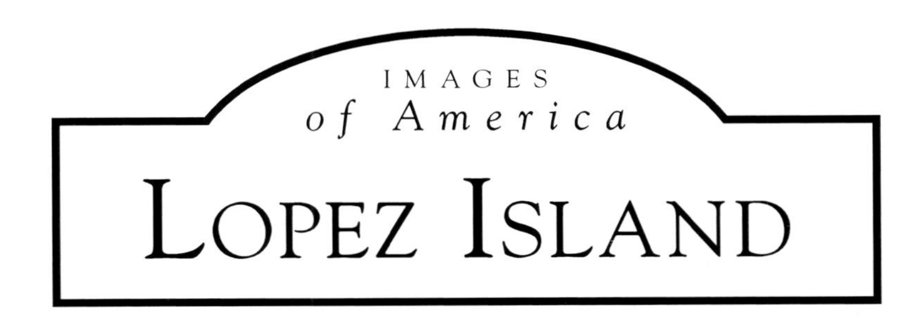

Susan Lehne Ferguson and
the Lopez Island Historical Society and Museum

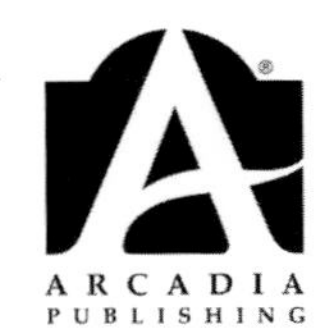

ISBN 978-0-7385-8030-2

Published by Arcadia Publishing
Charleston, South Carolina

Printed in the United States of America

Library of Congress Control Number: 2009936033

For all general information contact Arcadia Publishing at:
Telephone 843-853-2070
Fax 843-853-0044
E-mail sales@arcadiapublishing.com
For customer service and orders:
Toll-Free 1-888-313-2665

Visit us on the Internet at www.arcadiapublishing.com

We dedicate this book to the Lopez community,
beloved across the generations.

Contents

ACKNOWLEDGMENTS

We would like to express our sincere thanks to all those who made this book possible.

Thank you to Mark Thompson-Klein, director of the Lopez Island Historical Society and Museum, whose passion for Lopez history helps us understand and treasure our shared past.

Gertrude Boede deserves special recognition for her tireless dedication to preserving Lopez history and stories, as do Phyllis Lovejoy and Francis Kring, who have helped us to keep the memories alive.

Thanks to Gary Morris for his invaluable Web database chronicling Lopez's history.

Our gratitude goes to those who created and sustained the Lopez Island Historical Society and Museum and contributed to the preservation of Lopez history, including Christi Carter, Connie Kyser, Charles Givens, former curator Nancy McCoy, Amy Hildebrand, Delores Foss, society and museum founders, and many others.

Thank you to John Goekler, whose wonderful curiosity, tireless research, and countless fascinating articles captured so many Lopez Island stories.

Thank you to Lopez family descendants who generously gave of their time and shared their memories contributing to the book's content, including Clark Lovejoy, Melba Gaddis, Rochelle Fowler, Raelyn Dolton, Bob and Vivian Burt, Billie Burt, Duane Weeks, Mary Fagerholm-Reece, Donald Fagerholm, Linda Graham Rose, Mary Harris, Donna Graham, Nancy Wright, Marguerite Goodrow, Ona Jean Goodrow, Margaret Jenison, Gerald Davies, Cathy Clemens, Lisa Hummel, William Hummel, Robert Yates, Colleen Weeks Breeden, and many others.

We appreciate Bill Holm for allowing us to use his painting *Mexicana and Sutil in Guemes Channel, June 11, 1792.*

Special thanks go to Arcadia Publishing editor Sarah Higginbotham, whose consistent guidance and positive encouragement kept us on track.

And last, thank you to our families and to our extended Lopez family and friends, who together deepen the joy of being part of the Lopez community.

Unless otherwise noted, all images appear courtesy of the Lopez Island Historical Society and Museum.

INTRODUCTION

Nestled in the San Juan Archipelago, Lopez Island is a 29.5-square-mile mountaintop rising out of the Salish Sea. Lopez is a magical place, eliciting in many an ethereal response to its beauty, its substance, and its peace. Over the past two centuries, people from near and far discovered Lopez, were drawn by its beckoning, and made their lives here. Together they created and nurtured a special community spirit that has garnered islanders' lifelong affection and passed through generations to the present day.

This is the story of that community. Photographs introduce the people who came to Lopez when impenetrable woods met the shoreline, marshland was yet to be cleared, and life was carved out of wilderness. Given the gifts of phenomenal surrounding beauty, a mild climate, and abundant natural resources, the homesteaders and their descendents embraced their new life together.

The island was settled by Native Americans and people of European and American descent. They arrived on Lopez shores from Canada, Ireland, Sweden, England, Germany, Finland, Denmark, Norway, North Wales, and Scotland and from states as far east as Maine and west as California. They were Civil War veterans, gold prospectors, orphans, sailors, and violin makers.

They embraced an island life shaped by earlier historical events. Native Americans came to hunt marine mammals, fish, and birds 7,000 to 9,000 years ago, and over time, they developed strong social relationships and a continental trade network that extended as far as Alaska, Central America, and the Great Lakes. Many Native Americans came to the San Juan Islands, but those who spoke the Straits Salish languages represented today by members of the Lummi and Samish Tribes have the strongest ties to Lopez Island. Several Lopez settlers married women from coastal Native American tribes, and their children became the foundation of many island families. Traditional native fishing techniques were built upon and helped settlers wrest a living from the sea.

More than 400 years ago, the first Europeans appeared looking for the Northwest Passage linking the Atlantic and Pacific Oceans. Spanish place names in the San Juan Islands can be traced to the 1790s islands' exploration. Ships captained by Francisco de Eliza and piloted by Manuel Quimper and Gonzalo Lopez de Haro competed with the British ships of George Vancouver and others. Originally called Lopez Island in the 1790s after Lopez de Haro, the island's name was changed to Chauncey's Island in 1841 to honor the American naval commander Isaac Chauncey. In 1847, the British changed the name back to Lopez Island. The first people believed to arrive on Lopez Island from explorers' ships were crewmen of the *Sutil* and *Mexicana*, who landed near Watmough, as depicted in Bill Holm's painting on page 10.

No photographs exist of two of the earliest temporary Lopez settlers, William Pattle and Richard W. Cussans (or Cousins). Pattle, a British citizen and Hudson's Bay employee, was granted the first Lopez land license from the British territorial governor in about 1852. Pattle cut timber and traded with Native Americans on Lopez's southwest side. He left the island soon after to mine coal in Bellingham. American Cussans took over Pattle's land and made $1,500 worth of improvements before the British governor learned of it. Cussans was informed he was trespassing on British land and decided to leave by the end of the summer.

A boundary dispute between the United States and Britain arose following the signing of the Oregon Treaty of 1846, creating ambiguity as to San Juan Islands' ownership. The shooting of a pig on San Juan Island led to an escalation of the dispute, and both countries agreed to joint military occupation while the issue was decided. From that time through 1872, when the issue was resolved in favor of the United States, people who immigrated to Lopez Island were unsure whether they would ultimately be American or British citizens. James and Amelia Davis, for example, were loyal British subjects, and others who emigrated from Canada thought they were moving to a British-controlled territory.

Life on Lopez Island began to center around three hamlets: Port Stanley, Lopez Village, and Richardson. Families flourished, and people worked together to improve island life. They built houses with outhouses, dug wells, built barns, and planted orchards. They provided for community needs, founding and constructing schools, churches, stores, and post offices and served as county commissioners and school district board members.

Large families of 10 or more children were not uncommon, and most made their livings farming and fishing. The settlers raised cattle, sheep, pigs, chickens, and horses, as well as crops of fruit, potatoes, vegetables, berries, hay, oats, and grains. They made clothes, sold butter, wrote diaries, and played music. From 1894 to 1934, many worked on fish traps as pile drivers or watchmen, tarring nets or canning fish. In 1870, Lopez had 70 inhabitants. By 1920, the island was home to 750 people.

The Lopez story is richer and more detailed because of residents and visitors who observed island life, interviewed islanders, and told their stories before they were lost. Articles published from 1876 onward praised the island's productivity and the friendliness and generosity of its people. To this day, Lopez remains "the friendly isle," where newcomers learn to give old-timers their own characteristic waves as they pass by in a car, on a bicycle, or on foot.

Looking back at the lives of those who settled the island, several qualities stand out: bravery, generosity, capability, and public mindedness. Fear was somehow swept aside. Together Lopezians faced a diphtheria epidemic, tragic children's deaths, the Great Depression, and losses from World Wars I and II. They learned to do things, to make things, to invent things, and to eke out a living gathering the bounty of land and sea. They often shared any surplus they had with one another. Lopezians built a community that provided solace, hope, fun, and a true sense of belonging.

The Lopez Island Historical Society and Museum is the repository for about 10,000 photographic images taken by islanders, many long gone, that provide a window through which people today can view island life as it was lived then. From this collection, about 200 images were selected for this book. This pictorial history has been written as a fund-raiser for the museum to help contribute to the continuation of its good work. Sincere apologies are extended to anyone whose ancestor or friend has not been included.

One

Golden Shores

During the short-lived Fraser River Gold Rush in 1857 and 1858, thousands of prospectors passed through the San Juan Islands on their way to and from unproductive gold fields. By the 1870s, a few people began settling on Lopez, and at least one, Alex Sayre, was anxious for others to join him "on our golden shores."

In December 1876, a publication called *West Shore* printed Sayre's letter to the editor, extolling the advantages of relocating. "In regard to our beautiful island, there is, at this time, some seven or eight or ten families, and soon to arrive eight or ten more." Sayre urged women to marry island bachelors and become "queens of the log cabins of the great Northwest," assuring them household "necessaries" were stocked at Hutchinson's store.

Land was plentiful and free, and food was abundant. "Homes for the homeless can be had on Government land of one hundred and sixty acres" that yield "immense crops" of vegetables, grains, and fruits, he wrote. Fish, shellfish, and game offered nature's bounty. About 20 to 25 good land claims were left, and Sayre promised, "Settlers will take pleasure in showing seekers of homes the best locations." Surely society would soon "naturally spring up," including schools and churches.

Whether in direct response to Sayre's article or in response to other entreaties to move west, new settlers came to Lopez Island and began to discover together the true virtues of its golden shores.

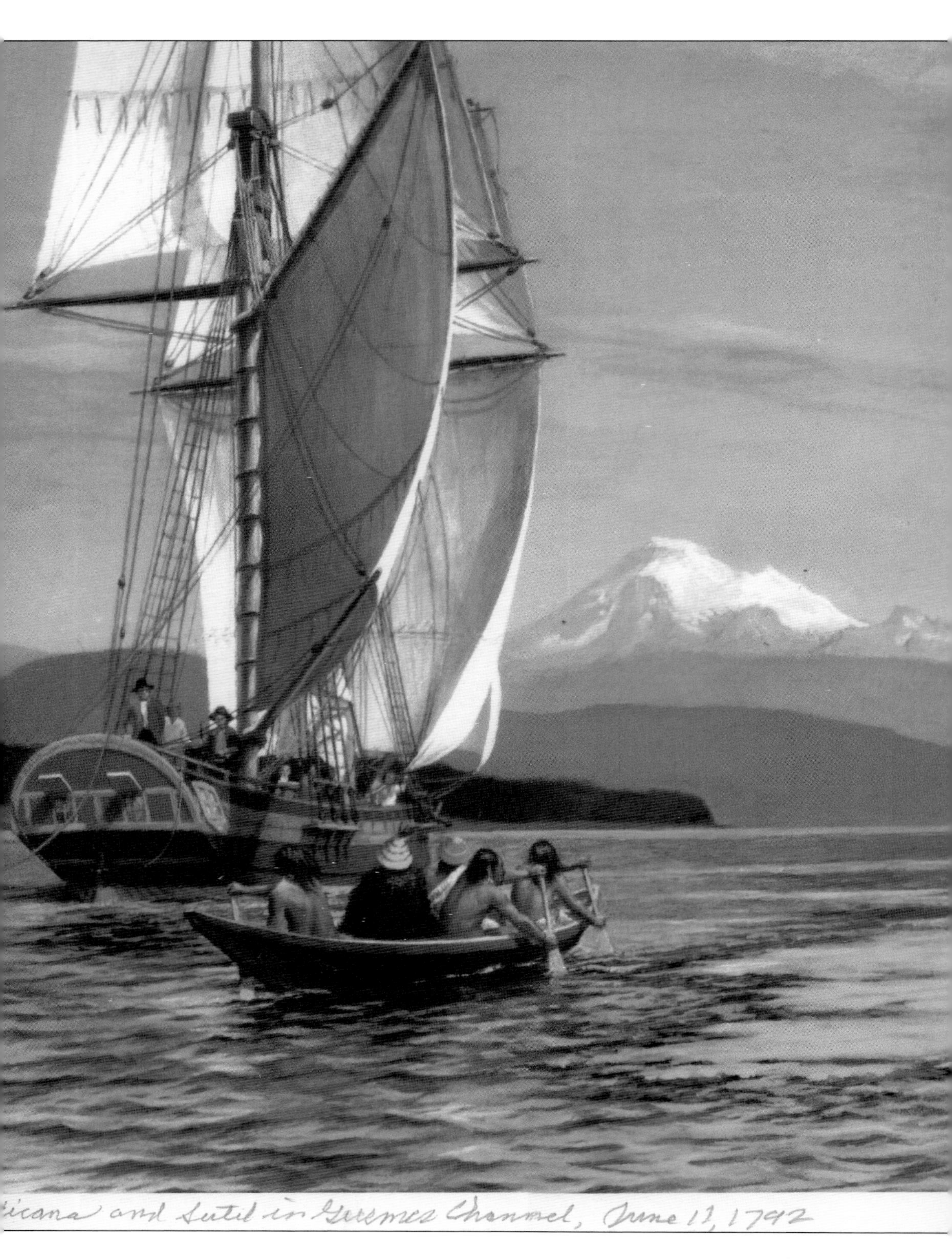
icana and Sutil in Guemes Channel, June 11, 1792

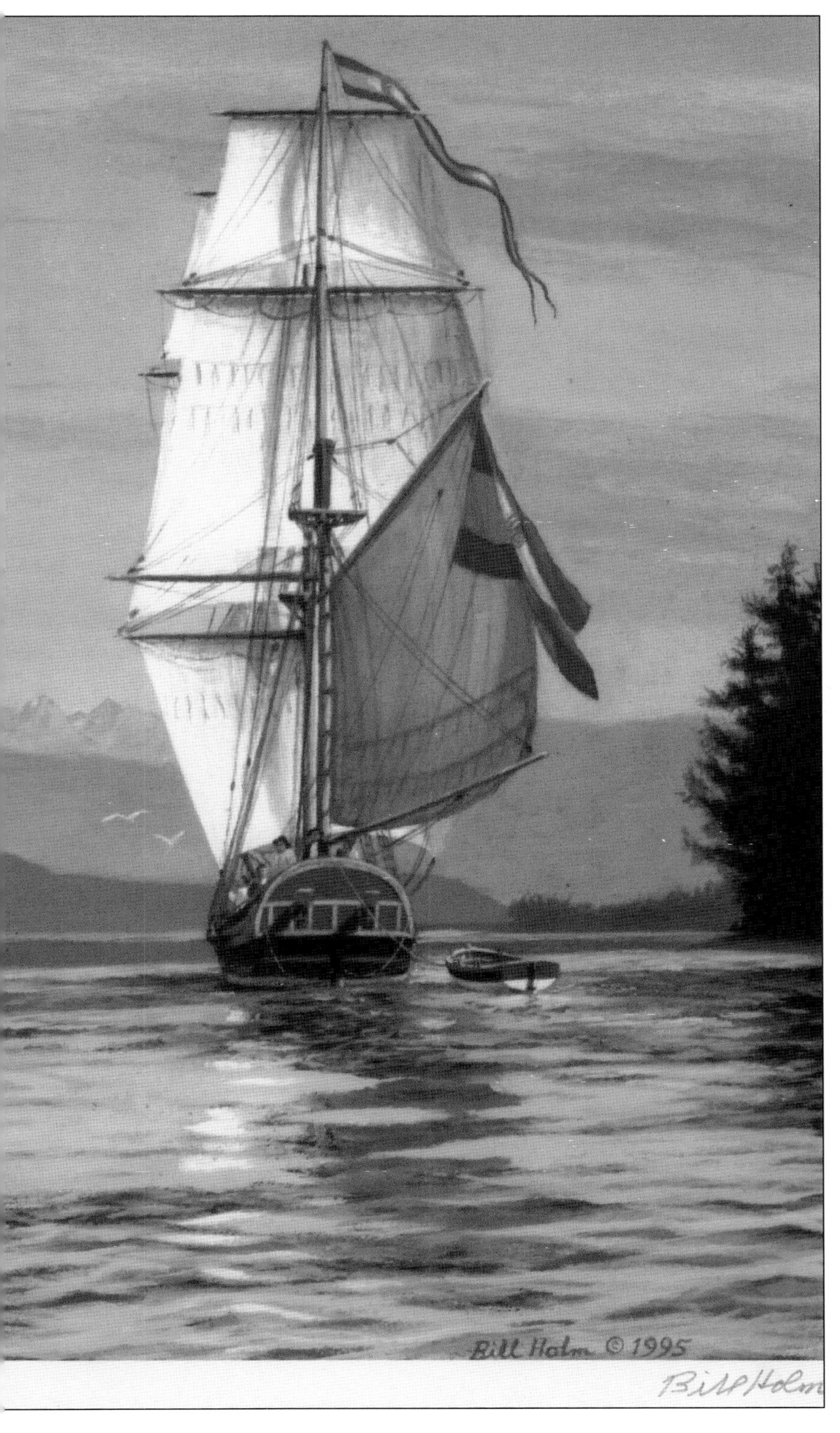

Native Americans approach two small Spanish ships, the *Mexicana* and *Sutil*, to trade blackberries, dried clams, and a dog-wool robe lined with feathers for buttons and beads on June 11, 1792, in Guemes Channel near present-day Anacortes. The ships' mission was to chart the waters in Juan de Fuca Strait and to search for the Northwest Passage to the Atlantic Ocean. One young artist on the *Mexicana*, José Cardero, captured this encounter in a spectacular painting now in Madrid's Museo Naval that inspired Bill Holm's painting. The evening before, the ships' landing party went ashore near Watmough Head on Lopez Island to observe the emergence of the first moon of Jupiter to correct their longitude. (Courtesy of Bill Holm.)

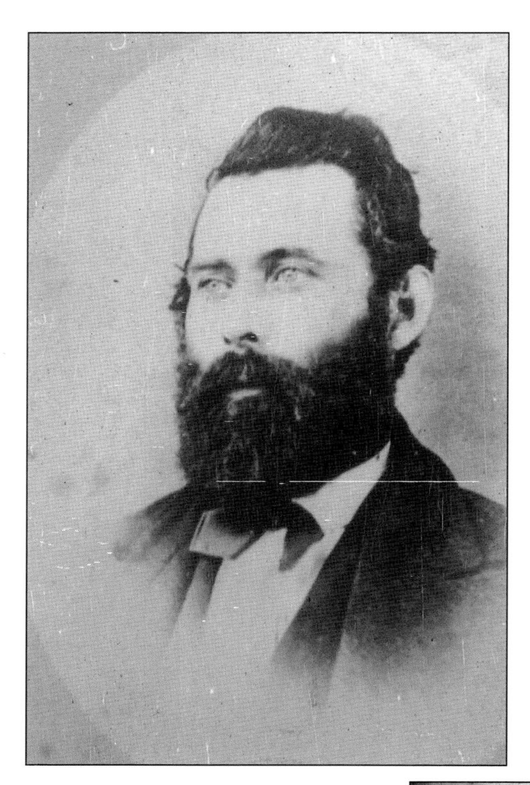

Hiram E. Hutchinson came to Lopez about 1850 in the midst of a clash between two Native American tribes, local Straits Salish people and a group from the north. Hutchinson shot his firearm to end the battle, and the locals welcomed him to settle in their village called Sxolect at Fisherman Bay. Hutchinson married a Tlingit woman, Mary, by tribal rights. Their son, Millard, was born about 1867.

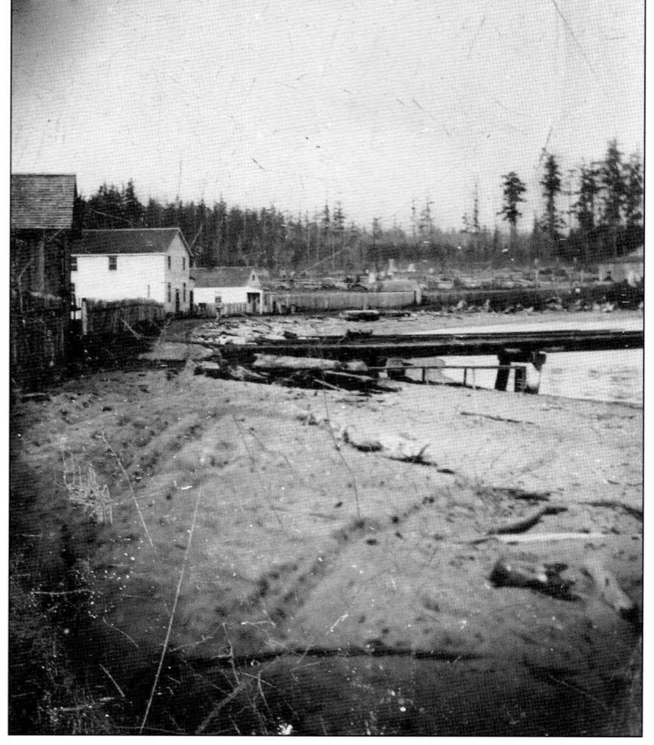

Hutchinson became the island's first postmaster and shopkeeper, selling or bartering everything from sugar and flour to shingles and soap. Names in the 1872 store records include Anderson, Brown, Chadwick, Nelson, and Swift. A visitor in 1871 described Lopez village, saying, "Nothing there, no fields or cleared land. Mr. Hutchinson had a small store on the beach." This early Lopez photograph was reproduced from a tintype.

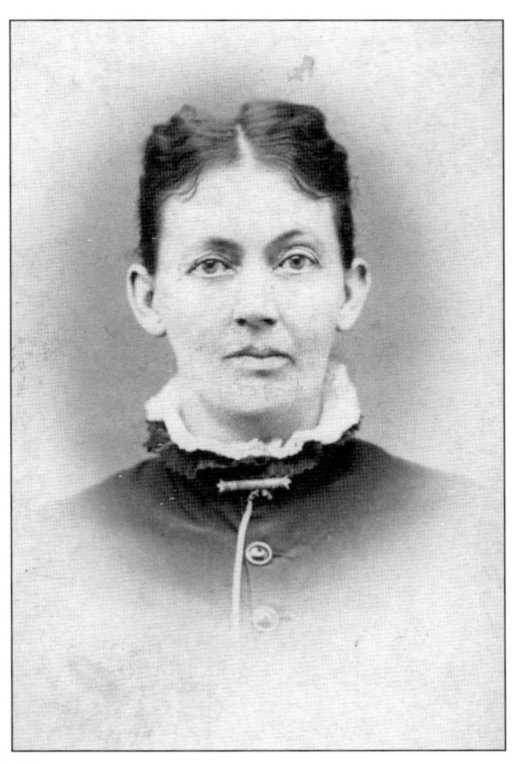

Hutchinson's sister Irene and her husband, Lyman Weeks, arrived on Lopez about 1873 with their son Oscar to help at the store. Some say that they also came to convince her brother to end his union with Mary. Washington Territory passed a law requiring settlers who lived with Native American women to either marry them before Washington statehood or send them back to their tribes. Hutchinson did not marry Mary, and according to descendant Duane Weeks, Mary and Millard went back to the Tlingit Tribe. Millard later returned to Lopez and Irene raised him, along with her five children, Edson, Bertram, Etta, Jennie, and Oscar. Irene became Lopez's first postmistress and died in 1926. Lyman was a farmer and died in 1900.

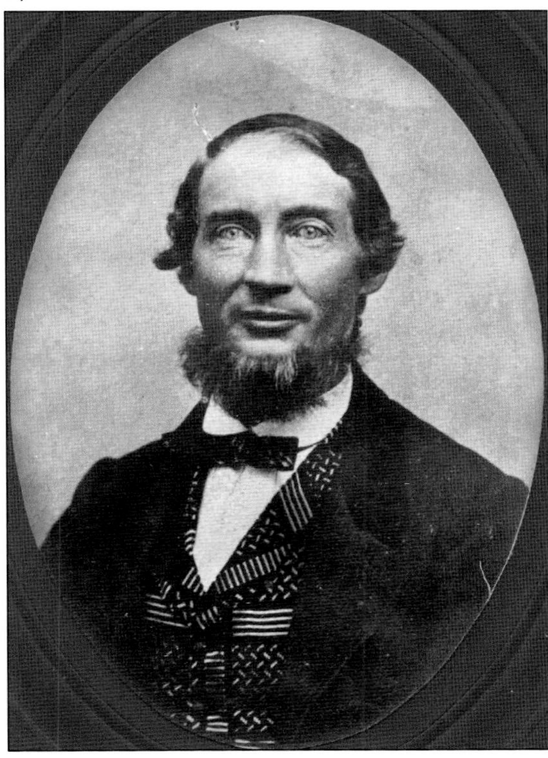

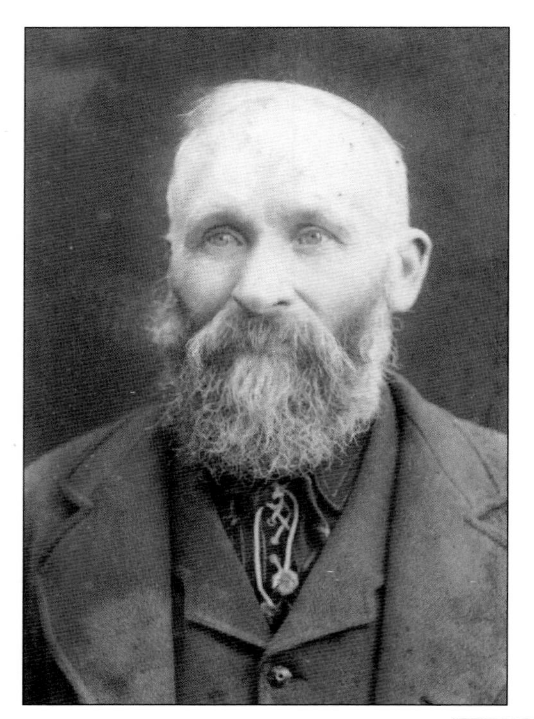

Charles Brown was born in Sweden, worked on British merchant ships, and arrived on Lopez in 1869. He met his future wife, Conna, whose name became Mary Jane, in Victoria about 1855 after she was left behind by her tribe. Brown originally was a shipbuilder and sailor and transported the mail from Puget Sound ports to American Camp soldiers on San Juan. He ultimately settled down to farming on Lopez.

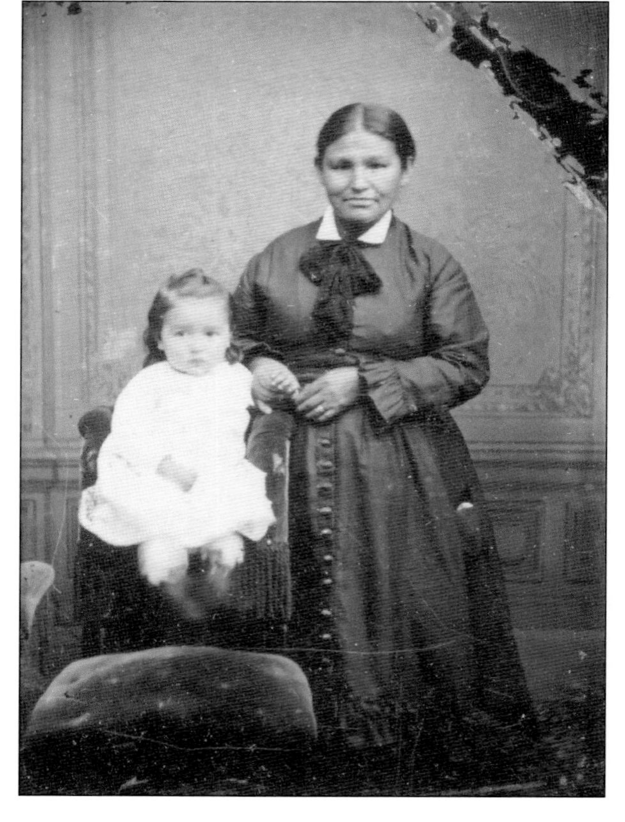

Mary Jane Brown, shown with her daughter Mary Jane, was a respected member of the Lopez community. Affectionately known as "Mother" Brown, she helped break down barriers among people. Grace Wood, whose parents moved to Mud Bay in 1884, said that her mother was "terrified of Indians . . . until she became friends with Mary Jane Brown." Charles and Mary Jane were officially married in 1872 at American Camp.

James Nelson, Charles's friend, came to Lopez in 1862 and settled near Port Stanley. Nelson sold land to Charles near the Port Stanley School where Charles planted fruit trees that still stand. Nelson remembered, "The wickedest shark he ever saw was one caught between Sperry Peninsula and Lopez Pass." Nelson sold his Lopez farm in 1903 and moved to Seattle's Georgetown, where he died in 1911 at age 91.

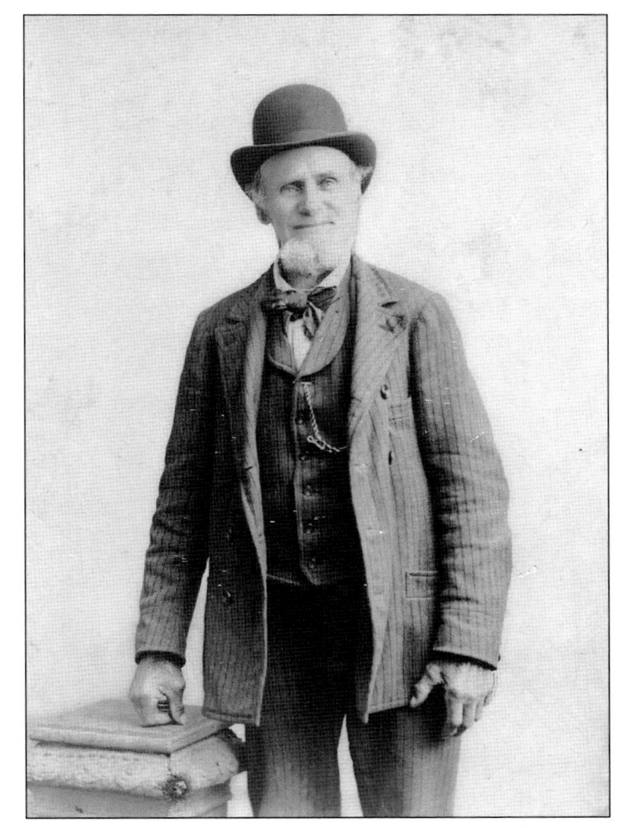

This c. 1905 photograph depicts the original Brown and Nelson houses after being moved and joined together, the left half being Nelson's and the right Brown's. Lopez historian Gertrude Boede commented that the houses were perhaps the first settlers' homes, noting a controversy existed as to whether Charles Brown or Nelson may have arrived on Lopez before Hiram E. Hutchinson.

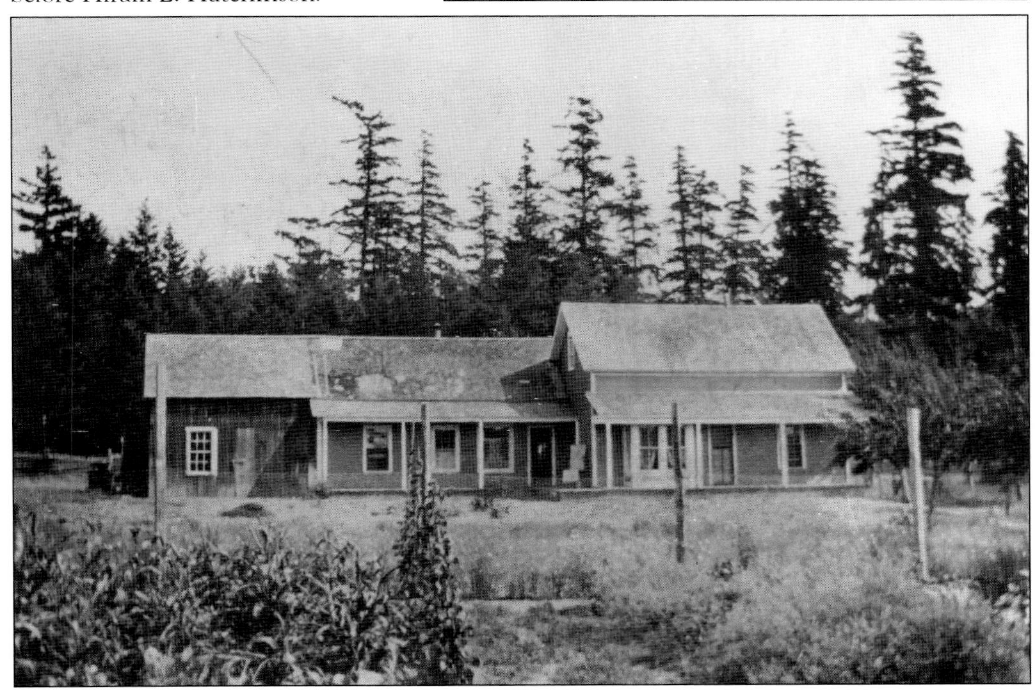

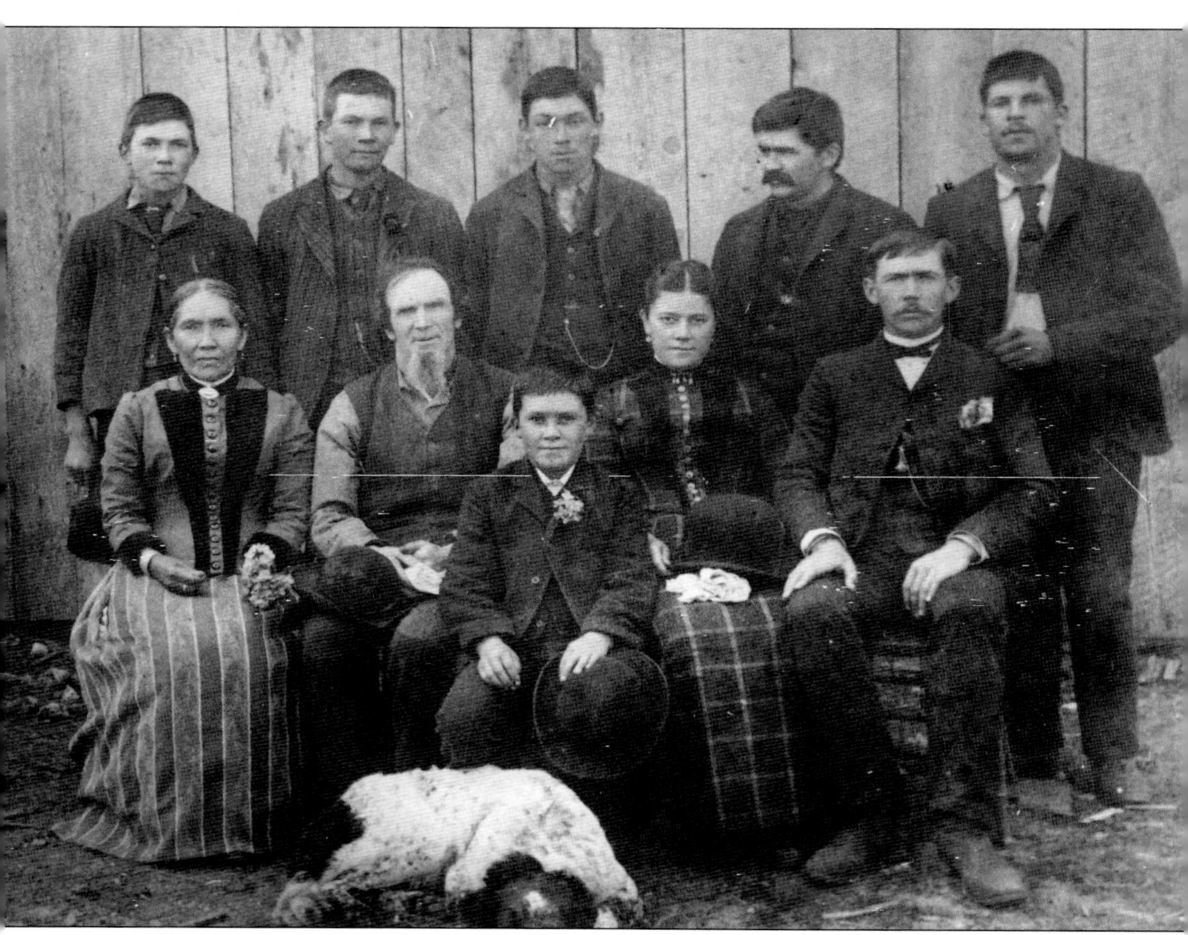

Legend says that while surveying waters aboard British warship HMS *Satellite*, Arthur "Billy" Barlow saw present-day Barlow Bay, described it as Eden, and vowed to return to claim it. Barlow jumped ship before the *Satellite* sailed for England and settled on the bay in 1856. Newspapers report that Lucy of the Stikine Tribe was brought to Lopez by a Haida canoe and offered for sale to Capt. Jack Shears. While Shears went to get his money, Barlow traded his gold buttoned military coat for her to be his wife. Lucy became the first woman to settle on Lopez. Barlow married Lucy at a ceremony in 1872 at American Camp at the same time as Charles and Mary Jane Brown. The Barlows are shown here with eight of their nine children. One son, Sam Barlow, became a renowned Puget Sound ship captain, and another, Harry Barlow, invented an elevator for ships called the Barlow Steam Elevator. Arthur Barlow lived at Barlow Bay until he died in 1898.

Elizabeth Mary O'Clain was born in Port Simpson, British Columbia, and married English naval officer Richard Davis of Nova Scotia. They came to Lopez Island in about 1868 and settled at Shoal Bay on Port Stanley Road. They had one daughter, Mary Elizabeth Davis, who married John Carle. Mary and John had six children, Sidney, George, William, Weldon, Anne, and Frank.

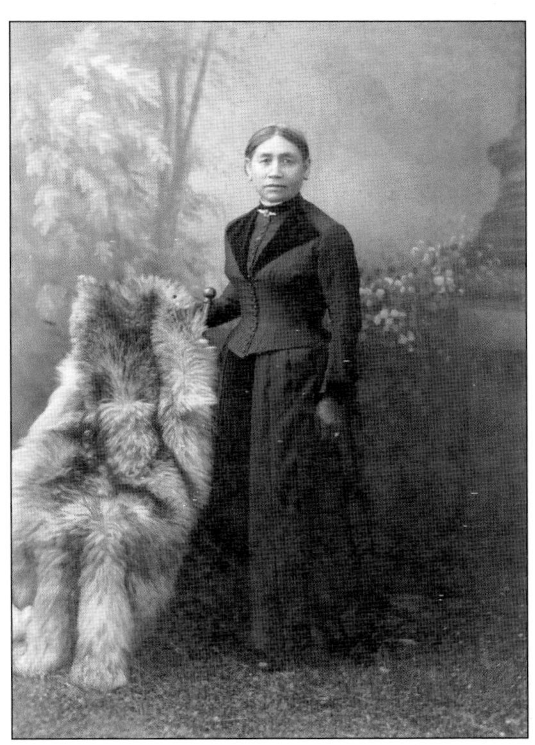

James Blake Sr. came to Lopez in 1883 and established a 250-acre farm. A widower with 13 children, Blake later sold and gave some of the land to his children. A 1901 writer found him to be "one of the prosperous and successful men of the island." Pictured are, from left to right, (first row) unidentified and Blake; (second row) Blake's sons: Thomas, Solomon, James, and John.

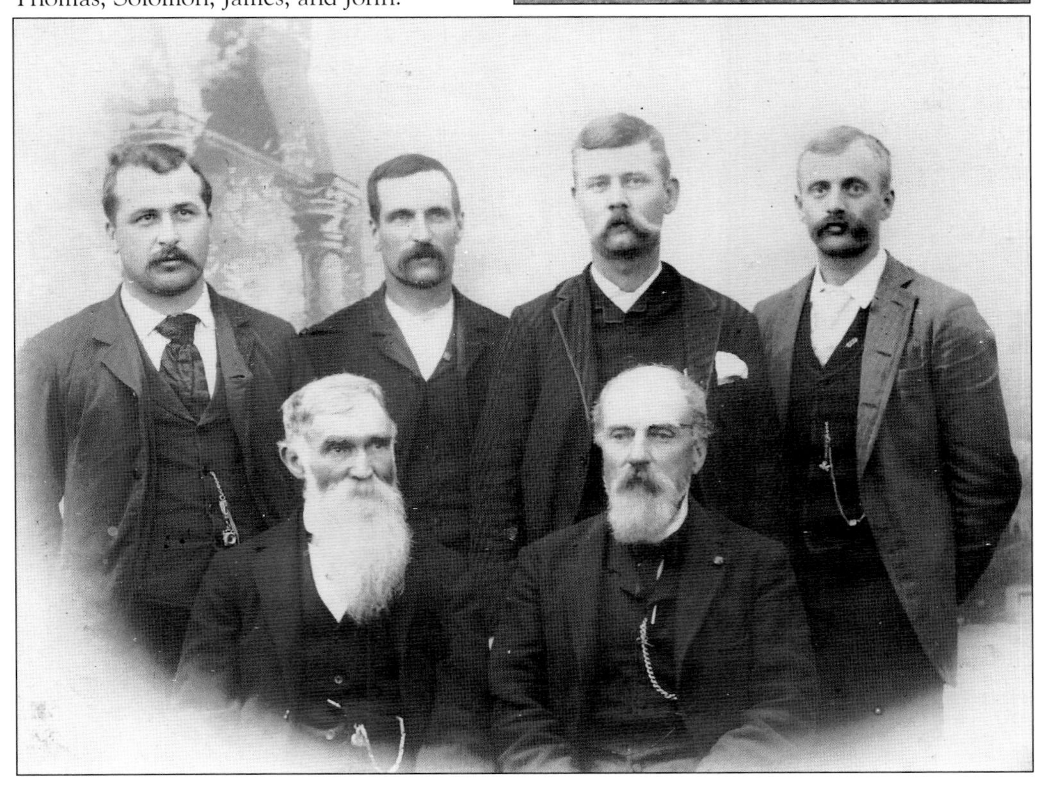

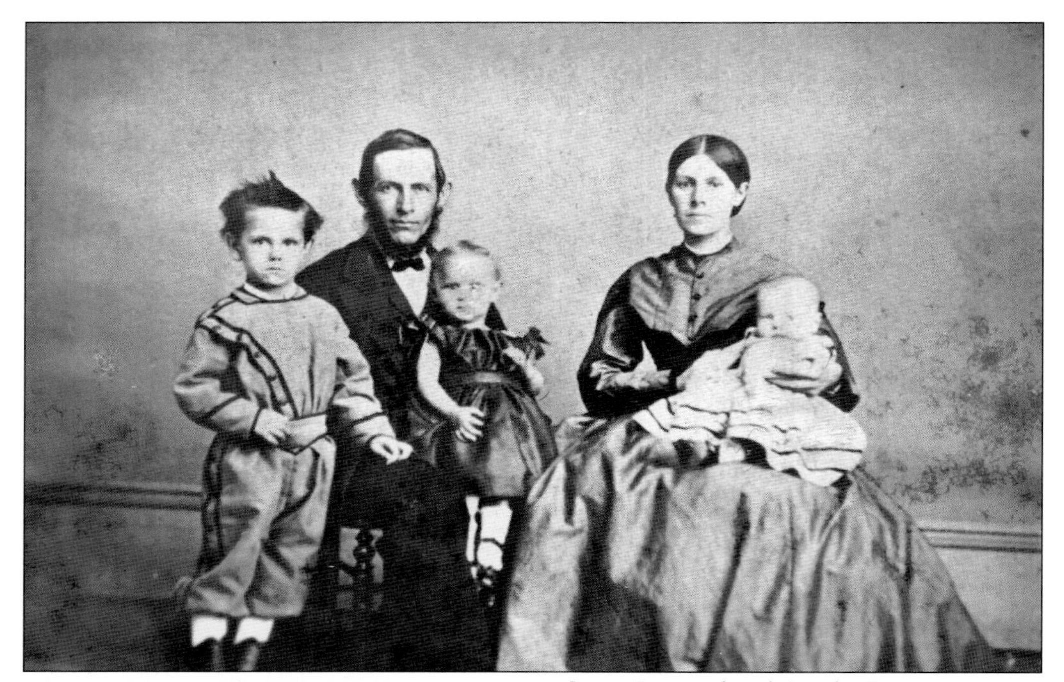

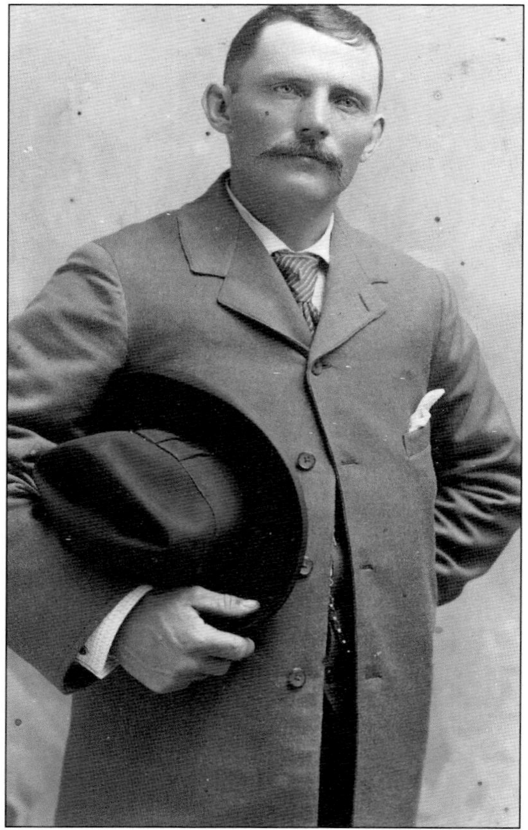

James Leonard and Amelia Barnum Davis followed James Davis Sr.'s father, Hezekiah Davis, to Dungeness from Ontario in 1868. Wanting to continue on, they hired Native Americans to row them across the straits to Lopez in a canoe, arriving with livestock, planks, and 40¢ in 1869. James and Amelia loved music and reading, and their home served the community as a post office, Sunday school, library, hotel, and dispensary.

Charles Anderson came from Finland to Lopez in 1869. He married Ella Brown, Charles and Mary Jane Brown's daughter, in 1873, settling on Lopez's south end. The Andersons had nine children, Emma, Ida, Elise, Mariah, Edna, Charles, Oscar, Amelia, and Adelia. Anderson and Philip Fagerholm both came from the Åland Islands and were possibly cousins. Their families are buried together in an Åland Islands cemetery plot.

John Cousins came to America from Ireland in 1866, married Helen Burt in Iowa, and moved to Lopez in 1873. The Cousins family bought a farm halfway between Lopez Village and Richardson on 464 acres and built "the largest and finest farm house in the county." Seen here, from left to right, are (first row) Helen and John; (second row) their children Robert, Isobel, Laura, and Joe. John died from a horse kick in 1905.

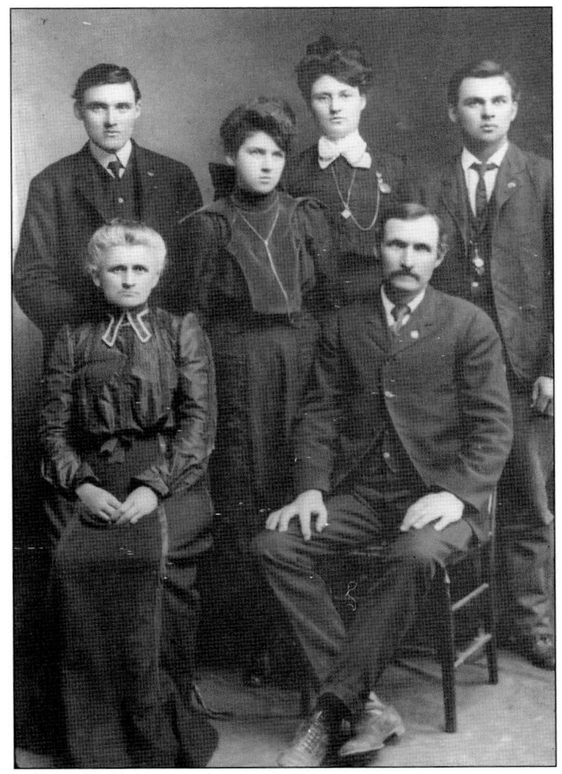

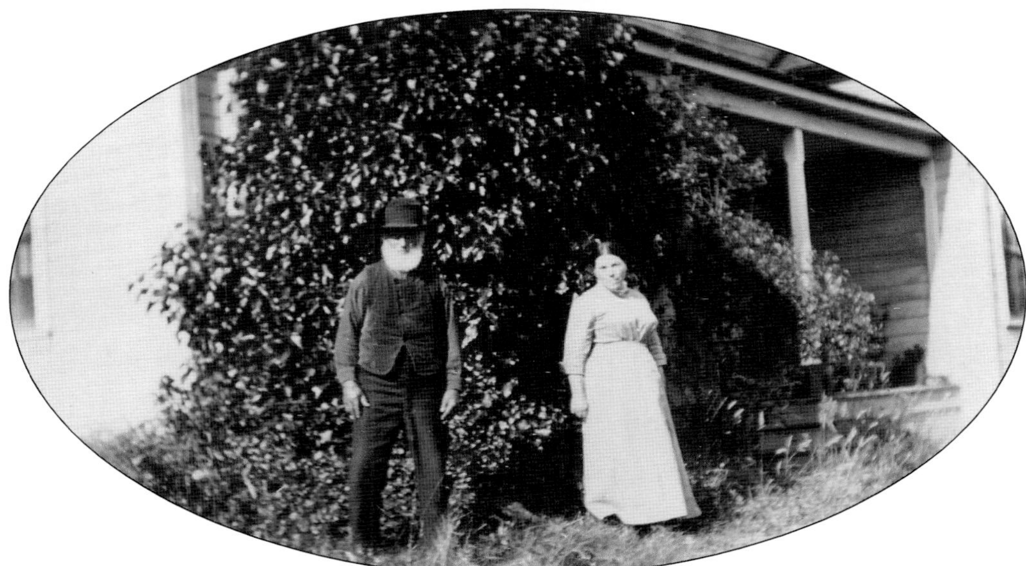

James Cousins (John's brother) moved from Ireland to Iowa and later sent for his wife, Margaret Heron, and their children John and Ella. Sons Willie and James were born in Iowa. The family moved to Lopez in 1883. Willie recalled his father "took 160 acres as a homestead and bought 80 acres more" at Hunter Bay. Shown here with his daughter, James produced fruit, grain, and cattle. He died in 1921.

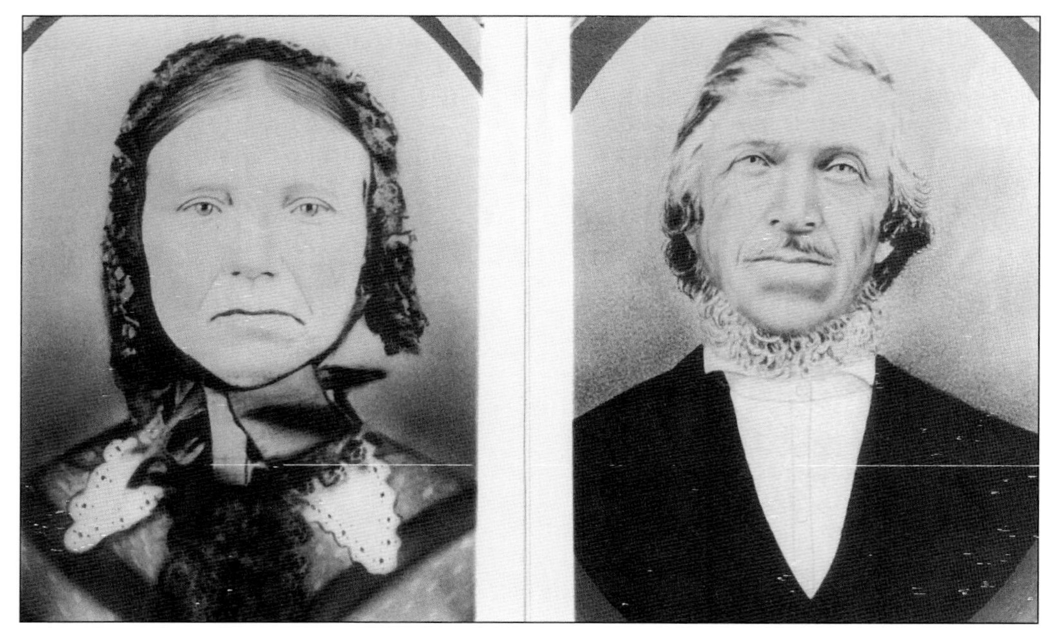

Thomas Graham married Jane Cousins in Ireland, moved to Estherville, Iowa, and then came to Lopez in 1877. They had six children, William, Ellen, Annie, John, Lizzie, and Thomas. Descendent Linda Graham Rose says Annie was the first to come to Lopez and encouraged family members to join her. Eleven family members came at once, including Grahams, Hodgsons (William Graham's stepsons), and Phillips.

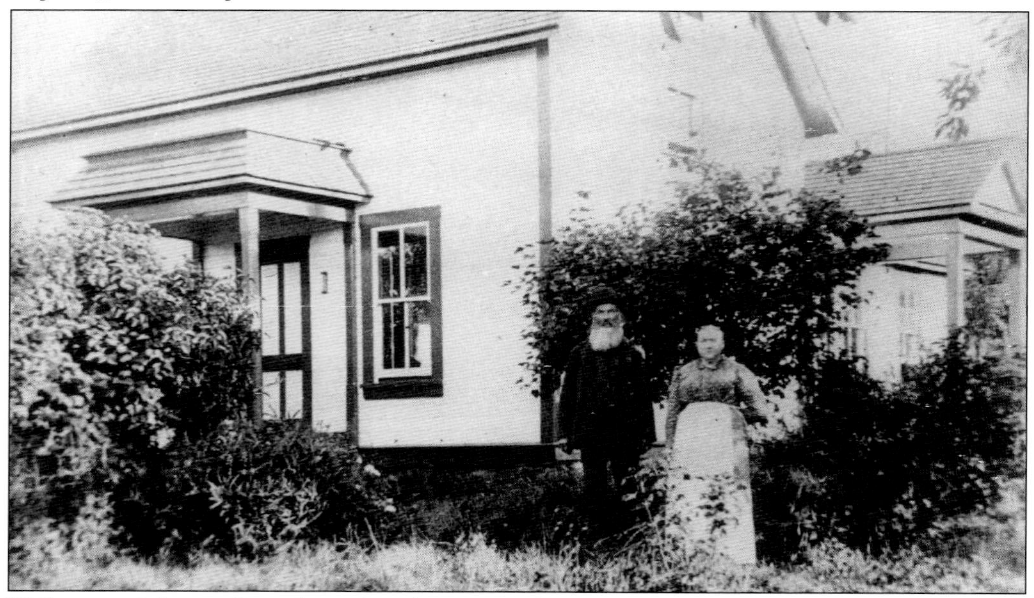

William and Annie Humphrey, for whom Humphrey Head is named, moved from Estherville, Iowa, to Lopez in 1876. They are shown here next to their house at Shoal Bay. William was Canadian, and Annie was the daughter of Thomas and Jane Graham and sister of Thomas and William Graham and Lizzie Ridley. The Humphreys owned 166 acres with an orchard of 600 trees, and raised wheat, hay, and chickens.

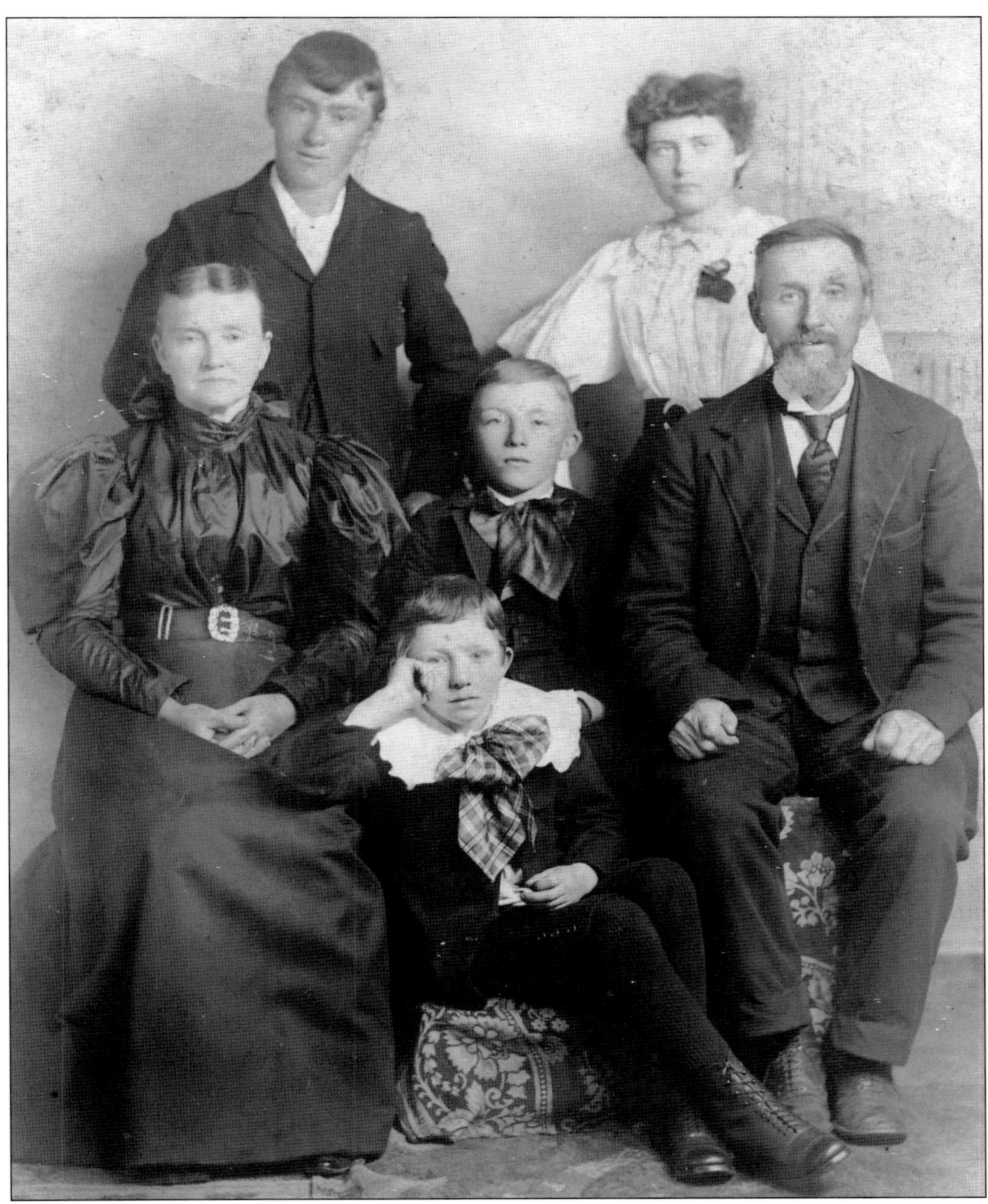

Born in Ireland, William Graham married Mary Wilson in Estherville, Iowa, and moved to Lopez at the same time as his parents, Jane and Thomas Graham, in 1877. William bought a farm built by Richardson's founder, George Richardson, and bought the Richardson store in 1899, turning it over to his stepson Norman P. Hodgson to run. Graham built the Salmon Banks Cannery (also known as the Hodgson-Graham Cannery) and sold the store, cannery, and other enterprises to Ira and Mary Lundy in 1916. He served as a county commissioner and school director for the Richardson district. Shown here are, from left to right, (first row) Claud Graham; (second row) Mary, Howard, and William Graham; (third row) Willie Graham and Mary Wilson. William and Mary's son John died by an accidental gunshot wound at a chivaree, a noisy mock serenade to newlyweds.

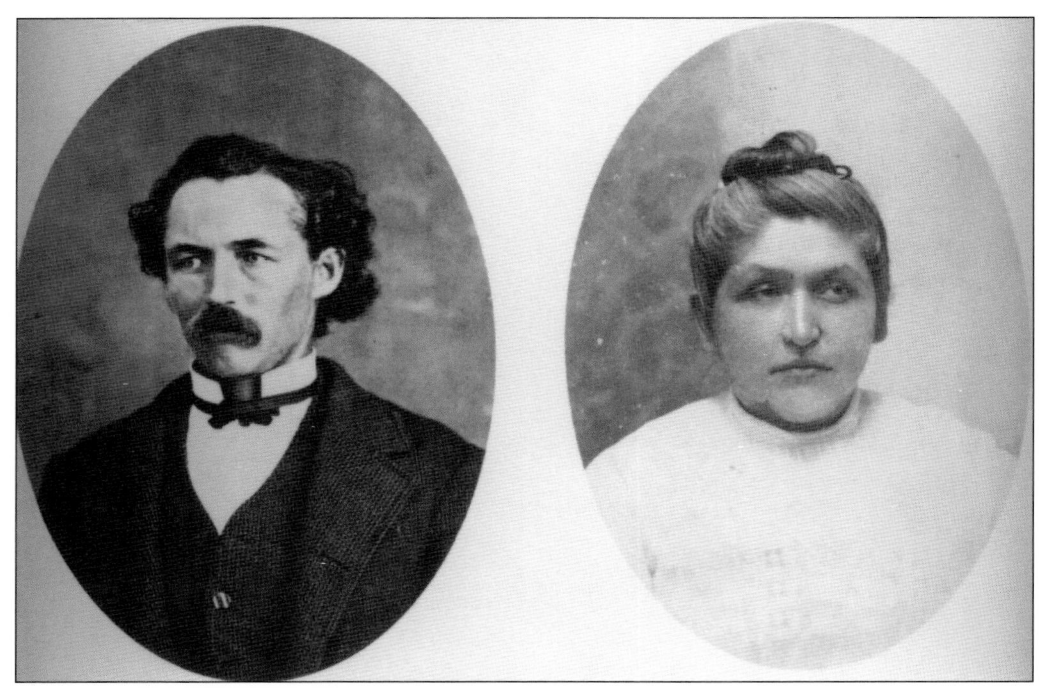

Sampson Chadwick came to Lopez about 1872 to tend 200 sheep for John Keddy. Adelia Bradshaw, daughter of a prominent Port Townsend attorney and a Clallam Indian woman, was sent to Lopez after her father married someone else. Chadwick called Adelia "the prettiest girl I ever saw." They married in 1876 and built a house overlooking the strait in an area now known as Watmough Head.

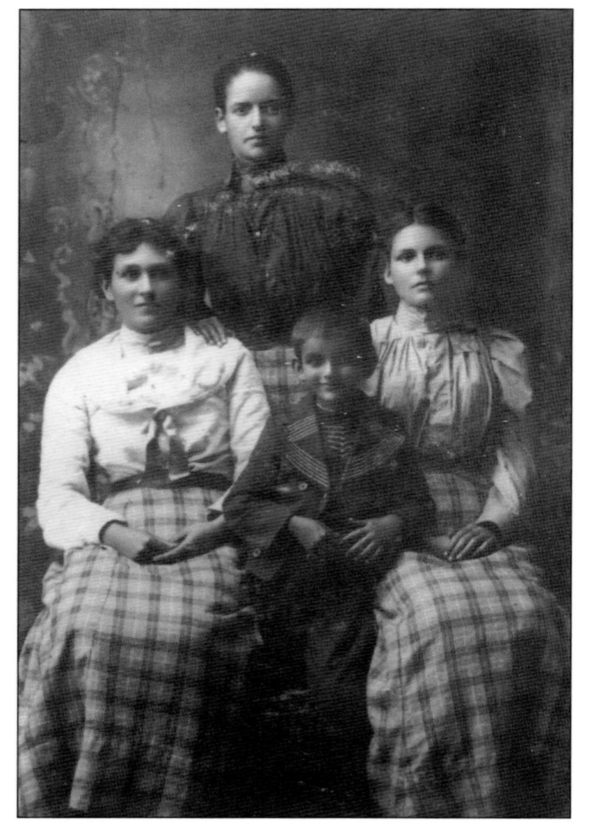

The Chadwicks had six children. Four lived to adulthood. From left to right are (first row) Fannie, George, and Minnie Chadwick; (second row) Addie Chadwick. A 1946 writer interviewed Addie and her nieces and nephews about the three Chadwick/Hume generations on Lopez. The interviewer concluded, "They love this place as if it were a person. They love it as few people in this world ever do love the place of their birth."

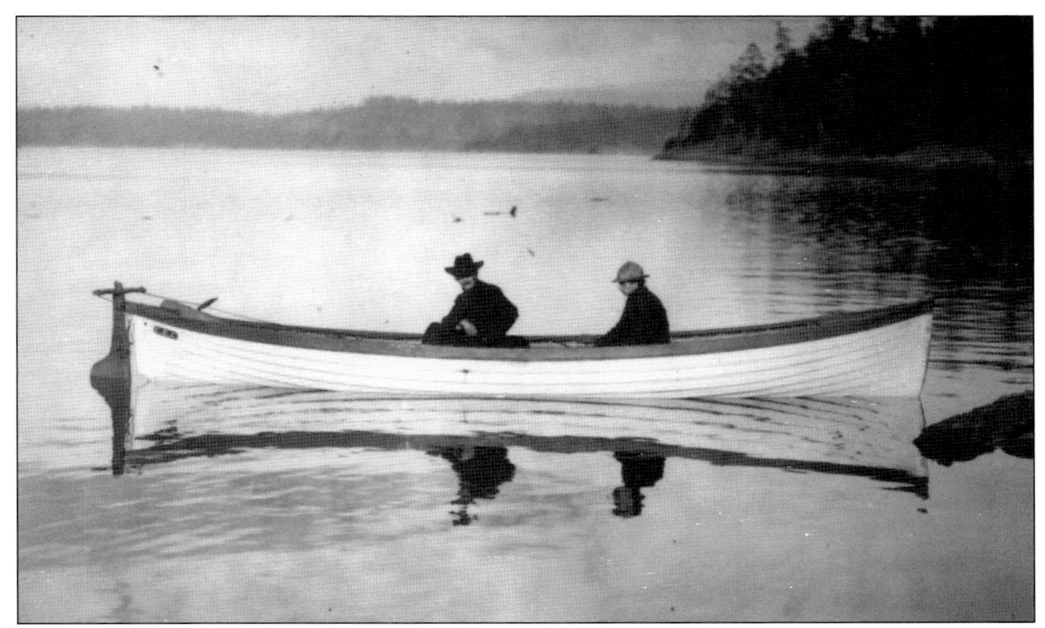

Stories conflict as to how Chadwick got this clinker-built boat, known as a captain's gig. Some say he purchased it for $10; others say he received it for helping deserting British sailors flee their ship. Seen here with son George, Sampson Chadwick ferried islanders across the strait to pick up supplies in Anacortes. Sampson was a dedicated reader, and he was a writer of poetry and articles submitted under the byline "Lopez W. T."

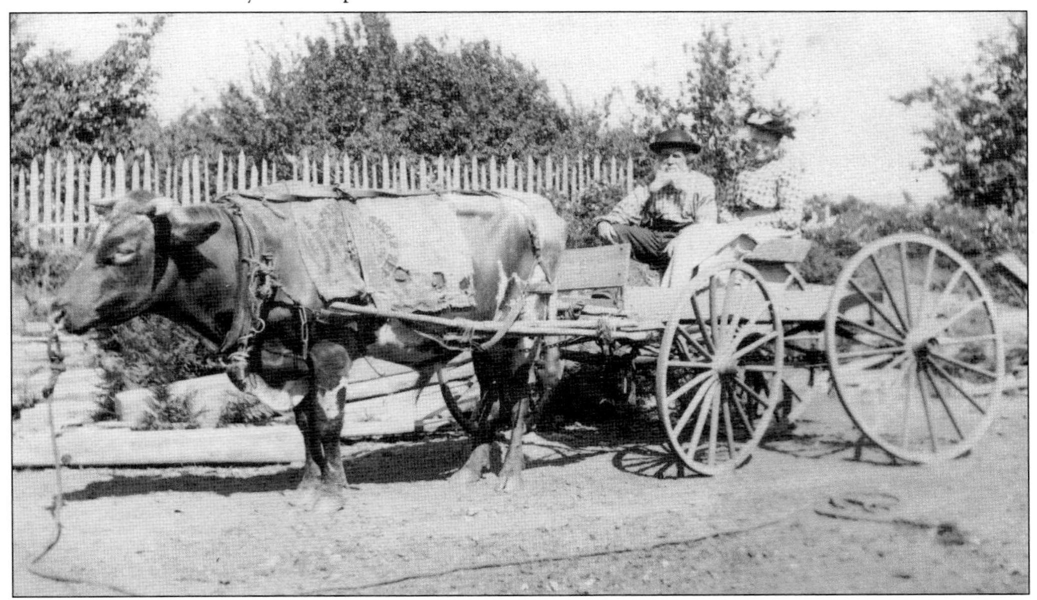

John and Eliza Sperry hailed from Illinois and moved to Lopez in 1879. Settling on land now known as Sperry Peninsula, records indicate they had four children, Orrin, Asa, May, and Minerva. John and Eliza frequently drove their ox-drawn wagon to the Hodgson-Graham store at Richardson. Sampson Chadwick and John Sperry tended sheep in partnership and protected them at night from prowling purse seine fishermen, who loved to steal them.

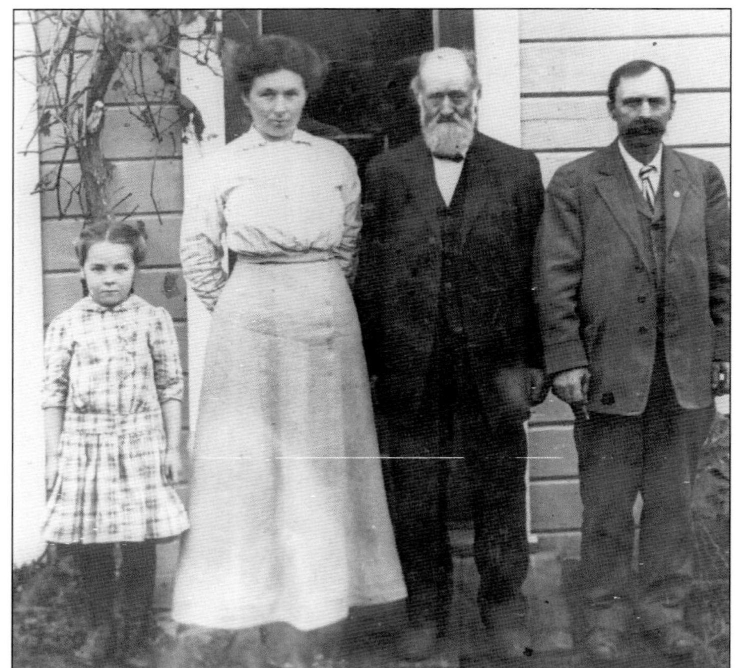

Robert Hummel came to Lopez in 1878 with a letter of introduction to Wesley Warner. He worked for the Warners for his board and "such help as they could give me to get my cabin in condition to receive my parents and sister when they arrived in the fall." Shown here, from left to right, are Hummel's daughters, Netta and Alice; his father, E. H. Hummel; and Robert.

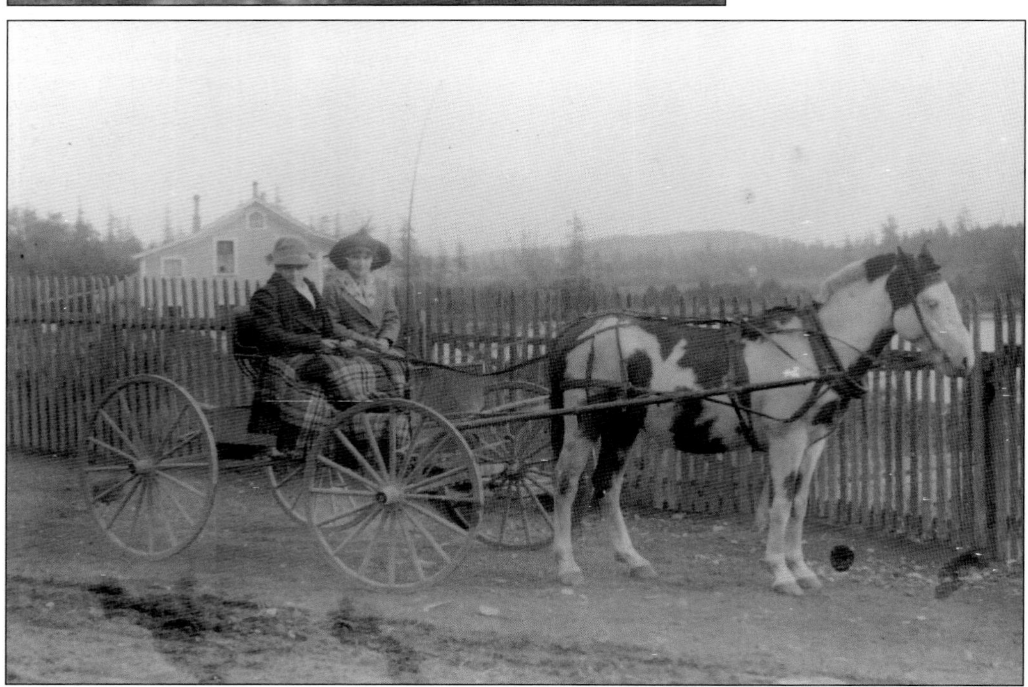

Hummel homesteaded Lake View Farm across from present-day Hummel Lake. He went back to Pennsylvania and returned with a wife, Mary Alice, shown here with daughter Helen. The Hummels had four children and moved in 1897 to Seattle for the children's education. After returning to Lopez later in life, Robert wrote, "It is a great privilege to have lived the life of a pioneer in such splendid surroundings."

Wesley Warner moved to Lopez from New York in 1876 and wrote to entice his wife, Mary, "The newcomers from Iowa say I have the best place on the island." Mary and two daughters arrived in 1879. With only three months of school available annually, community dances raised school funds. The Warners built a log house, outbuildings, and, with neighbors' help, a barn, on the east side of Ferry Road.

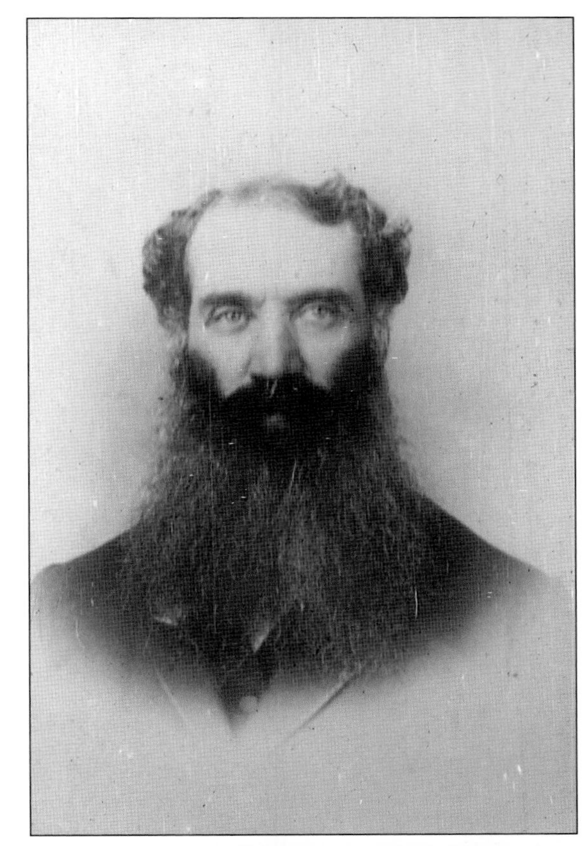

Jasper Coffelt, patriarch in this family photograph, came to Lopez with his mother from Missouri in the 1870s. Coffelt married Rosella Richey, whose father, George Washington Richey, came to Lopez in the 1870s as well. The Coffelts had 10 children who married members of the Wilson, Barton, Gawley, Kendall, and Weeks families, among others. Roy Butler remembered Coffelt as a "fine family man" and admired his "inventiveness and persistency."

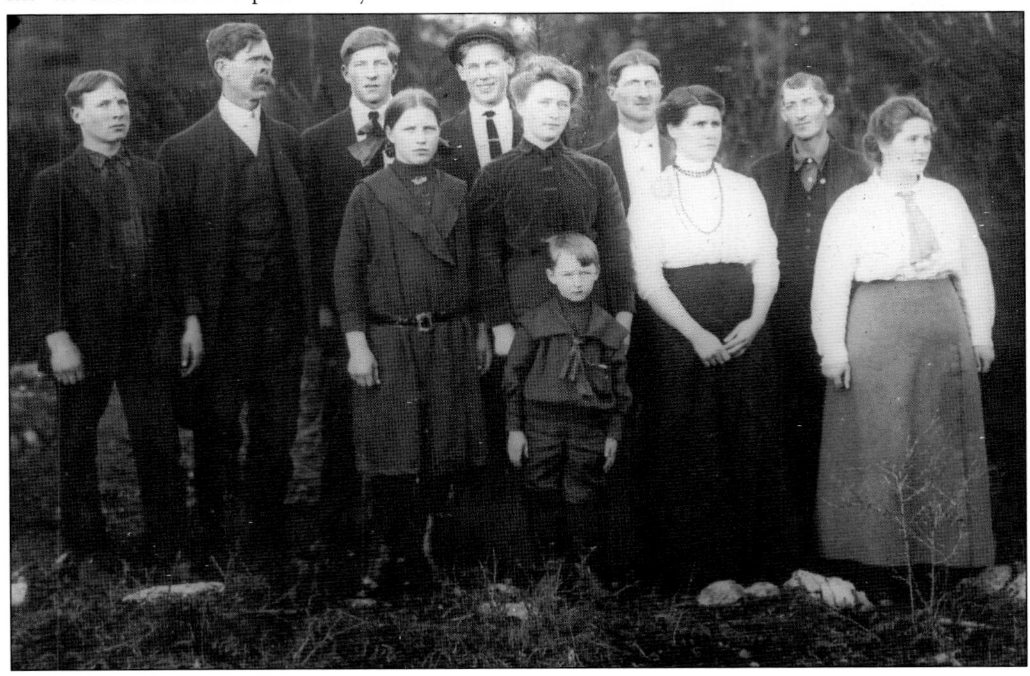

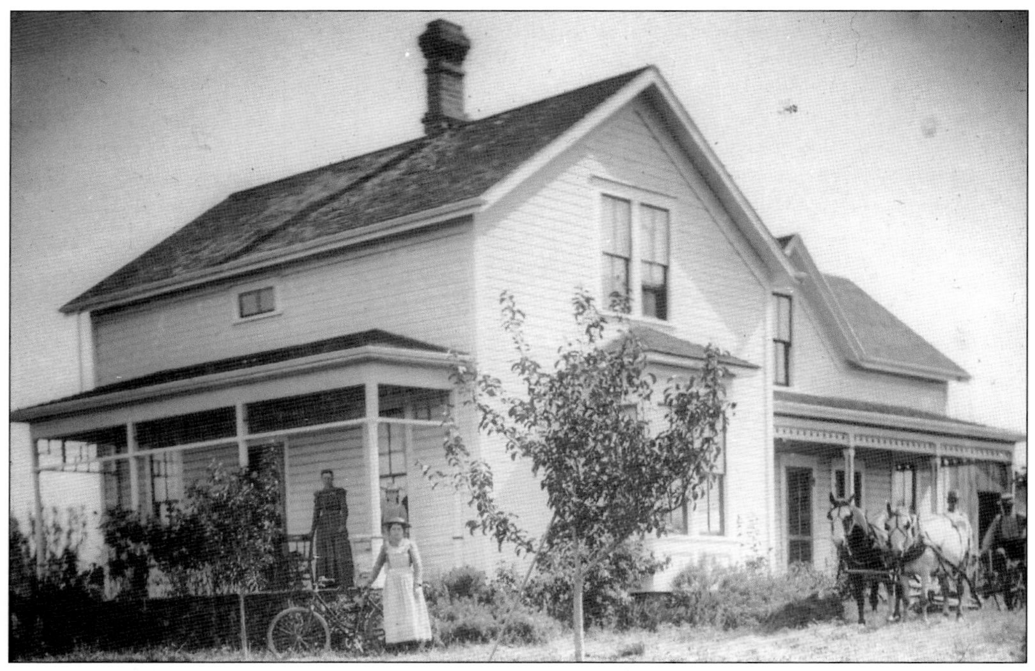

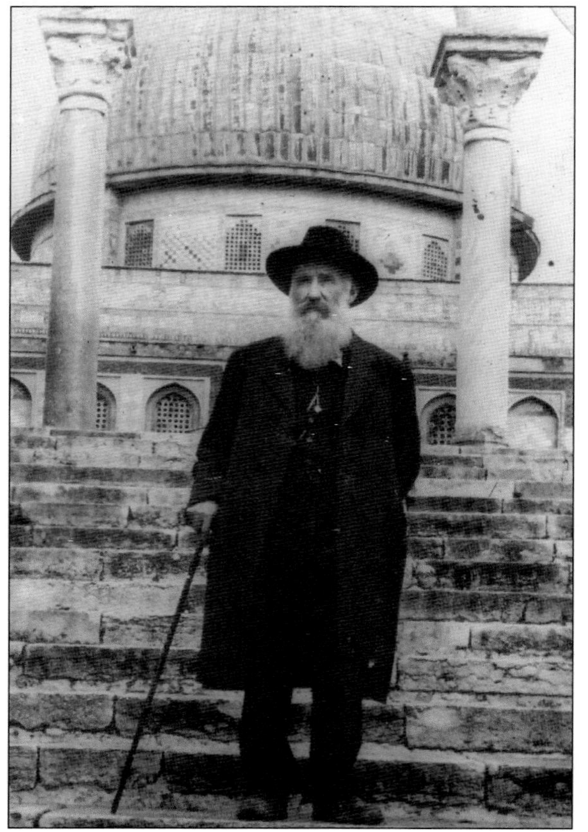

Thomas Upston, a native of Canada, moved to Lopez in 1880. In 1883, he married Eleanor Cousins and they had two children, settling on 160 acres in the island's Center Valley. Upston raised hay, grain, produce, sheep, and cattle and was considered an "esteemed and honored" man of the county, serving for many years on his district's school board.

According to "Uncle" Phil Hastin, his grandfather George Henderson Hastin came to Lopez in 1885 and homesteaded 160 acres on Lopez Hill. George was the first butcher in the county and ran shops in Friday Harbor and Anacortes. He later purchased two 40-acre parcels on the south end of the island with his son, also named George. They cleared the acreage with horse teams.

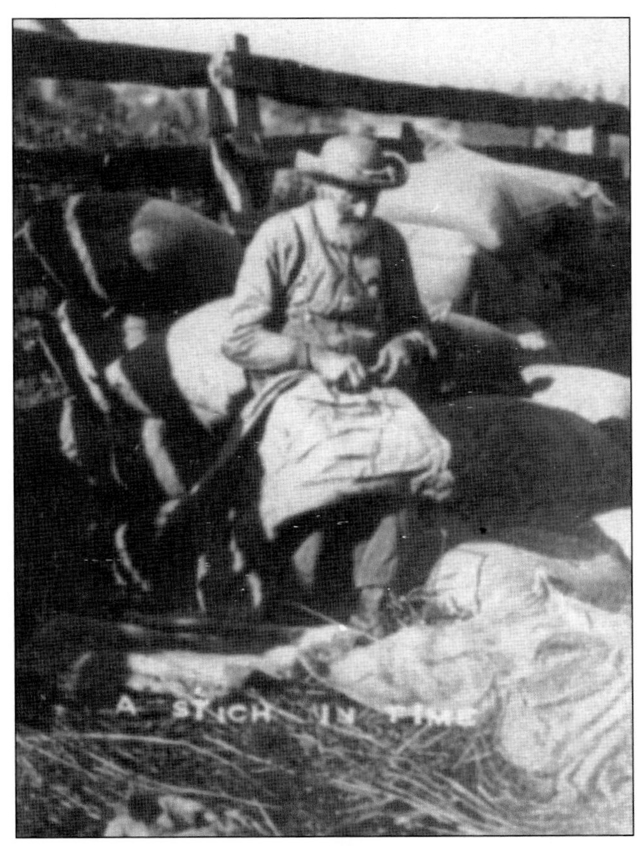

Born in Maine, John Bartlett married Ellen Clancy from County Cork, Ireland, and moved to Lopez in 1874 from Port Townsend. The Bartletts cleared and then farmed 143 acres in Center Valley just north of Center Church and raised hay, grain, produce, cattle, and fruit. They reported that the soil was ideal, better than on the mainland or other nearby islands, and planted an orchard of about 1,000 trees.

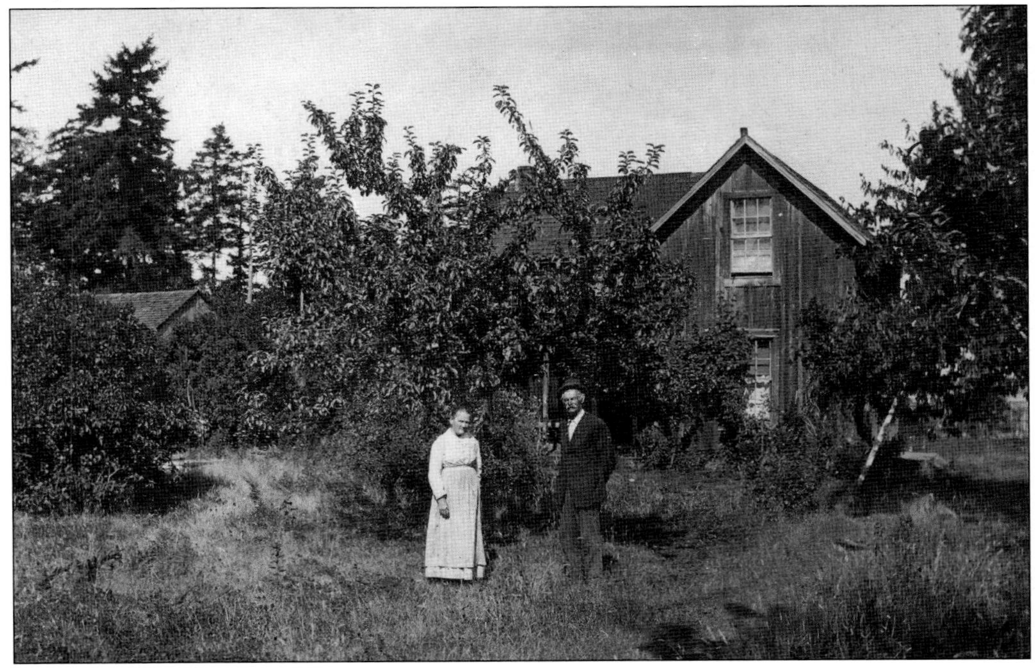

Benjamin Franklin and Salinda Wood moved to Lopez in 1884 and are shown here at their home in 1916. The 1900 census shows the Woods had two daughters, Grace, born in 1885 on Lopez, and Estelle (Stella) born in 1883 in Kansas. Descendent Raelyn Dolton recalls that Stella married Norman Blake and kept a diary for many years chronicling her life. Dolton recently donated the diary to the Lopez museum.

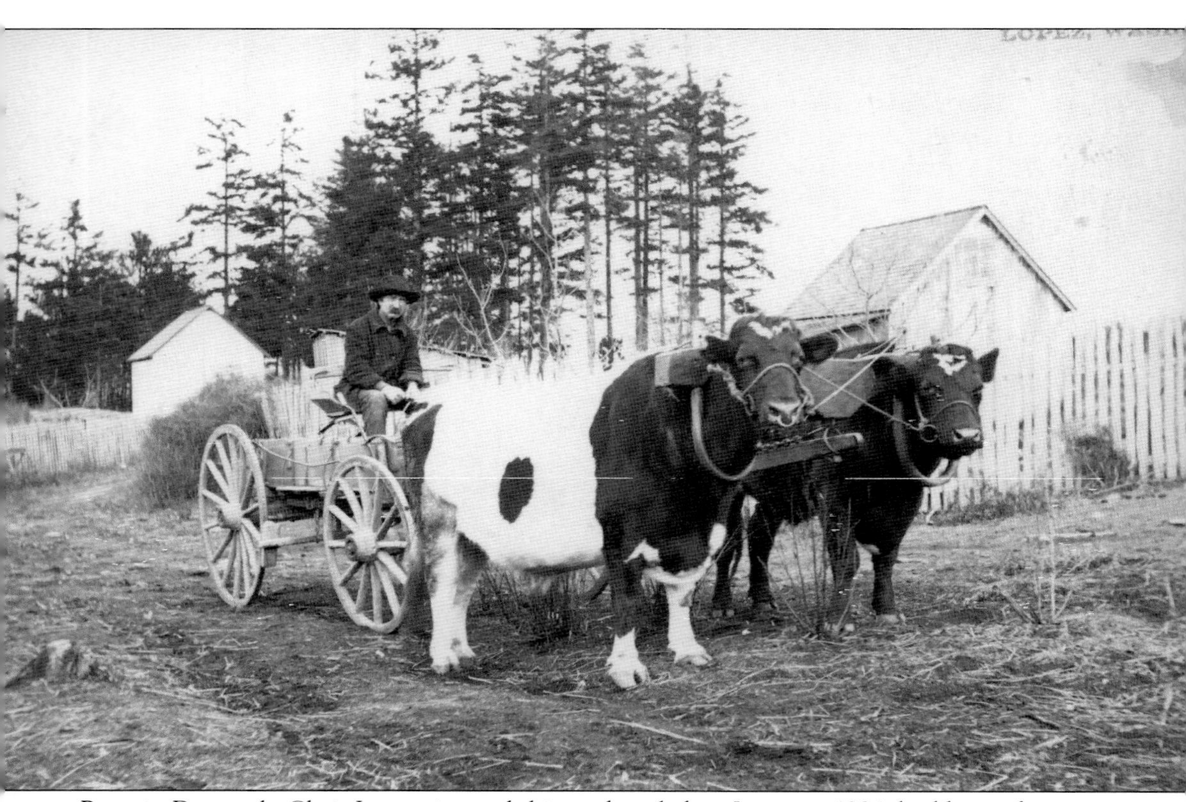

Born in Denmark, Chris Jensen jumped ship and settled on Lopez in 1884, building a farm on present-day Kjargaard Road. He and his friend Pete Asplund each homesteaded 160 acres in Center Valley. When he died a bachelor in 1913, Jensen divided his land between niece Anna Kjargaard and nephew Niels Nielsen. Kjargaard's children were Carl, Juhn, Anita, Amalia, Alma, Harold, Otto, and Nina. Nielsen's children were Anna, Eva, Hazel, Johanna, and Peter.

Two

Hamlets Grow and Families Flourish

In a 1903 article, Honor L. Wilhelm, editor of the magazine *The Coast*, captured the spirit of the Lopez community at the time. "The people of Lopez are most hospitable and entertaining. It is a saying that no one on Lopez, be he stranger or friend, knocks in vain when seeking food or shelter."

By 1903, the island had become quite prosperous, centered on three hamlets, Port Stanley, Lopez, and Richardson. Lopez Village served as a "lively trade center," with a wharf and warehouse. Richardson grew as the epicenter of a thriving fishing industry.

"Extensive and profitable farms" surrounded the three hamlets, and all benefitted from the twice-daily steamboat service that took products to markets north, east, and south. "Beautiful homes, well-kept orchards, fine horses and vehicles . . . tell the tale of prosperity here better than words," the article said. Visitors who came "a summering" found "delectable rest and restoring solitude."

What the 1903 writer could not have known on a more personal level were the many Lopez families who worked together to create the generous and hardworking community the writer experienced. This chapter tells some of their stories and that of Lopez's three hamlets.

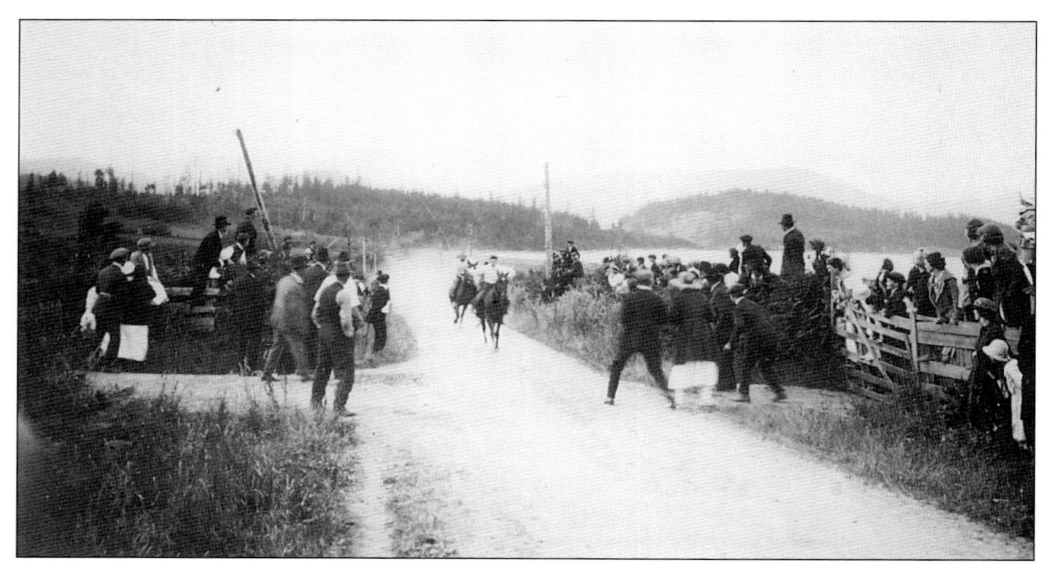

The Port Stanley community gathered to celebrate the Fourth of July in these two early photographs. Above, riders kick up dust in a horse race down Port Stanley Road, as onlookers watch with excitement. Below, women gather their skirts to run a footrace following the Port Stanley picnic. On one side of the road lies the Puget Sound Potash and Kelp Fertilizer Company, built to process kelp into potash and iodine. On the other is what is described as "Tom and Hannah Bell's store." Thomas Bell operated the Port Stanley Post Office for almost 30 years and managed the store on behalf of the Rochdale Company. In 1878, Wesley Warner wrote, "We had a celebration on the Fourth of July . . . Our company was small, but good for this place, there being something more than two hundred present."

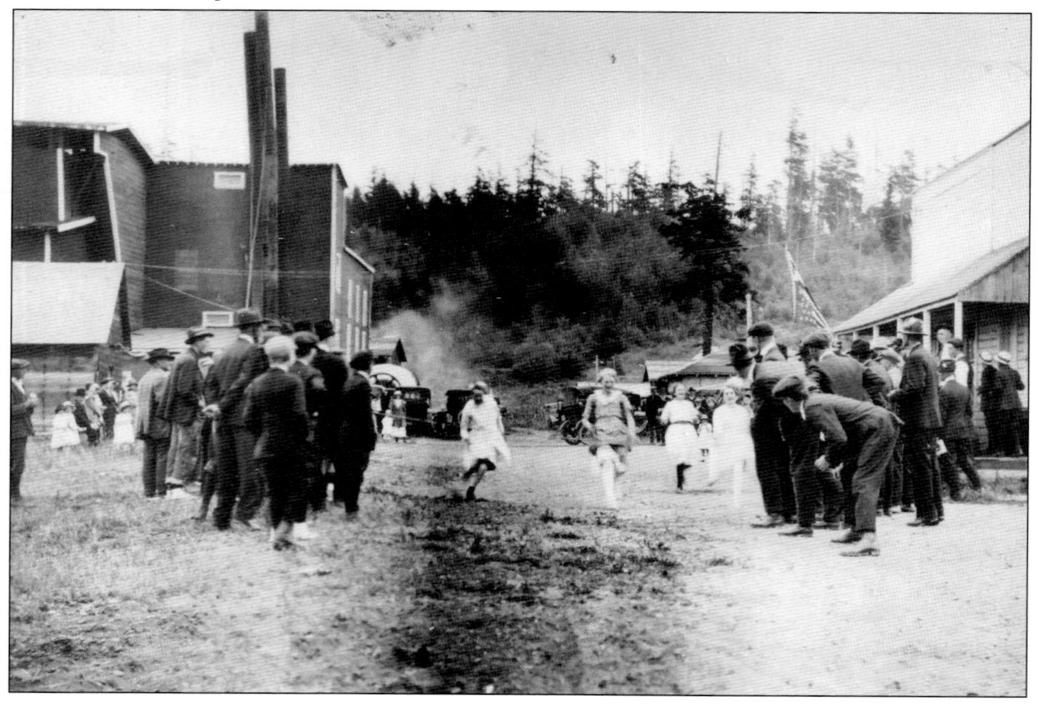

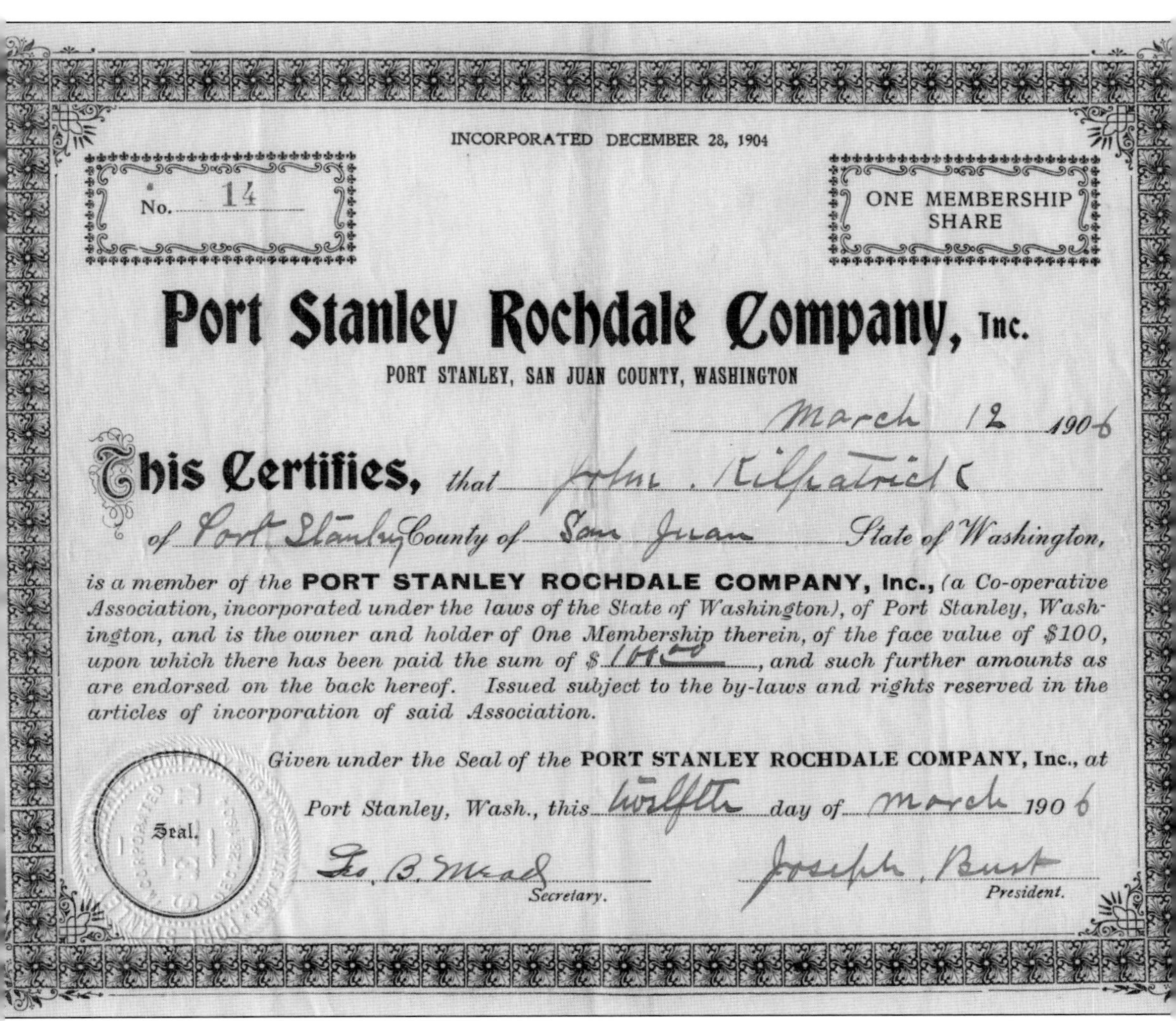
INCORPORATED DECEMBER 28, 1904

No. 14

ONE MEMBERSHIP SHARE

Port Stanley Rochdale Company, Inc.

PORT STANLEY, SAN JUAN COUNTY, WASHINGTON

March 12 1906

This Certifies, *that* John. Kilpatrick

of Port Stanley *County of* San Juan *State of Washington,*

is a member of the **PORT STANLEY ROCHDALE COMPANY, Inc.,** *(a Co-operative Association, incorporated under the laws of the State of Washington), of Port Stanley, Washington, and is the owner and holder of One Membership therein, of the face value of $100, upon which there has been paid the sum of $* 100.00*, and such further amounts as are endorsed on the back hereof. Issued subject to the by-laws and rights reserved in the articles of incorporation of said Association.*

Given under the Seal of the **PORT STANLEY ROCHDALE COMPANY, Inc.,** *at Port Stanley, Wash., this* twelfth *day of* March *190*6

Seal.

Geo. B. Mead
Secretary.

Joseph Burt
President.

Cooperative efforts are a long-standing Lopez tradition. Perrin I. Whitman owned Port Stanley's first store, and when it floundered, north end farmers and ranchers decided to take concerted action and pool their resources to buy it. The Rochdale Company borrowed the name and principles from England's Rochdale Society of Equitable Pioneers of the modern cooperative movement. Founded in 1844, the society promoted sustainable development under democratic control for the betterment of the community. Port Stanley's farmers and ranchers formed a cooperative with membership open to all. Each of its 50 members bought one share and had one vote. The co-op sold food, clothing, and tools, and dividends were paid in proportion to each member's purchases. Although no credit was permitted, the rule was broken more often than enforced, which led the co-op to be disbanded in 1914. The store and inventory were sold for $4,680.73.

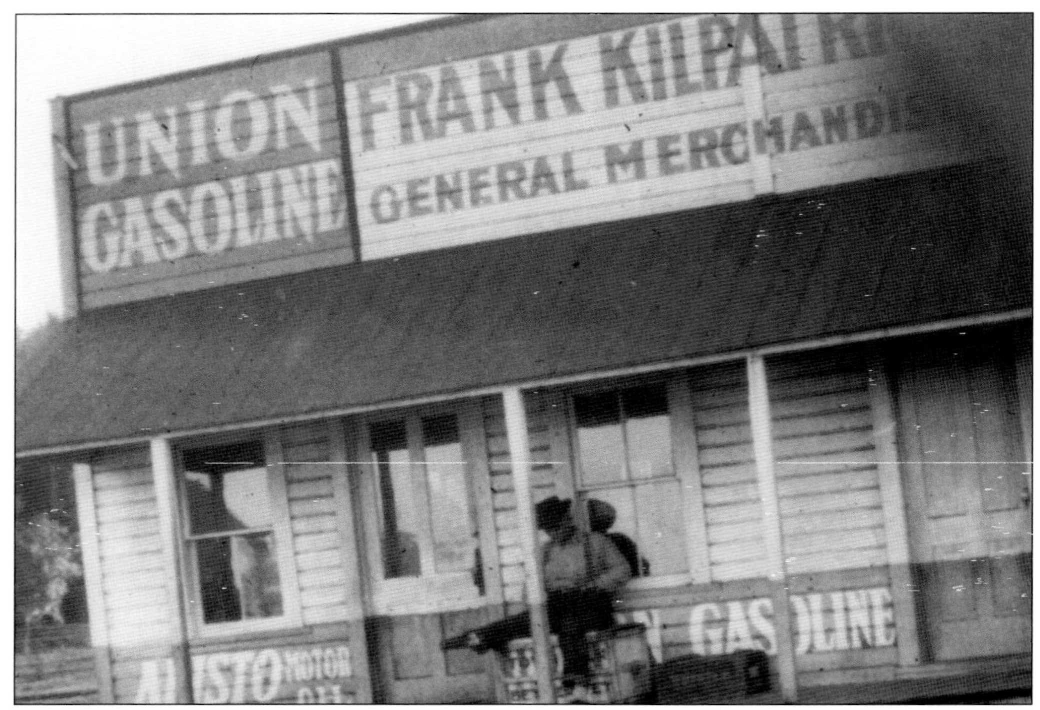

Moonshiner "Pegleg" Joe Leveque of Blakely Island sits on the porch of Frank Kilpatrick's Port Stanley store around 1915. Kilpatrick bought the store in 1915 after the Rochdale cooperative folded and carried on business there until the building burned about 1934. After the fire, Kilpatrick moved Port Stanley's mortuary building to the old store location and reopened the store in it, shown here with a car parked in front. Lopez historian Gertrude Boede recalled, "They had only two customers as a mortuary." Stores often served as community meeting places, and neighbors gathered to share stories when they came to pick up their mail from the post office located within the store.

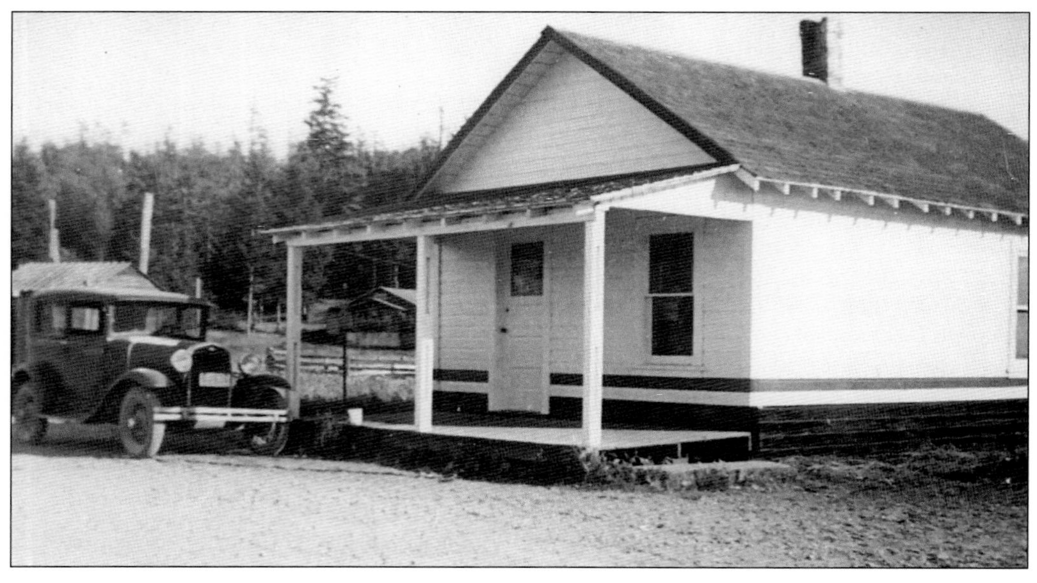

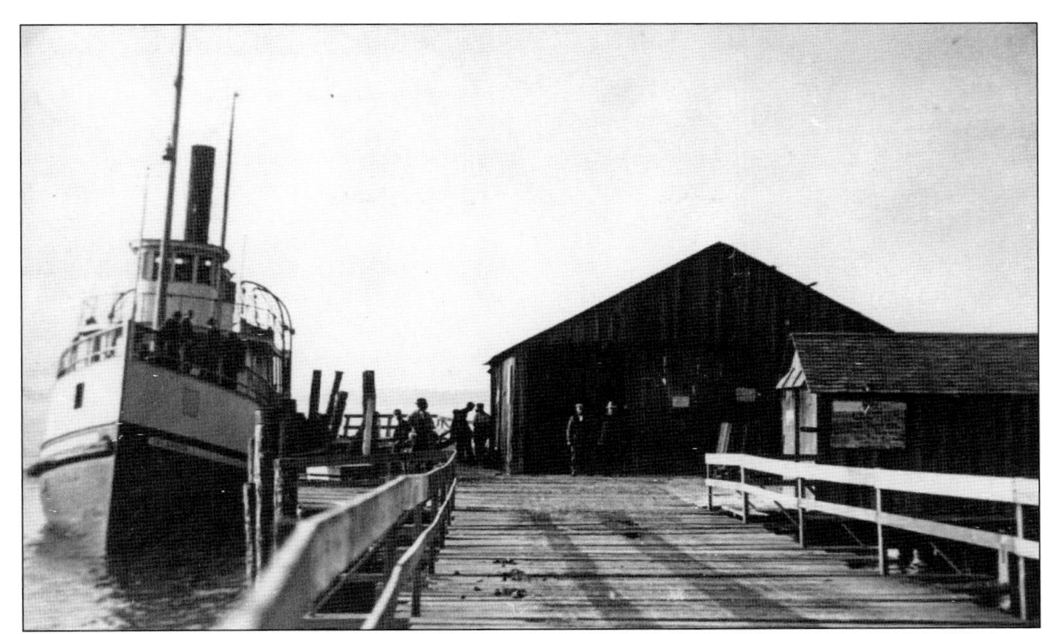

An industrious man, Kilpatrick owned the Port Stanley dock that served the north end farmers' shipping needs. With few island roads in the early days, boat travel was an indispensible link to markets, friends, and family on other parts of the island, the mainland, and beyond. This photograph is of a Seattle freight boat stopping by Kilpatrick's dock about 1920.

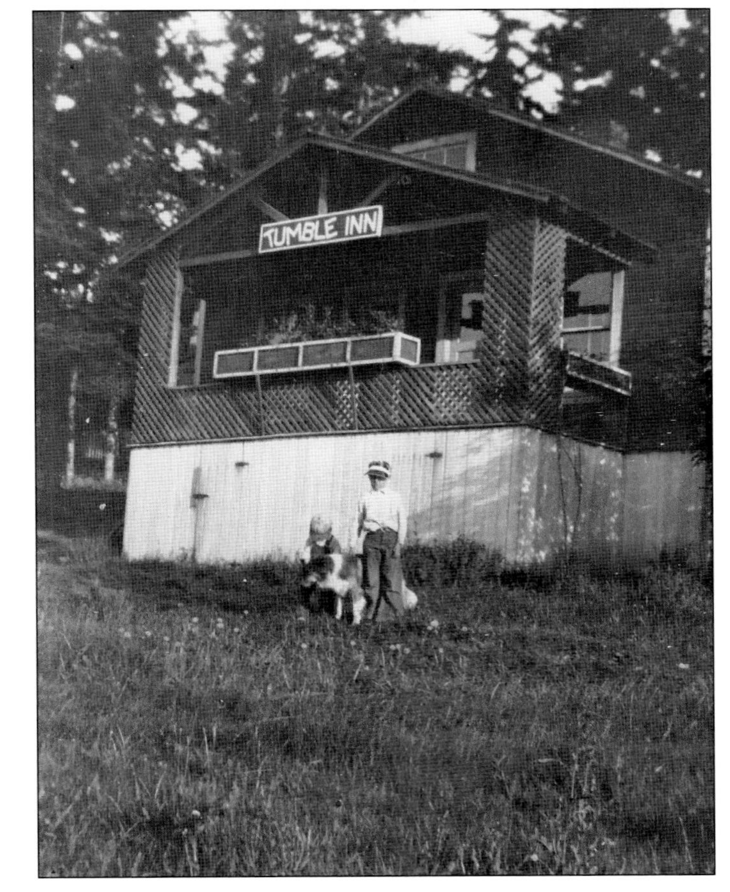

Nicknamed "the Stagger Out," Port Stanley's Tumble Inn served multiple roles in the community. It not only was an inn and restaurant, but it also served as the kelp plant office. The inn was operated by Kilpatrick's daughters Dorothy and Patricia. This photograph is identified as possibly being Bruce, left, and Arthur Kilpatrick and their dog Sparky in the 1930s.

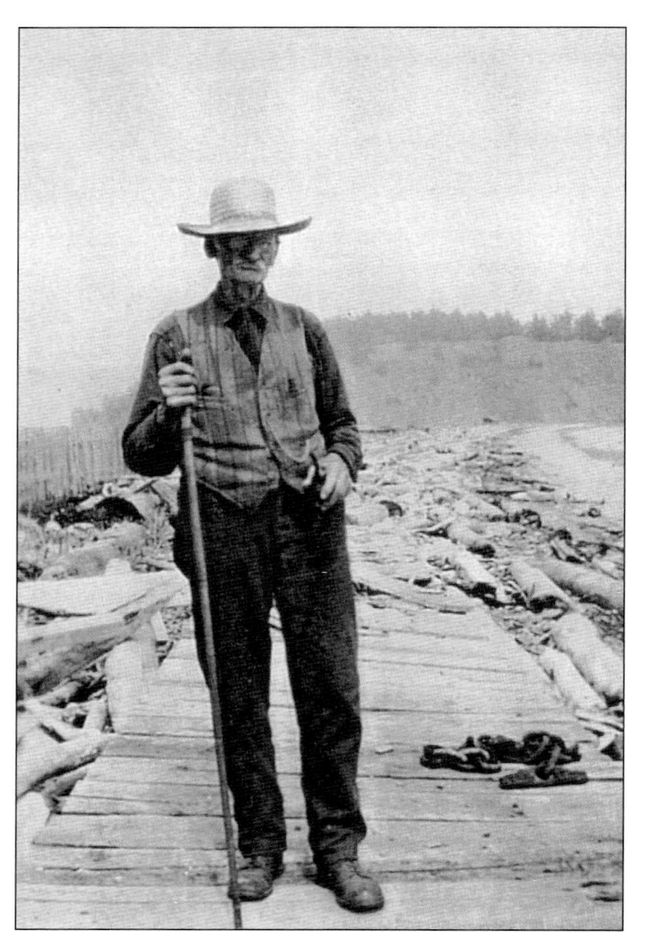

Theodore Spencer moved west by wagon train from Ohio as a young boy. In this photograph, he stands on the spit that bears his name. Franklin Troxell homesteaded Spencer Spit and then sold it to Rev. Isaac Dillon, who then sold it to Spencer. Spencer later moved to Blakely Island and ran a sawmill, which his son Ross later took over. In 1967, the Spencer family sold the land to Washington State. It is now a state park.

Judging by this photograph, Billy Carle, left, and Harry LeMaister must have been best friends. Carle's mother died trying to save his drowning brother, and he was raised by his father and grandmother. LeMaister, son of John LeMaister and Maggie Brown, became an early Lopez reefnetter. Marguerite LeMaister Hutchison fondly recalls her uncle Harry walking her to Port Stanley School from Hummel Lake, where he ran a sawmill.

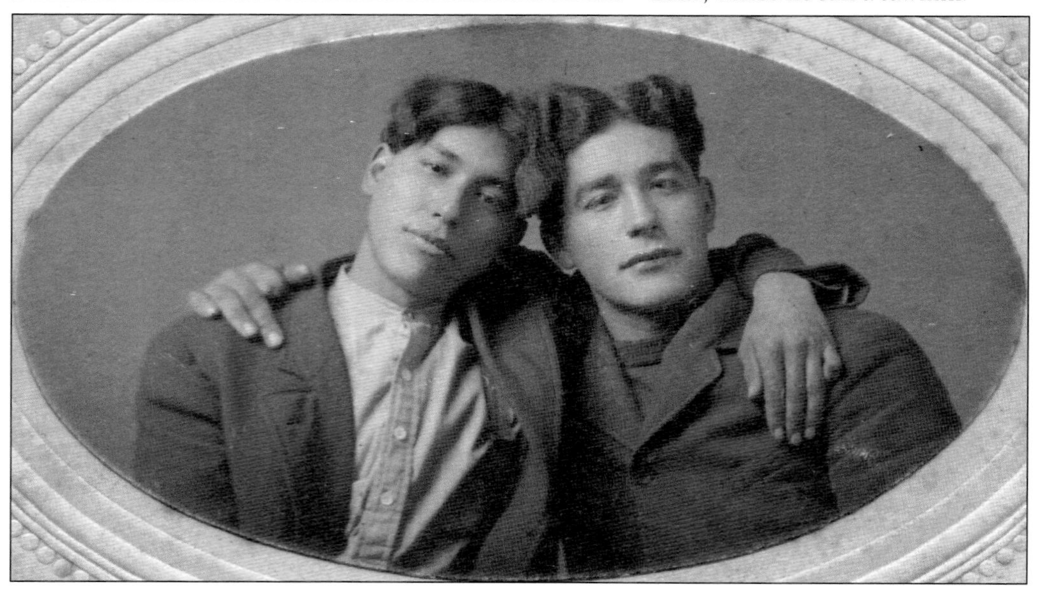

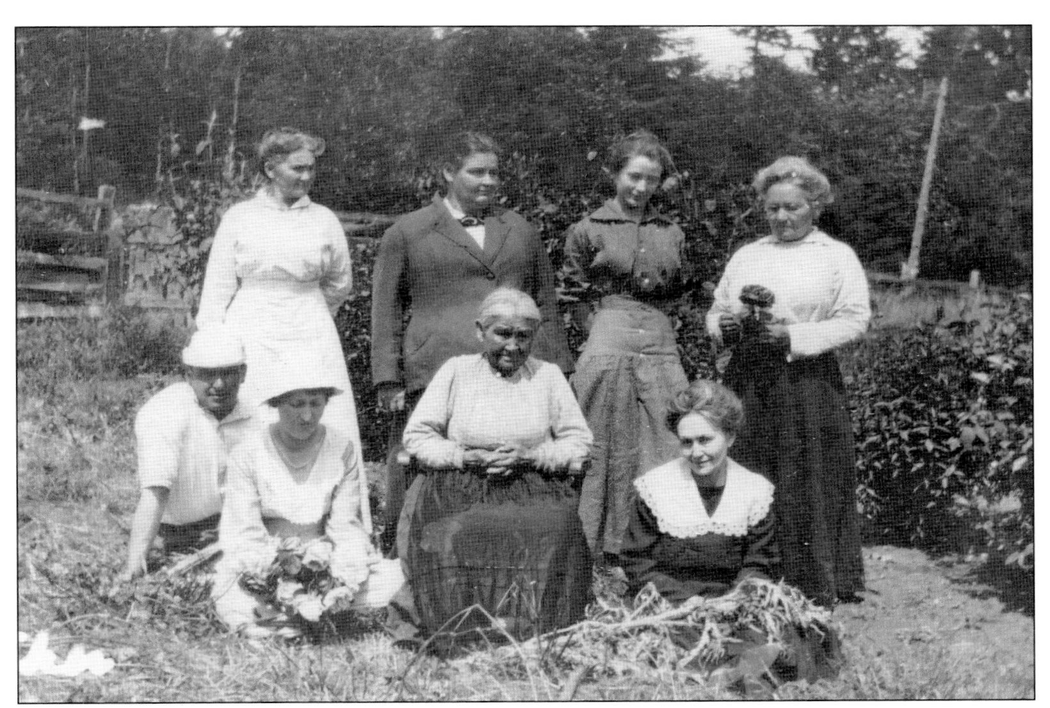

Mary Jane "Mother" Brown had 10 children, Ella, Maggie, Maria (pronounced like *Mariah*), Mary Jane, Sarah, Catherine (Kitty), Emily, Henry, Willie, and Nettie. The younger Mary Jane (second row, left) homesteaded 40 acres at the corner of Mud Bay and Aleck Bay Roads as an unmarried woman, built a house, and married Erwin Eaton in 1893. Nettie and Henry died unexpectedly in their 20s. The surviving Brown children became the foundation of many island families.

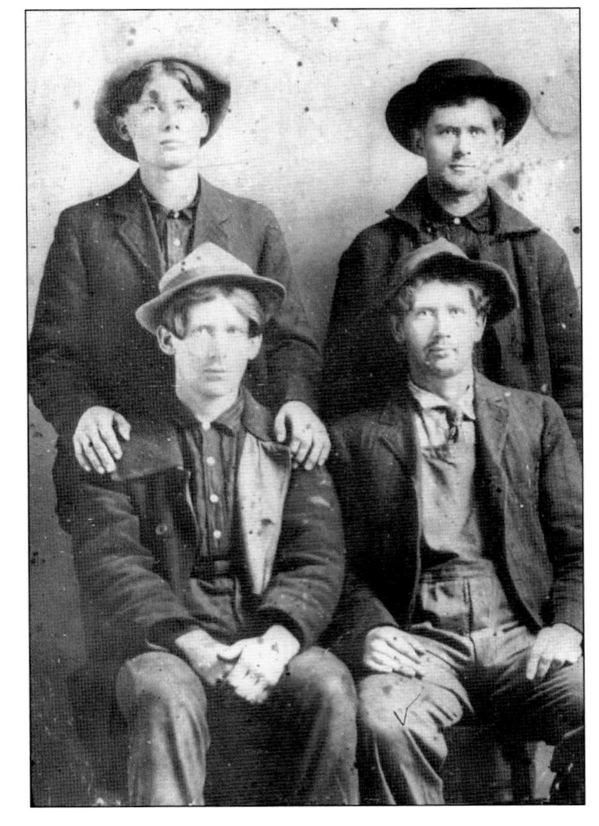

Thomas, Oliver, Frederick, and Edmund Cochran were the sons of Edmund and Antilla Cochran, who moved to Lopez about 1884, settling near Port Stanley. The brothers' sister Susie Cochran Gallanger Arnett remembered that their father taught school in the 1880s in a rough log building that was so "thoroughly ventilated by cracks and crevices in the chinking that both pupils and teacher were almost constantly taking colds."

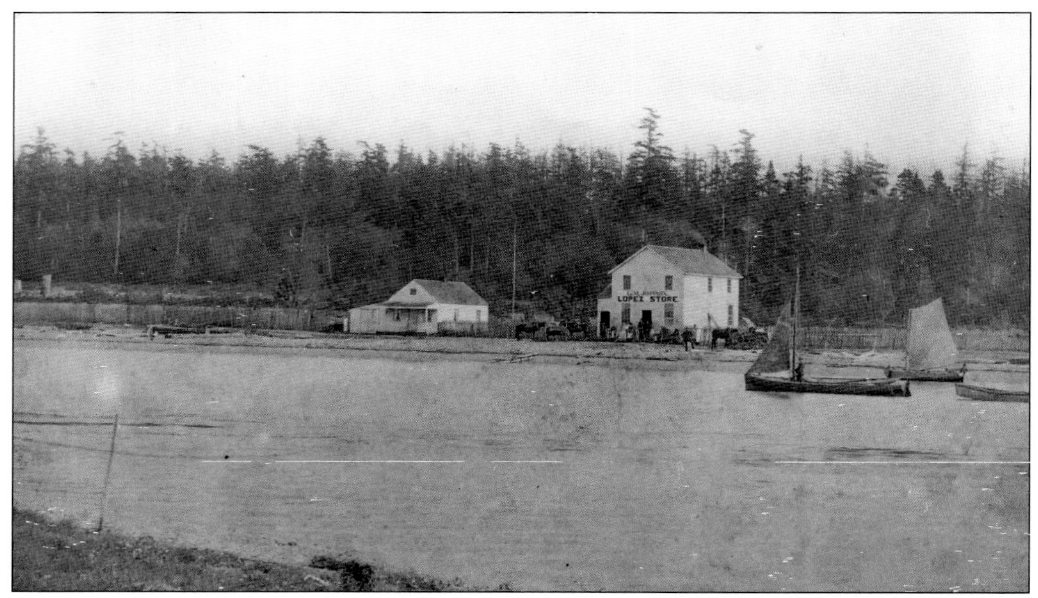

Started by Hiram E. Hutchinson and then run by his sister Irene Weeks, the Lopez store, shown here in the 1880s, was sold to G. M. Johnson. Irene's son Oscar remembered rowing out to steamboats to trade aboard ship before the dock was built. Legend has it the store burned in 1923 as Oscar's grandson, Eldon Weeks, was born 50 feet away.

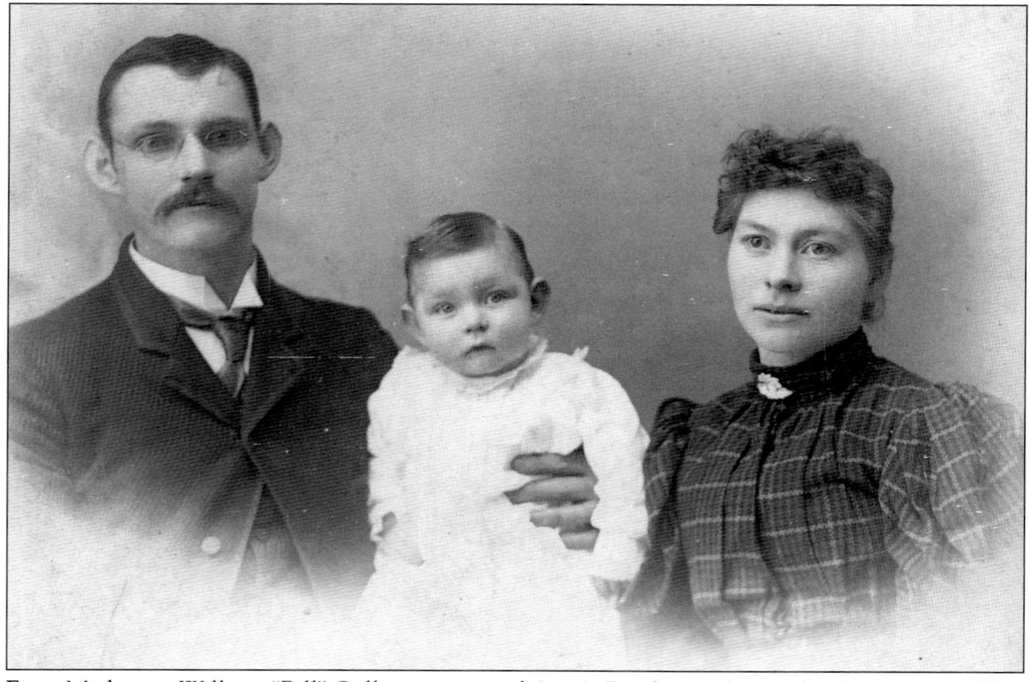

From Michigan, William "Bill" Gallanger married Annie Bartlett and moved to Lopez about 1891. Shown here with his son, Walter, the Gallangers had nine children, eight of whom were born on Lopez. Bill and Walter started a diary together, and Gordon Buchanan recalled, "They had 90 cows here one time. Walter and Bill used to milk all 90 cows. Bill was a hard workin' ol' brute."

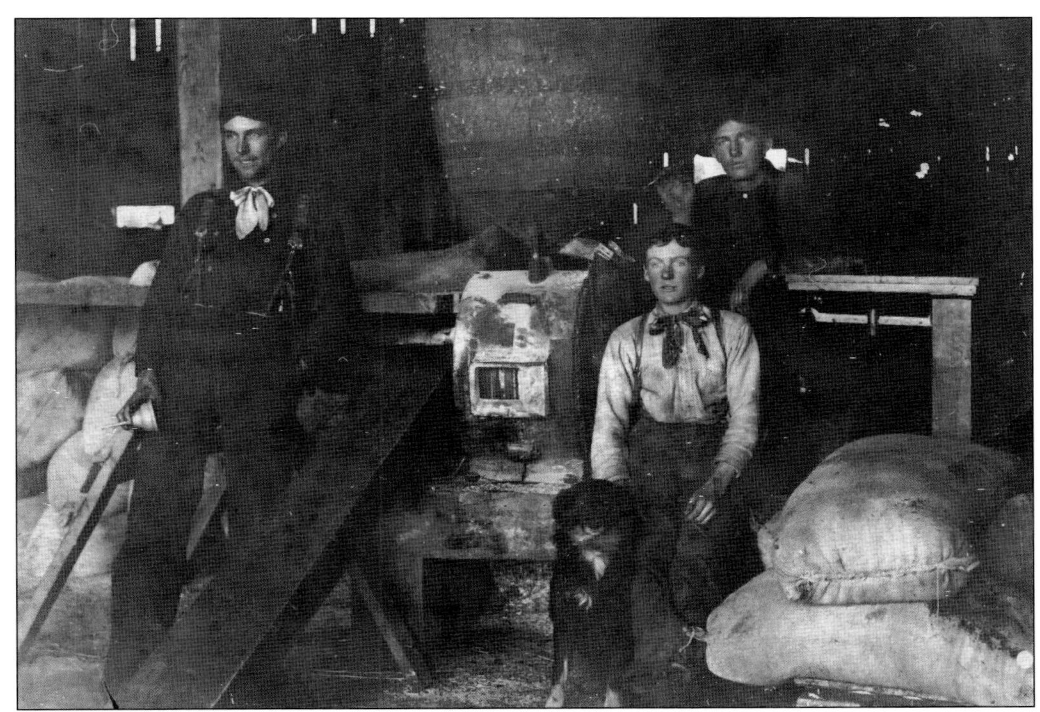

James, Eddie, and Charlie Buchanan sit inside a grain warehouse in this November 1900 photograph. Their father, James Buchanan, married Maime Shewin (or Sherwin) and then settled on Lopez about 1886. Maime died about 1893. James Sr. married Jennie Hodgson, and they had many more children together. Recognized as a leading rancher, James Sr. kept some of the finest pedigreed horses in the Northwest.

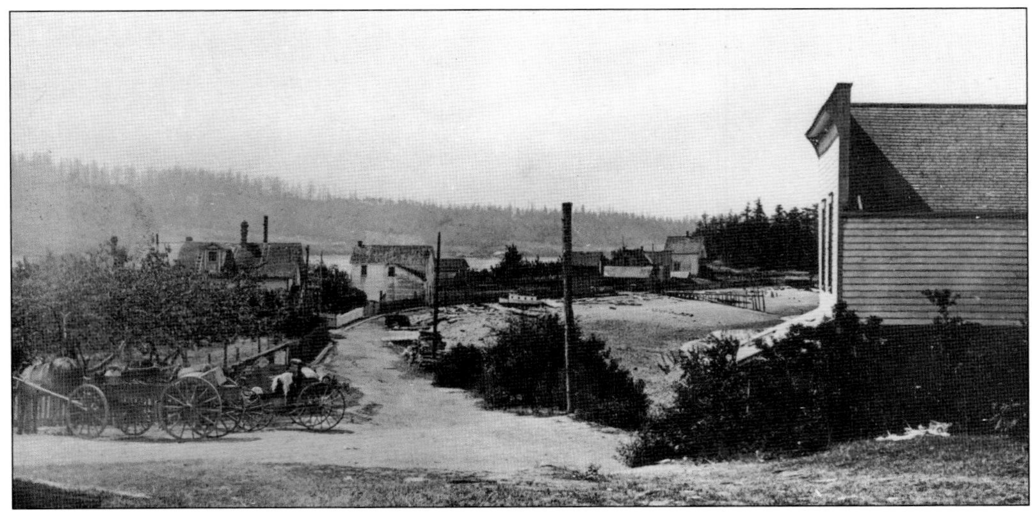

This early photograph of Lopez Village depicts the Lopez store, a clam cannery, and a creamery building among the structures looking south along the shore. The store's upper floor was used for Sunday school and church services until the Lopez Congregational Church was completed in 1905. In addition to the store, cannery, and creamery, villagers also operated a blacksmith shop and livery stable.

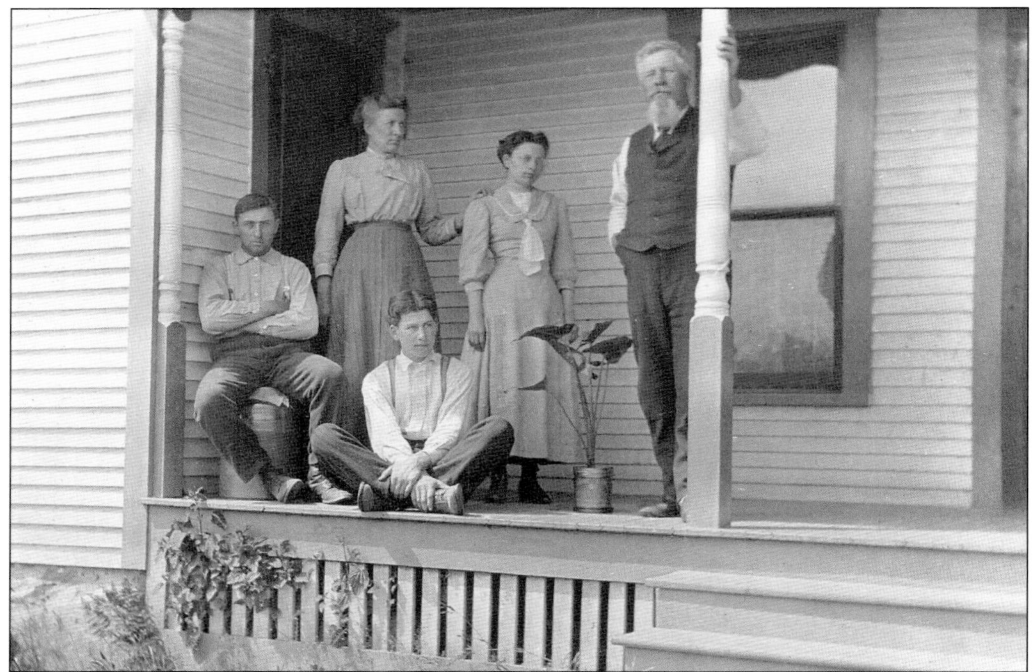

Joseph Burt, relaxing with his family on their front porch, was born in Scotland, farmed near Estherville, Iowa, and moved to Lopez in 1902. By 1905, his brother John and his family arrived. They are posing by the beach in this 1905 photograph. From left to right are (first row) Dorothy and Lillian; (second row) Harry, Hazel, John, and Ray. In addition to farming, Joseph and John were master carpenters and worked together to build Center School (now the Lopez Grange) and Mud Bay School. Joseph, John, and brother Peter were also skilled violin makers. Joseph died in 1941 while shocking hay at the age of 90.

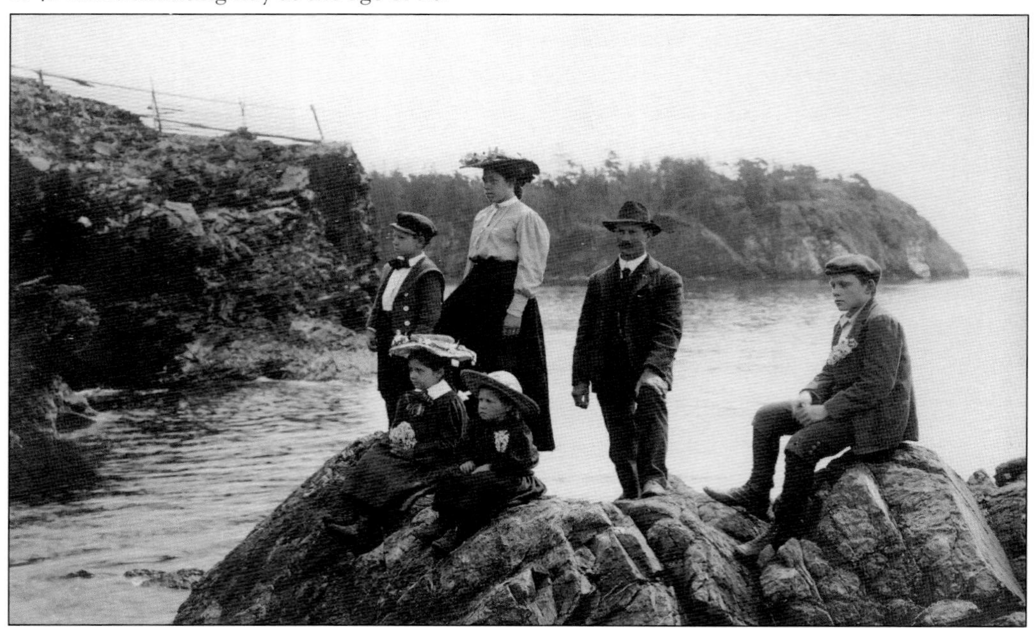

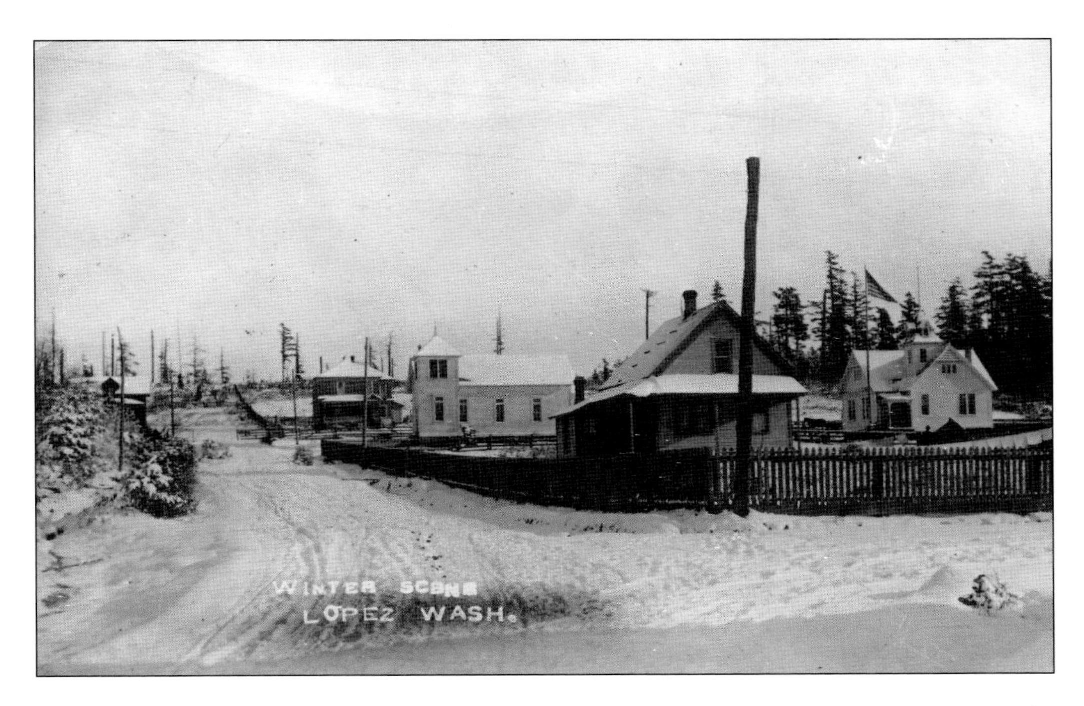

These juxtaposed photographs of Lopez Village show development before and after about 1904. The winter scene above was taken before 1904 because the Lopez Congregational Church, completed in 1905, is not in the photograph. The scene looks east with the Methodist church, its parsonage, and Lopez School (later relocated) covered with snow. The photograph below, called a "Bird's Eye View of Lopez after 1904," looks toward the sound. It identifies, from left to right, horse stalls for people attending the Lopez Congregational Church, Lopez School (built about 1894), Lopez Congregational Church, Oscar Weeks's home, the Methodist parsonage, Lopez Methodist Church (built about 1889), and the home and outbuildings of J. A. Paine (built about 1901).

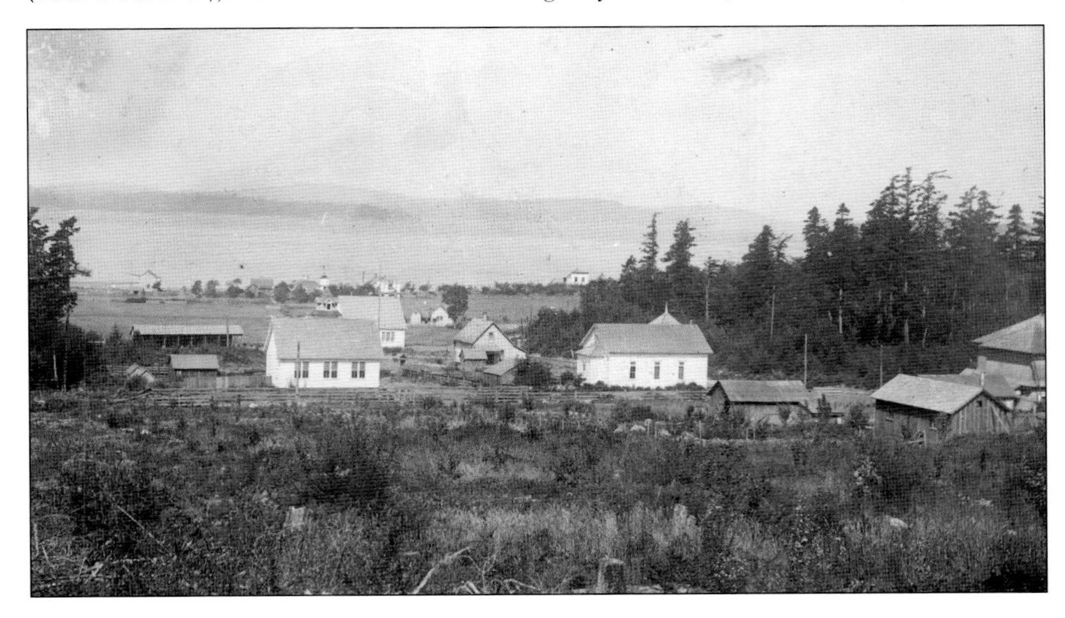

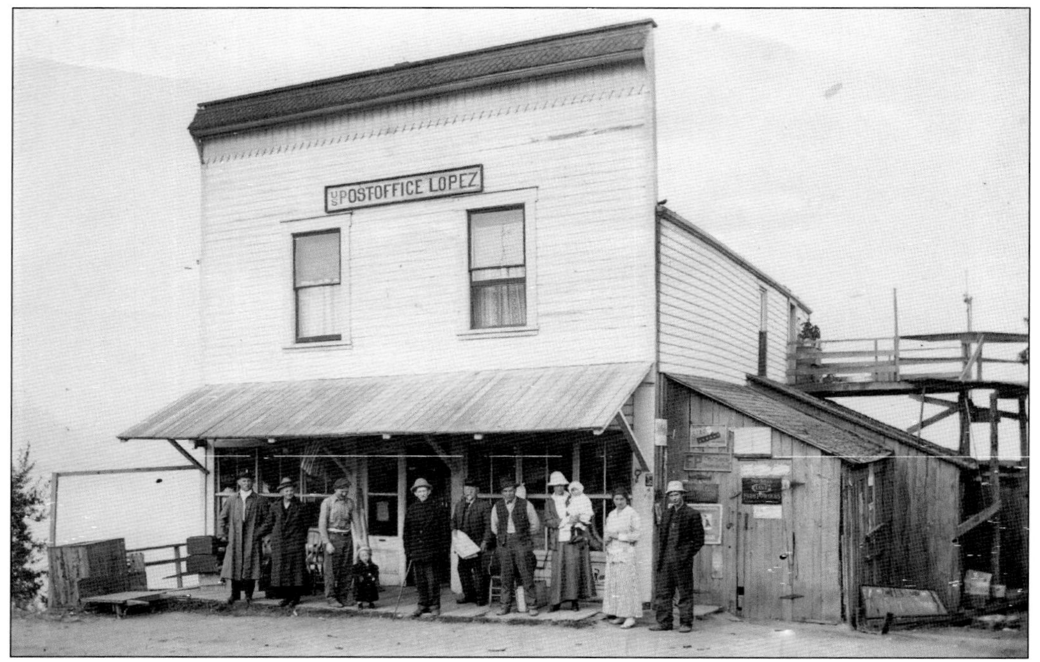

Lopez historian Gertrude Boede identified this photograph as the Lopez store at the time it was run by C. T. Butler. Butler came to Lopez in 1891, and in 1901, he owned the store, warehouse, and wharf in the village. In 1898, he was appointed postmaster. The store burned in a mysterious fire about 1923, and a new building, which has served as a store, tavern, sewing shop, and restaurant, replaced it.

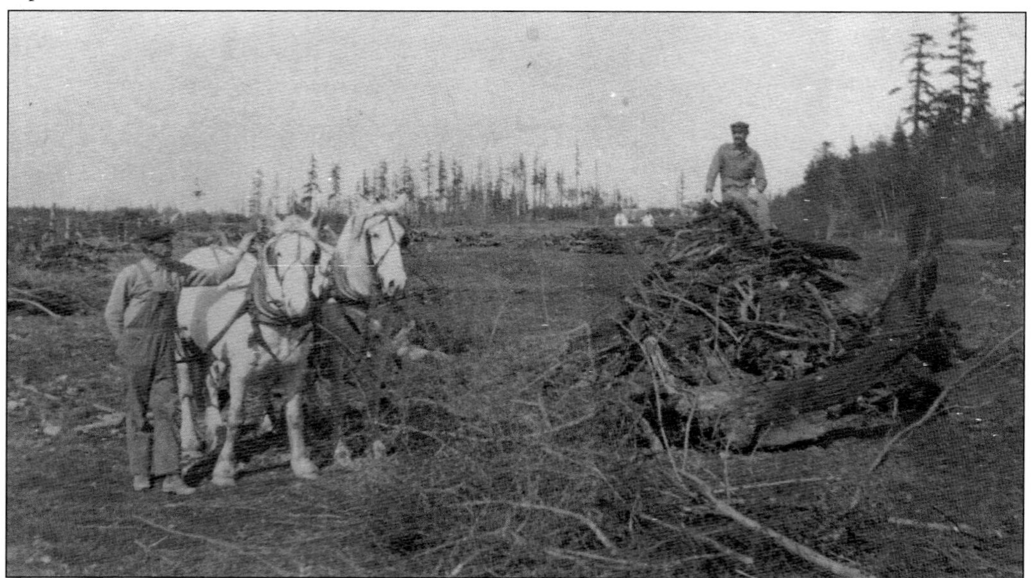

In this 1913 photograph, Oscar Weeks holds horses Grace and Betsy while clearing land in Lopez Village. His brother Bert sits on the slash pile. The Lopez Island Medical Clinic now stands near this site. Oscar and Bert were sons of Lyman and Irene Weeks. Oscar, Bert, and their older brother, Edson, built the three water towers still standing in the village.

Albert Dill, a bachelor, sits at his house located on what is now known as Dill Road. His aunt came to see how he was getting along, was not pleased by his bachelor housekeeping, and decided to stay. Marguerite Goodrow said that her parents, Jim and Barbara McCauley, rented the Dill house when they first came to the island. The Dill house was later moved to Fisherman Bay Peninsula for restoration.

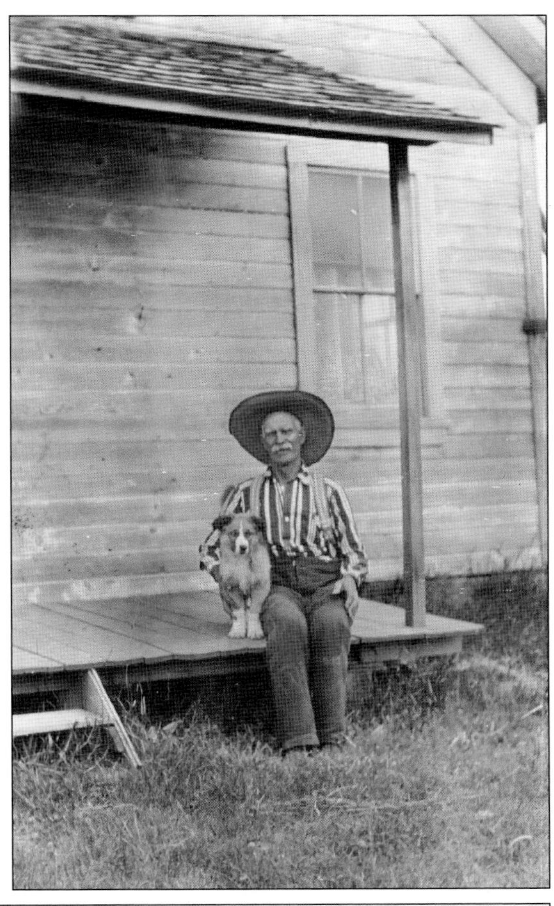

Uncertainty exists as to the date of this Lopez Village street scene, but descendent Duane Weeks believes it is from about 1916. Identified from left to right are Lincoln Weeks (carrying a shotgun), Irwin Blake (on a bicycle), C. A. Kent and wife (in the buggy), and George Hastin Sr. (on the sidewalk). The man standing in the street is possibly Guy Kent. The old blacksmith shop on the left was run by Jack Larson.

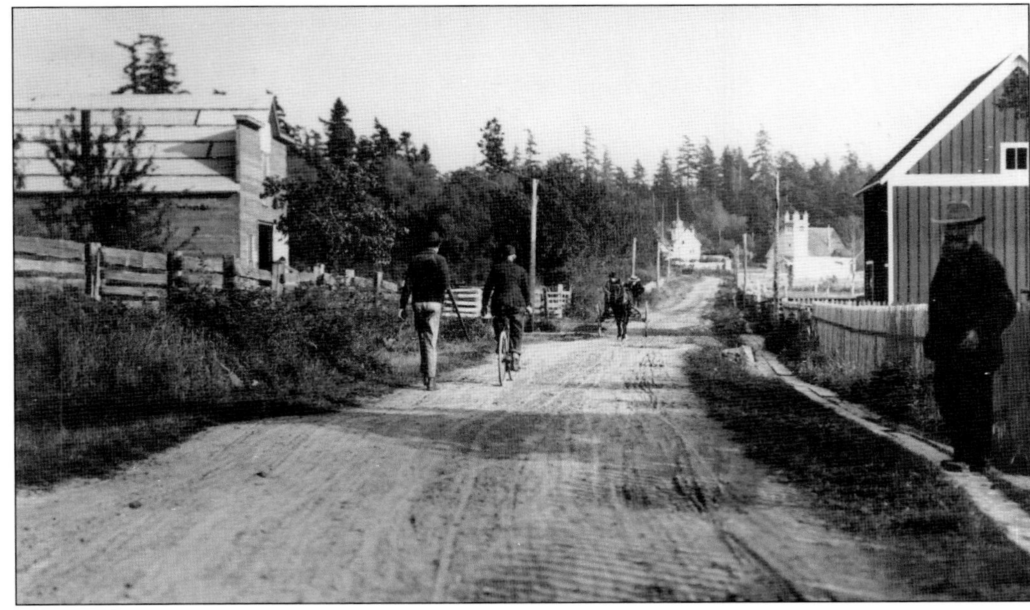

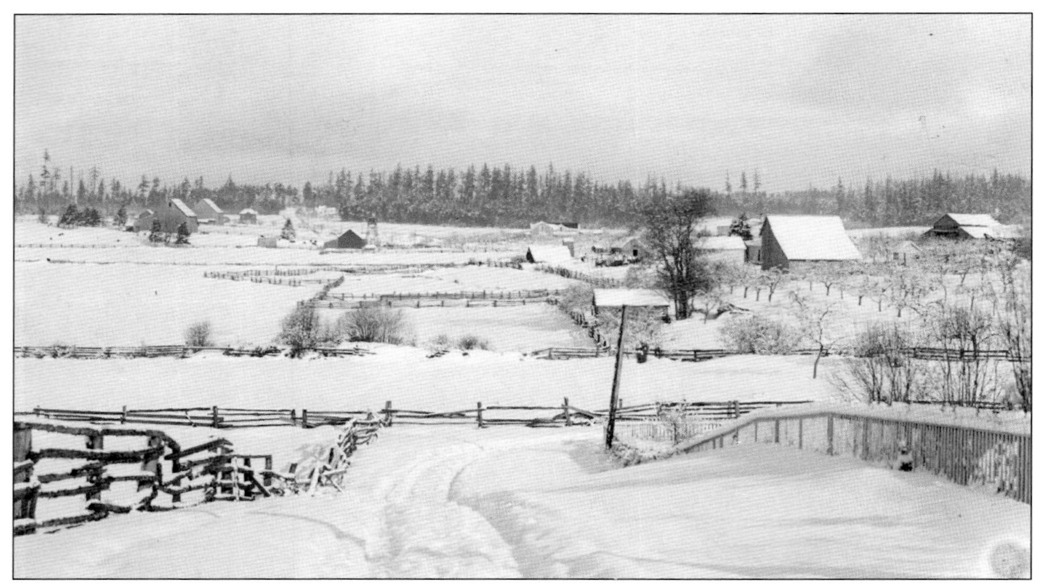

This photograph shows the big snowstorm of 1916 blanketing the island's Center Valley, looking north from Center Church. Beryl Mason recalled schools closed for 10 days, and "Grownups collapsed from fatigue and slept hard and long for several days when it was over." They broke trails through 4-foot drifts to reach animals and fed them warm mash to keep them alive.

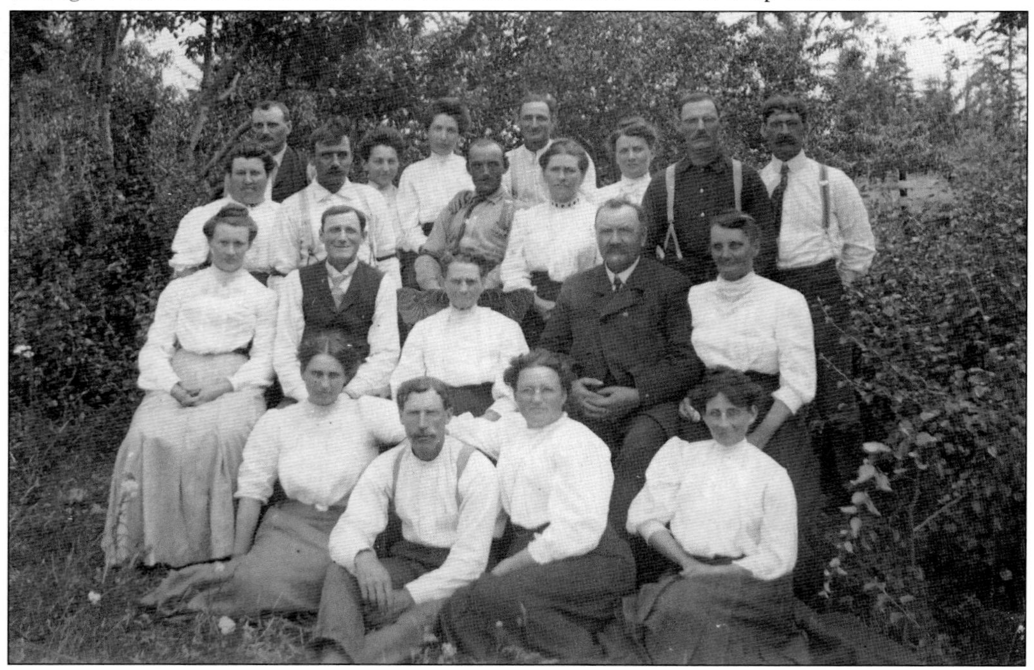

Grandmother Anne Gallanger (in the rocker) is surrounded by her family. Pictured are (first row) Hattie and Bert Whalen, Jessie Sharp and Mary Trescott (sisters of Will Gallanger); (second row) Susie and Joe Gallanger, Anne Gallanger, Sam and Liza Wilson; (third row) Lena and John Wilson, Norman Wilson, Anna and Will Gallanger; (fourth row) Ed Wilson, Gladys Wilson, Sarah and George Gallanger Sr., and Agnes and Joe Thornton.

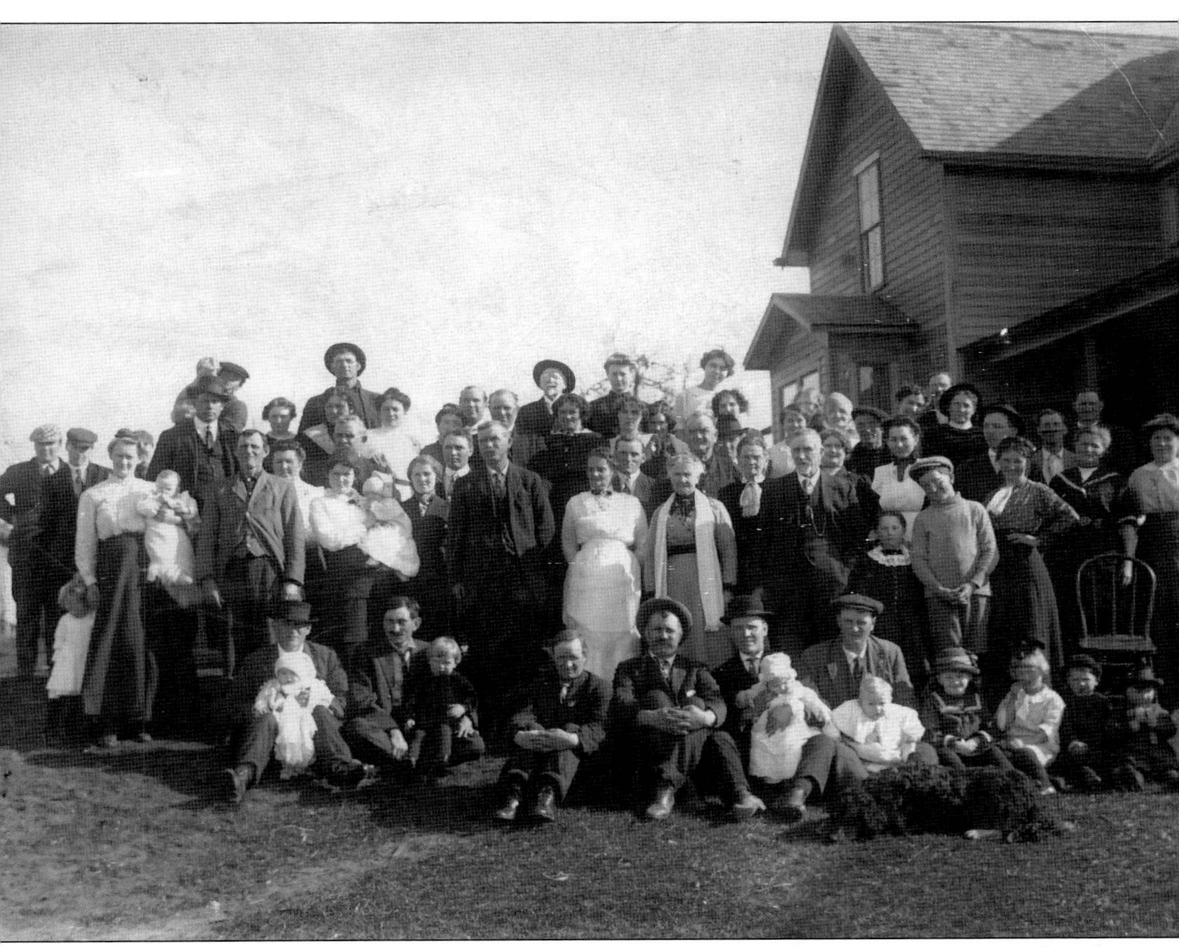

Pausing to be photographed during a joyful birthday celebration, the large group gives some idea of island families' interconnectedness. This 1913 photograph identifies 58 people, whose last names include Wilson, Graham, Walrod, Thornton, Gallanger, Buchanan, Butler, Bolton, Stedelin, Weeks, White, Krieg, Whalen, Burt, and Towell. The occasion marked Grandmother Anne Gallanger's 72nd birthday and that of Sam Graham's brother who was visiting from Michigan.

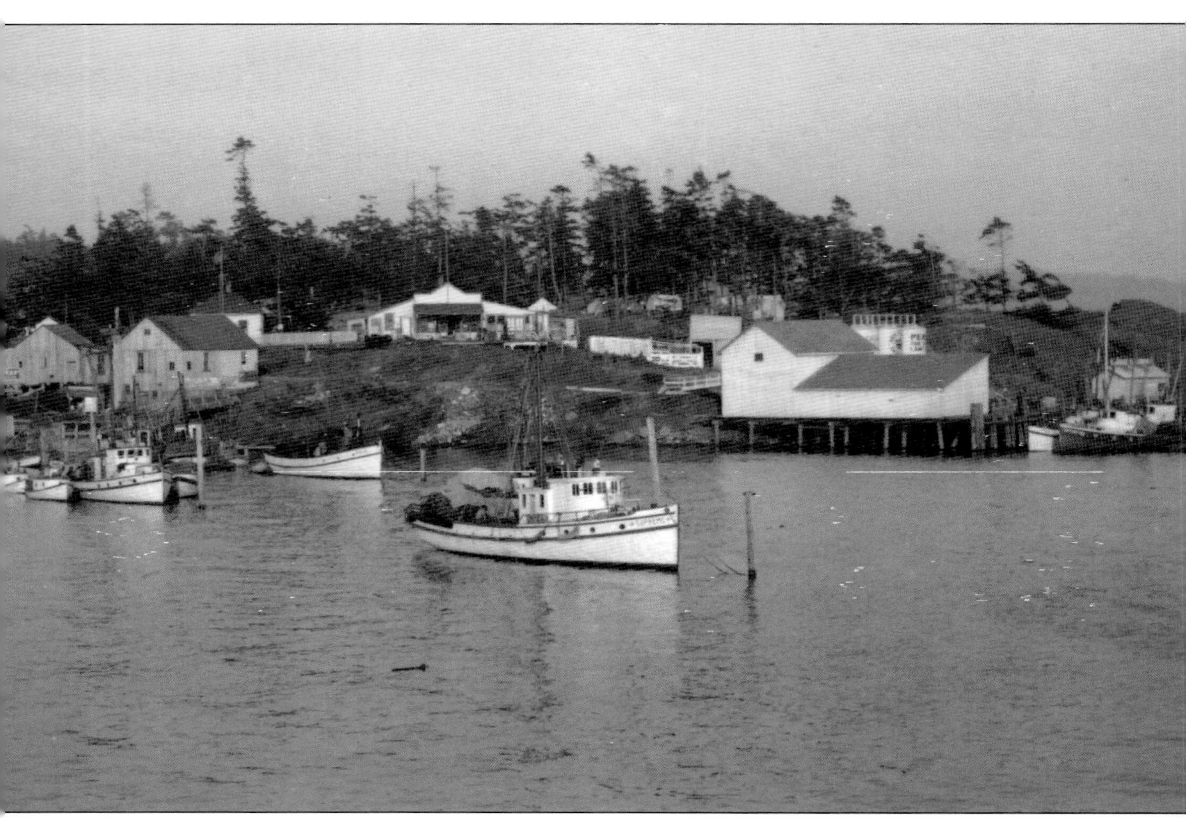

This Richardson postcard captured the hamlet in its heyday. Seen from left to right are the pool hall and bakery, Hodgson barns, N. P. Hodgson family house, Hodgson-Graham store, chicken house, slaughterhouse, warehouse, gas tanks, and oil house. The fishing boat *Supreme*, owned by someone named Hansen, is in the bay, and two others are tied up to floats. The postcard was addressed to Stella Blake.

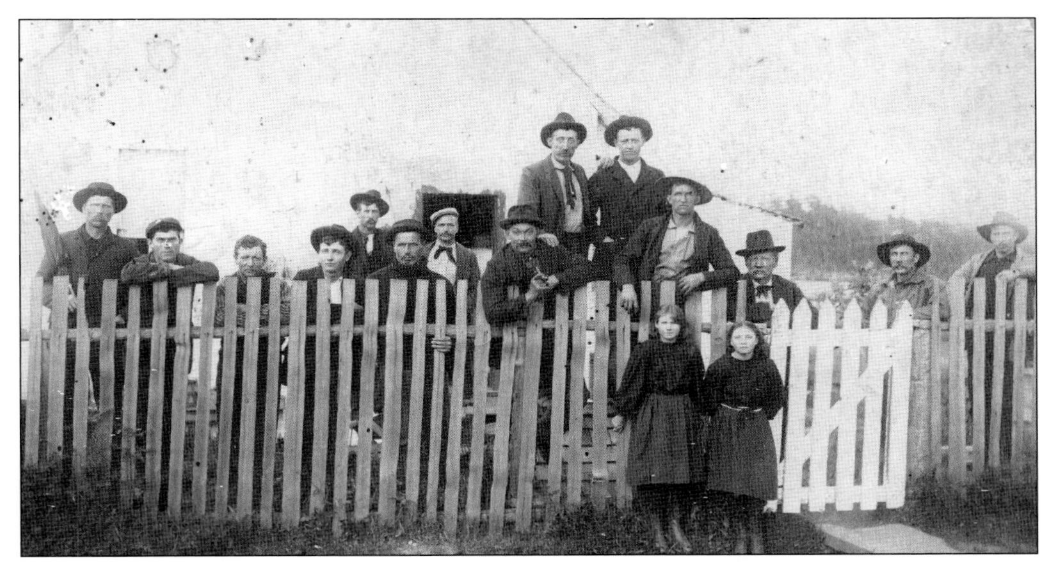

The back of this photograph is captioned, "Boarders, Richardson." Taken about 1897, the men behind the picket fence are identified, from left to right, as James Buchanan, unidentified, John Standley, Frank Brown, Emmet Ruger, Nick Davidson, Al Biggs, Sam Barlow, unidentified, unidentified, John Lanterman, Pete Landon, Erv Eaton, and Bat Clancy. The girls in front are Lulu (left) and Cora Standley.

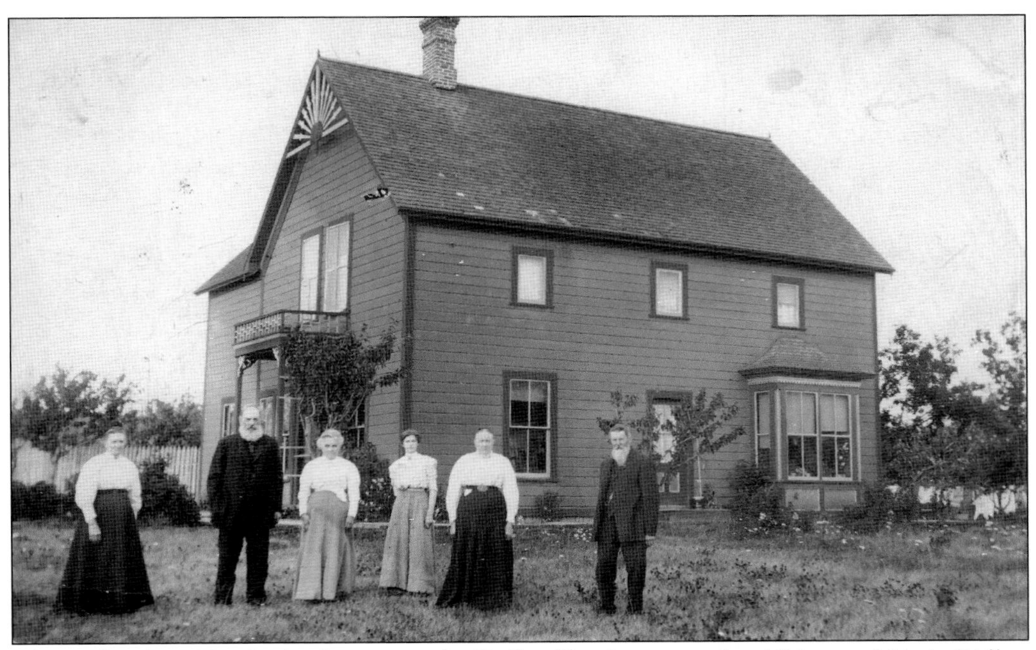

The Richardson Hotel, also known as the Ridley Hotel, was run by Albion and Lizzie Ridley. Lizzie was the sister of Annie Humphrey and William and Thomas Graham. Standing in front of the hotel from left to right are Lizzie, Albion, and two cousins from Iowa, Annie Humphrey and her husband, William Humphrey. The hotel was built in 1890 by Hamilton Carr and sold to the Ridleys in 1902.

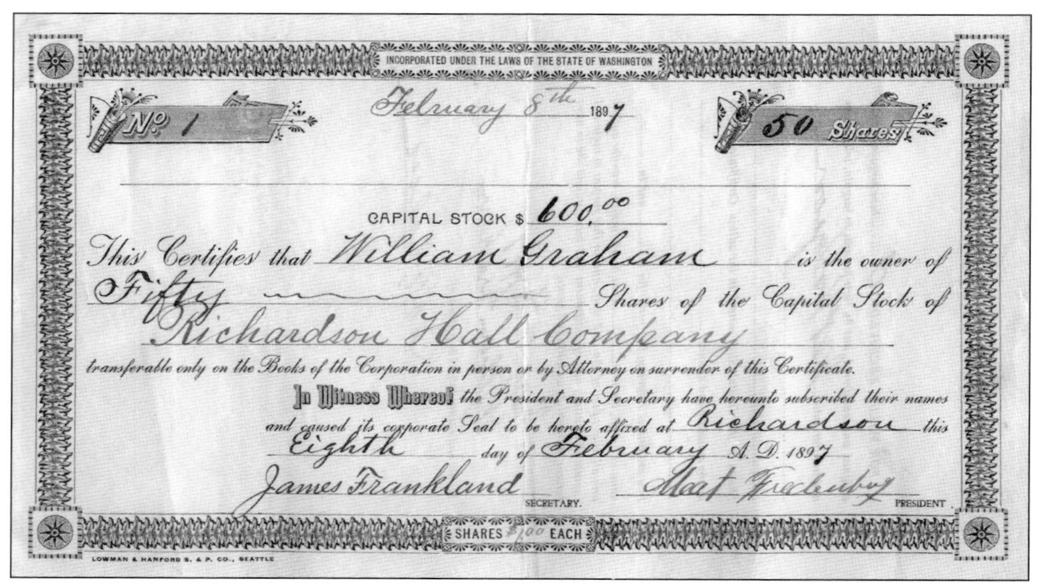

INCORPORATED UNDER THE LAWS OF THE STATE OF WASHINGTON

No. 1 — February 8th 1897 — 50 Shares

CAPITAL STOCK $ 600.00

This Certifies that William Graham is the owner of Fifty Shares of the Capital Stock of Richardson Hall Company transferable only on the Books of the Corporation in person or by Attorney on surrender of this Certificate.

In Witness Whereof the President and Secretary have hereunto subscribed their names and caused its corporate Seal to be hereto affixed at Richardson this Eighth day of February A. D. 1897

James Frankland, SECRETARY. [illegible], PRESIDENT

SHARES $100 EACH

LOWMAN & HANFORD S. & P. CO., SEATTLE

In January 1897, the community at Richardson decided to build a hall and pooled its resources, combining money raised by stock subscription and donated materials and labor. The two-story structure was built in a month. On February 4, most of the island's population and people from surrounding islands attended the first supper and dance. Later used as a school and for church services, the hall still stands at Richardson.

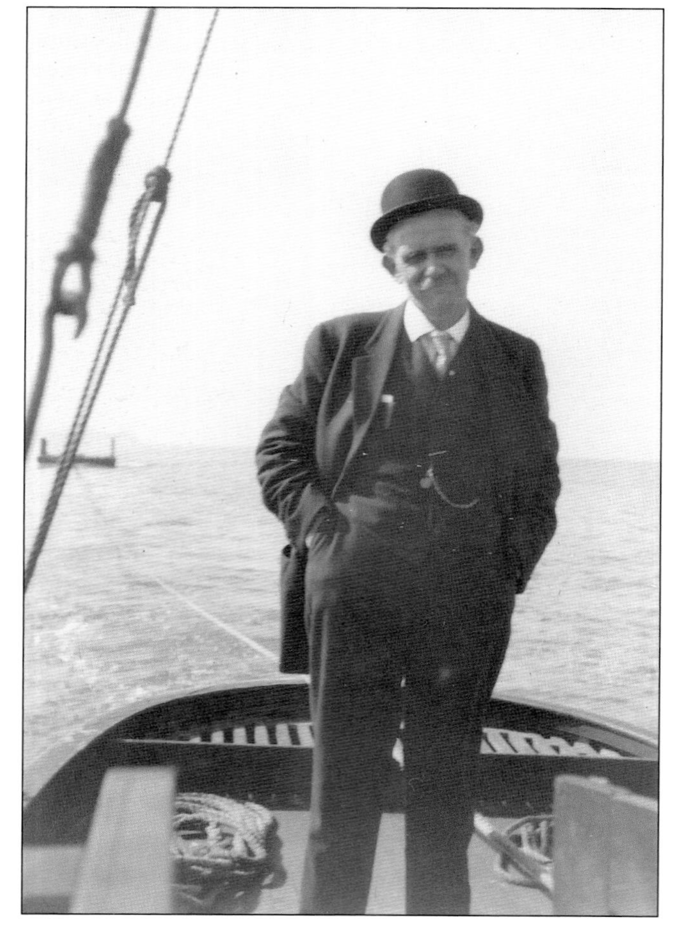

Norman Peter Hodgson, known as "N. P.," was born in Ontario, Canada, and came from Estherville, Ohio, to Lopez about 1878 with his mother, Mary Wilson; stepfather, William Graham; and brother Thomas Pearson Hodgson, known as "T. P." After Graham bought the Richardson store about 1899, N. P. ran it, while T. P. served as postmaster. N. P. married Charlotte (Lottie) Schmaling in 1895, and they had three children, Gertrude, Rita, and Norman William.

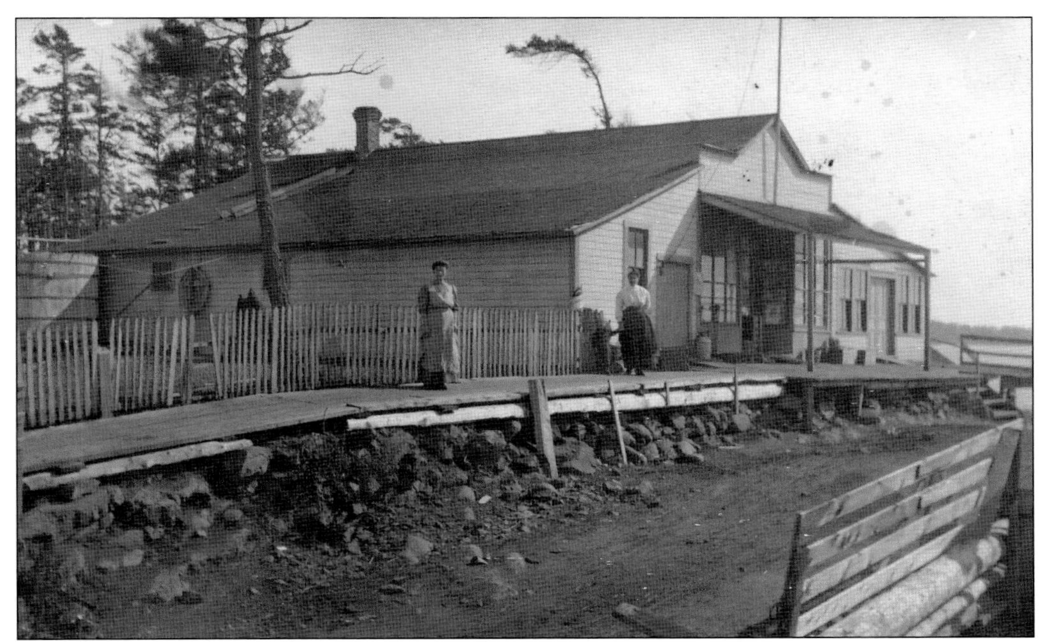

A 1901 supplement to the *San Juan Islander* described Richardson store as carrying "a well-assorted stock of dry goods and notions, boots and shoes, ladies' and gents' furnishings, tin ware, glassware . . . fancy and staple groceries . . . flour, food, fruit, candles, tobacco, cigars . . . and all goods of a general nature." Identified in this *c.* 1909 photograph, from left to right, are Bertha Benson (N. P. Hodgson's "hired girl"), young Norman W. Hodgson (holding hand), and Lottie Hodgson.

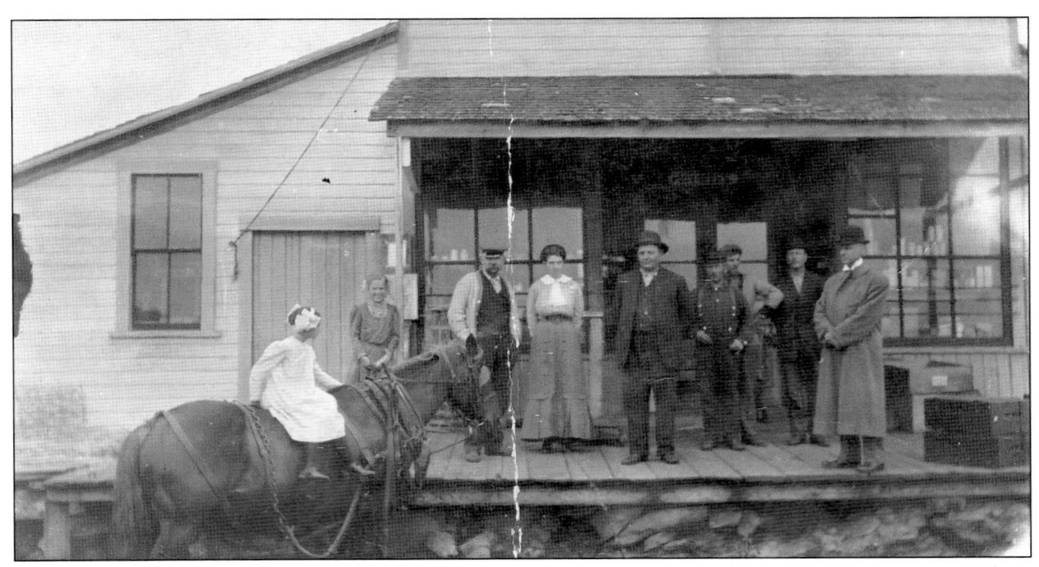

This postcard of the "Old Richardson Store" depicts, from left to right, Gertrude Hodgson riding William Graham's horse Maggie, Rita Hodgson, N. P. Hodgson, and Isobel Cousins. The men to Cousins's right are unidentified, except the one on the far right might be a "drummer," or salesman. Gertrude Hodgson, later known as Gertrude Boede, collected and annotated many historical Lopez photographs. Her father traded store keeping for dairying in 1916.

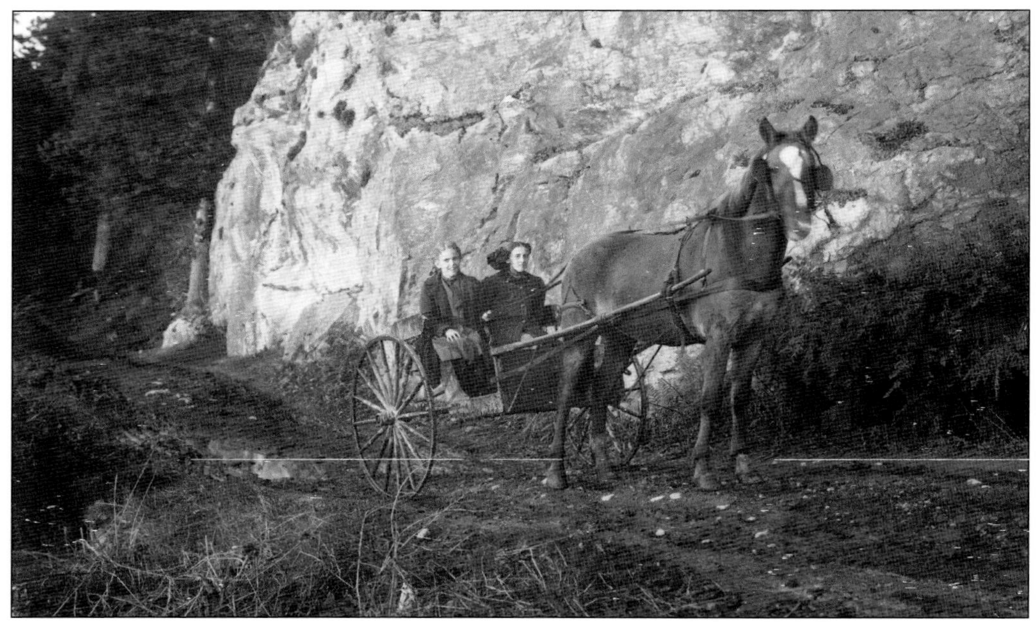

These photographs capture Hodgson and Graham family members with Prince, the Hodgson's horse. Above, Gertrude and Rita Hodgson are driving Prince to Center School (later the Grange Hall) on Richardson Road between 1909 and 1912. Gertrude remembered she and her sister rode Prince bareback to school until their father got them the cart. The photograph below shows Willie Graham, son of William and Mary Graham, holding Prince, as Gertrude and Rita's younger brother Norman William Hodgson sits on his back. When he grew up, Norman married Anna Bergman of Friday Harbor.

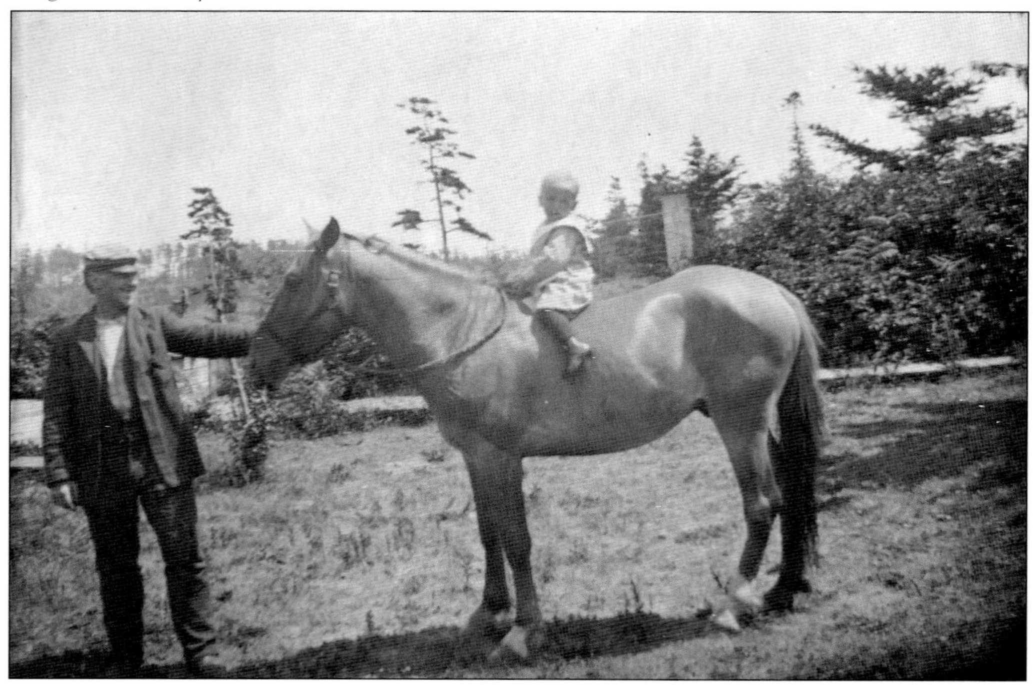

The Lopez Improvement Company of Seattle divided 750 acres at Islandale into quarter-acre lots to sell for $50 each, with $5 down and $5 payments each month, anticipating a land boom. A 1908 *Everett Morning Tribune* article noted, "Many well known people in all parts of Washington have bought tracks to take advantage of Islandale's cool summers and ocean breezes." In reality, the boom failed to materialize.

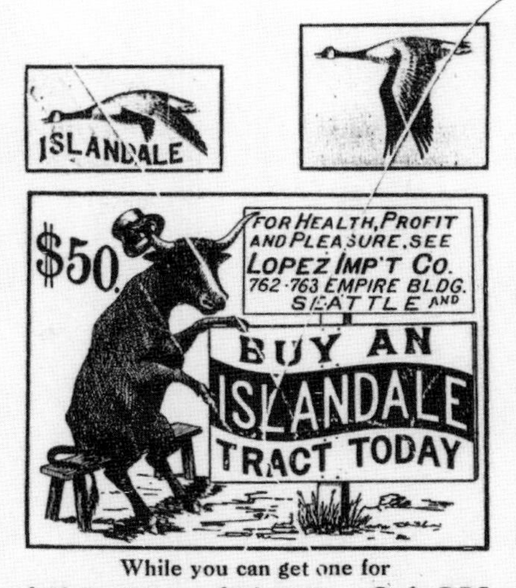

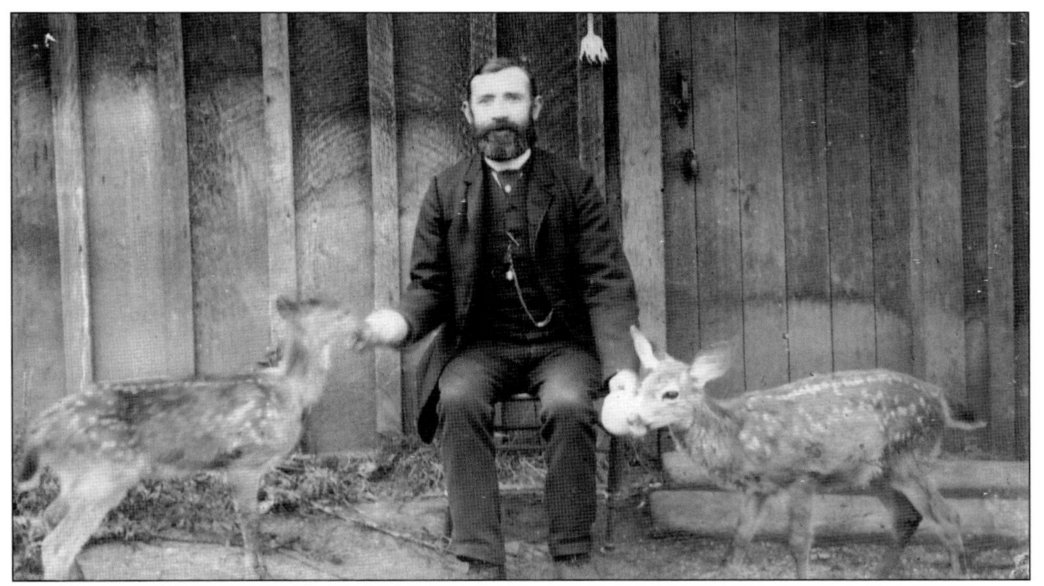

Capt. John Edwards moved to Lopez in 1889, and according to Willie Cousins, he was an old sea pilot who owned the Wood farm at Mud Bay. Edwards died about 1894. A 1964 article says "Cap" Edwards willed land to George Hess, who established a post office and store there. The Mud Bay Post Office was named Edwards, but its name was changed to Otis after confusion with Edmonds.

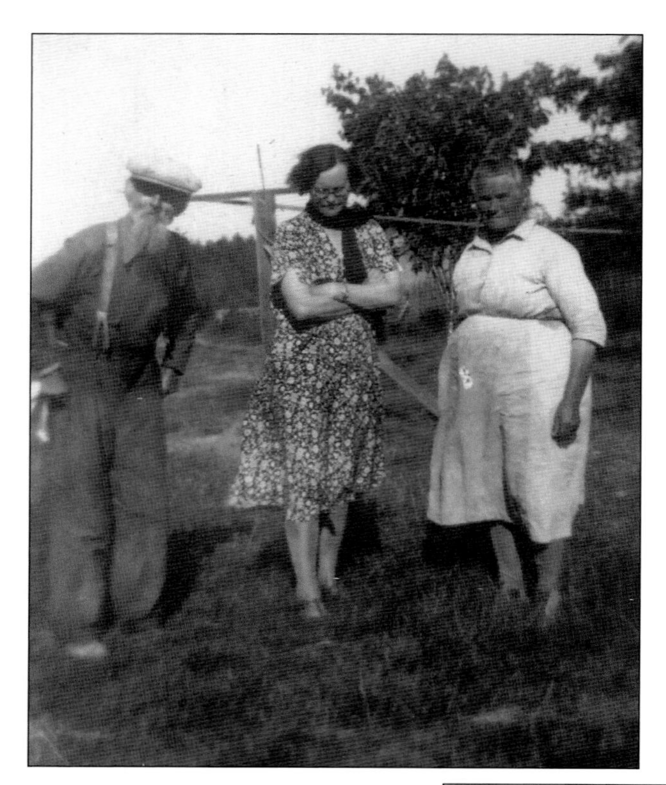

Michael and Dorothea Norman, seen at far left and far right, moved to Lopez about 1889. The Normans came from Norway, changing their name from Jorgenson to Norman. Their son Arthur skippered the fish tender *Fenwick*, and father and son built boats, including the *Peggy Sue* and *Silver Fin*. Arthur married Violet Vogt, who came to Lopez in 1909 to visit her uncle Willie Weir at the Gourley Camp, a religious community.

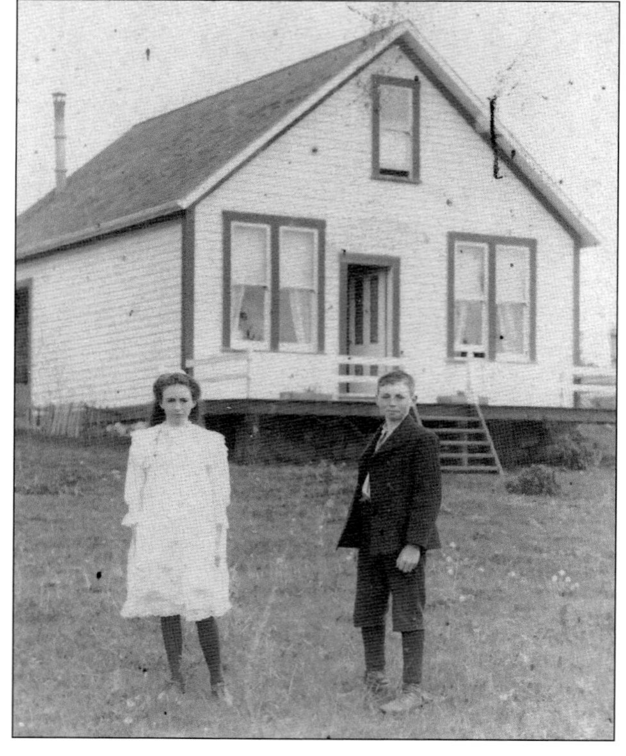

James Higgins came west in 1884 from Holyhead, North Wales, where he worked as a locomotive engineer. In 1891, he married Emma Thomas and moved to Lopez in 1894, settling near Richardson. They had two children, Mary and Owen, shown here. Owen married Eva Weir, whose family came to Lopez about 1917. Community-minded, Eva was described as a person who "gave so freely just for the love of giving."

Philip Fagerholm was born in the Åland Islands in Finland and came to the United States in 1887. He sent for his future bride, Maria Bergman, and they married in 1891. Charles Anderson may have sponsored Fagerholm to come to Lopez. The Fagerholms had five children, Julius, Edwin, Amoe, Jennie, and Albert (not pictured). They homesteaded 160 acres on Cole Road, raising livestock, hay, produce, and amazing strawberries.

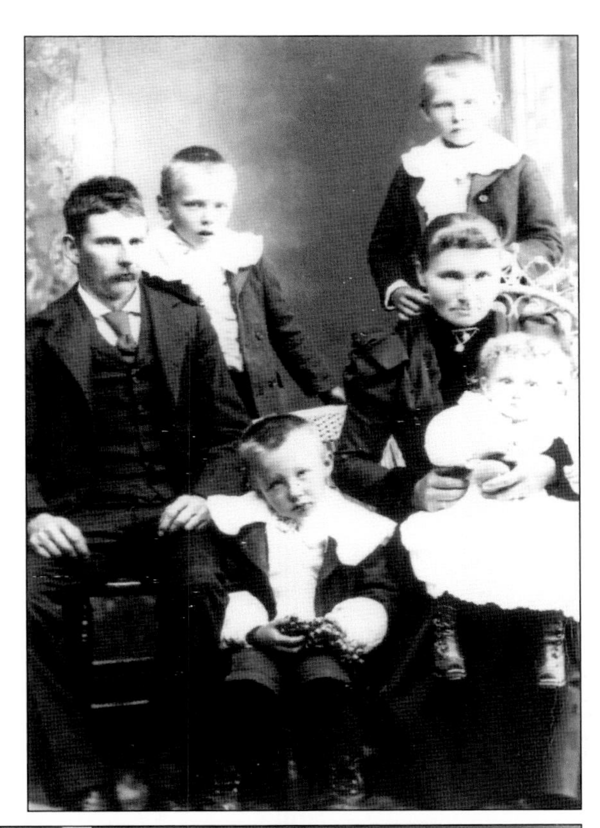

John Troxell, pictured here with his wife, Eunice Davis, was the son of Franklin and Katurah Troxell. John was born in Texas before the family moved west, settling on Lopez in 1885 on land near Spencer Spit. John was a well-known "fish trap man," who started working in the industry at age 17 and went on to locate, own, and operate fish traps until they were outlawed in 1934.

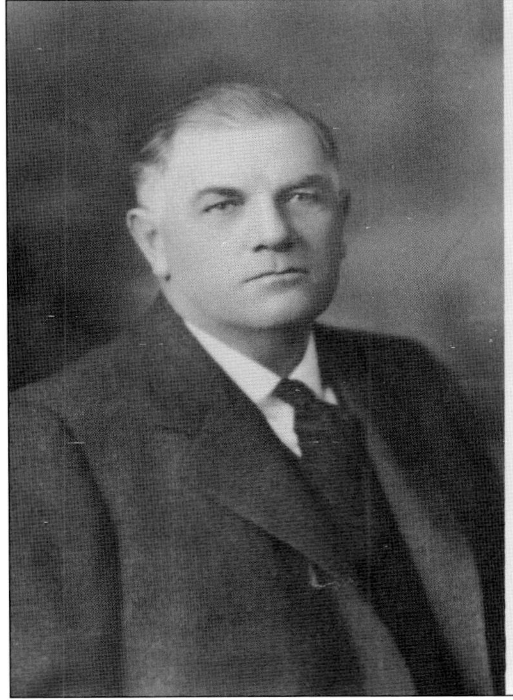

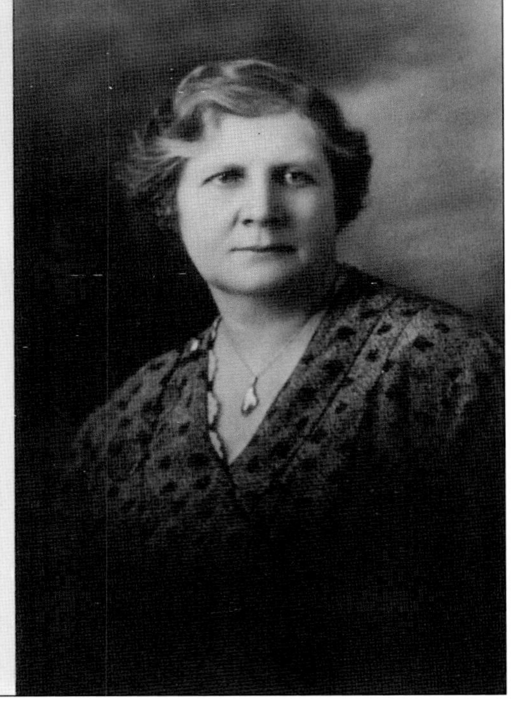

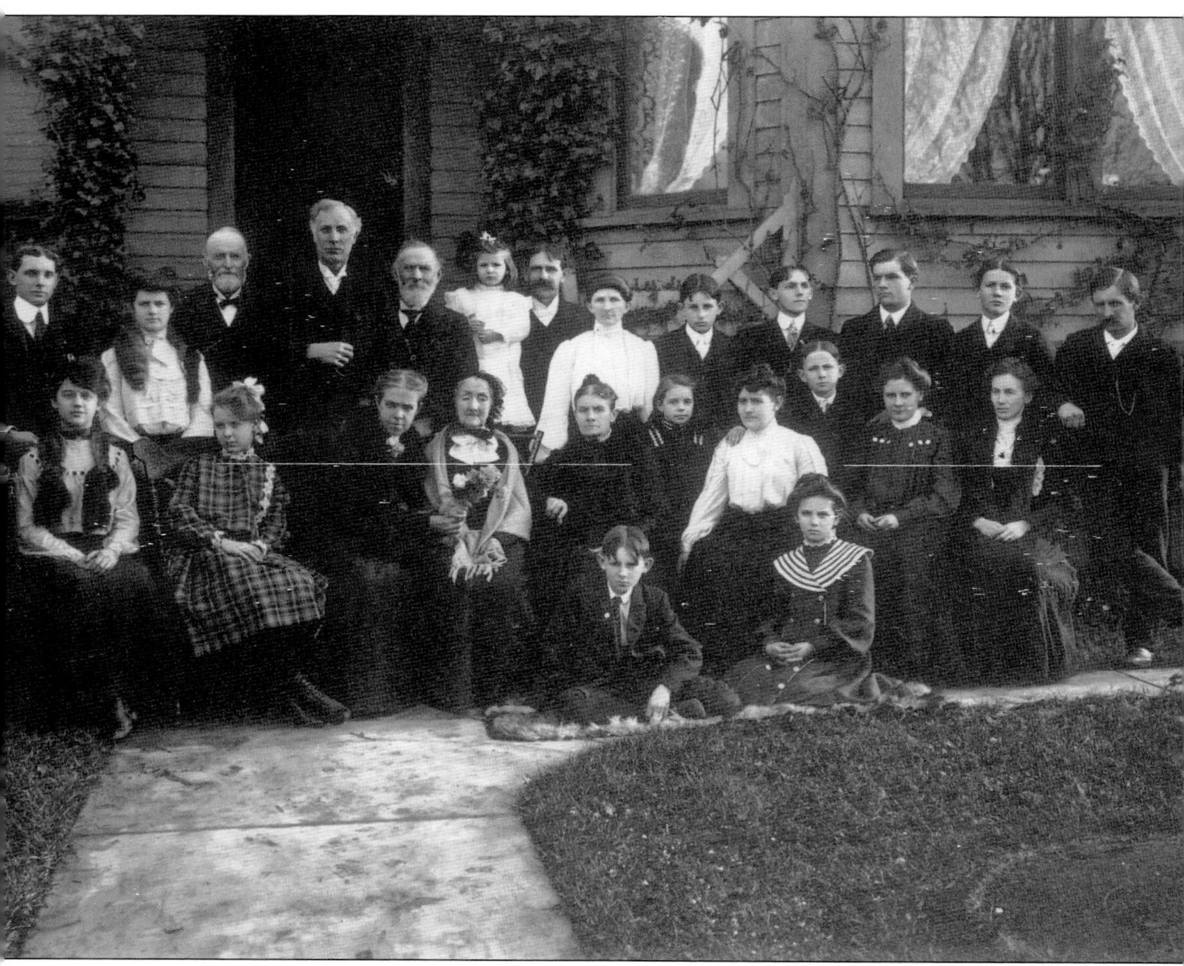

The Barnum, Davis, Tudor, Randles, Boynton, Middleton, and Troxell families are celebrating the 100th birthday of Grandma Eva Barnum in 1904 in Victoria, British Columbia. Large families were commonplace. Eva Barnum was the mother of eight children. Her daughter Navereign married James Leonard Davis and had a son, Rowland. After Navereign died in 1863, Davis married her sister Amelia Culver Barnum (first row, fifth from left), and they had 10 children. Four died young.

Three

Neighbors, Friends, and Community

Whether due to the nature of islands themselves, the remoteness of rural locations, or an inexplicable special community character, from its inception, Lopez Island's culture cultivated compassion and a community-minded spirit that endures today.

The catalyst that brings the Lopez community together often starts with a perceived need or an idea about how to improve island life. From those sparks, great things have come. People donated property, services, labor, and materials to build schools, churches, a library, a parsonage, a museum, the Richardson Community Hall, Woodmen Hall, a medical clinic, and more recently a community center and cooperative preschool.

Lopezians organized socials, wrote cookbooks, issued stock subscriptions, and created a birthday club to raise money for community projects or people who needed help. They made quilts and named halls to honor those among them who had contributed to community life or sacrificed for the betterment of all. They fought fires together and then rebuilt together.

They had fun, played baseball, played instruments, danced upstairs at John Wilson's blacksmith shop, and held midnight potlucks and wedding parties called chivarees.

An old-timer once remarked that even though Lopezians may seem a bit different from one another on the surface, all chose to make Lopez home, so they really must have a lot in common at heart.

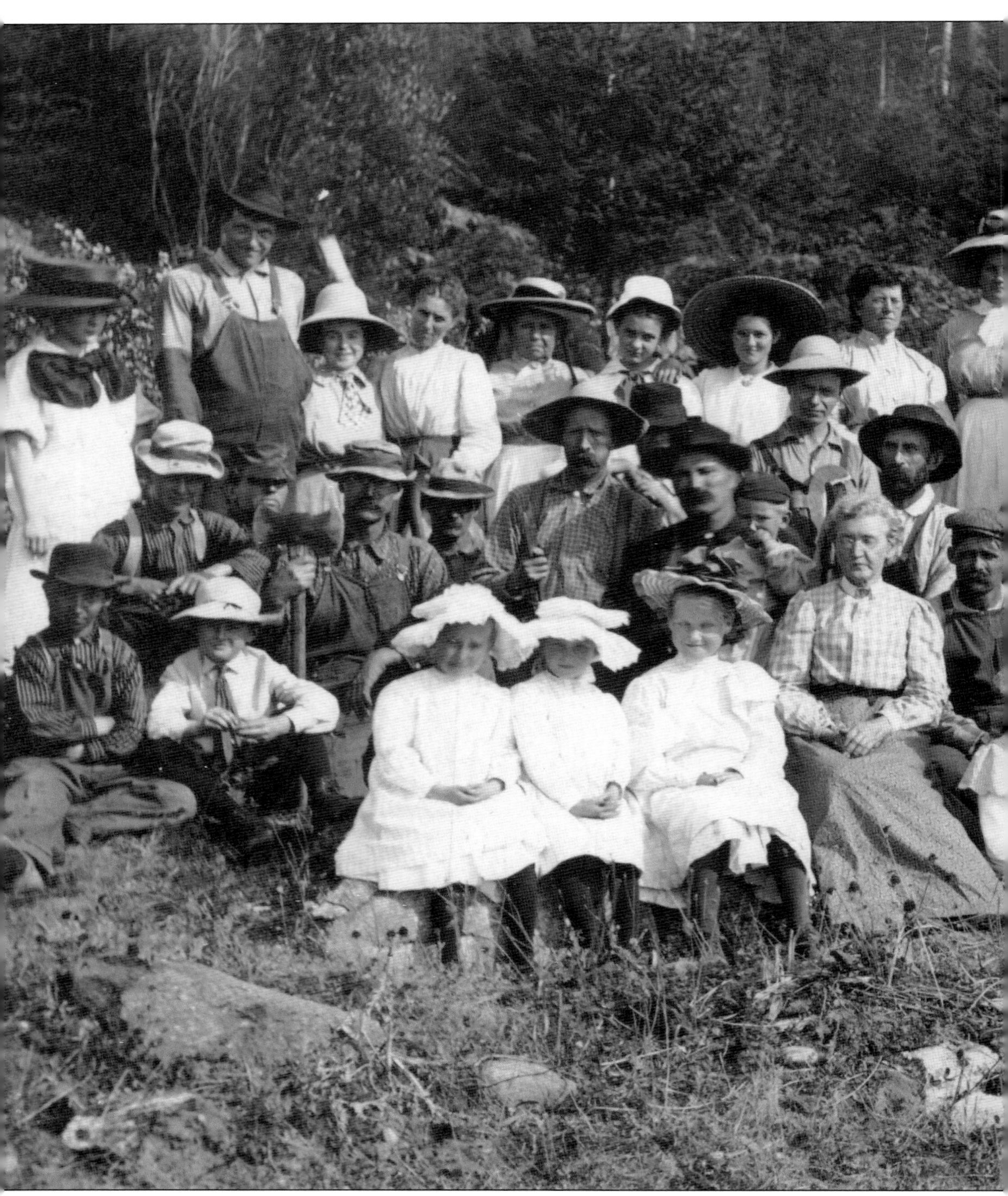

Knowing that many hands make light work, families, friends, and neighbors gathered at the Pierce's on Fisherman Bay Road for a work bee to slash, or clear land. A 1901 newspaper article mentions the bee and reported Fred Bolton bruised and sprained a leg after a log rolled on it. Work bees for sewing, harvesting, barn raising, and clearing helped establish the community

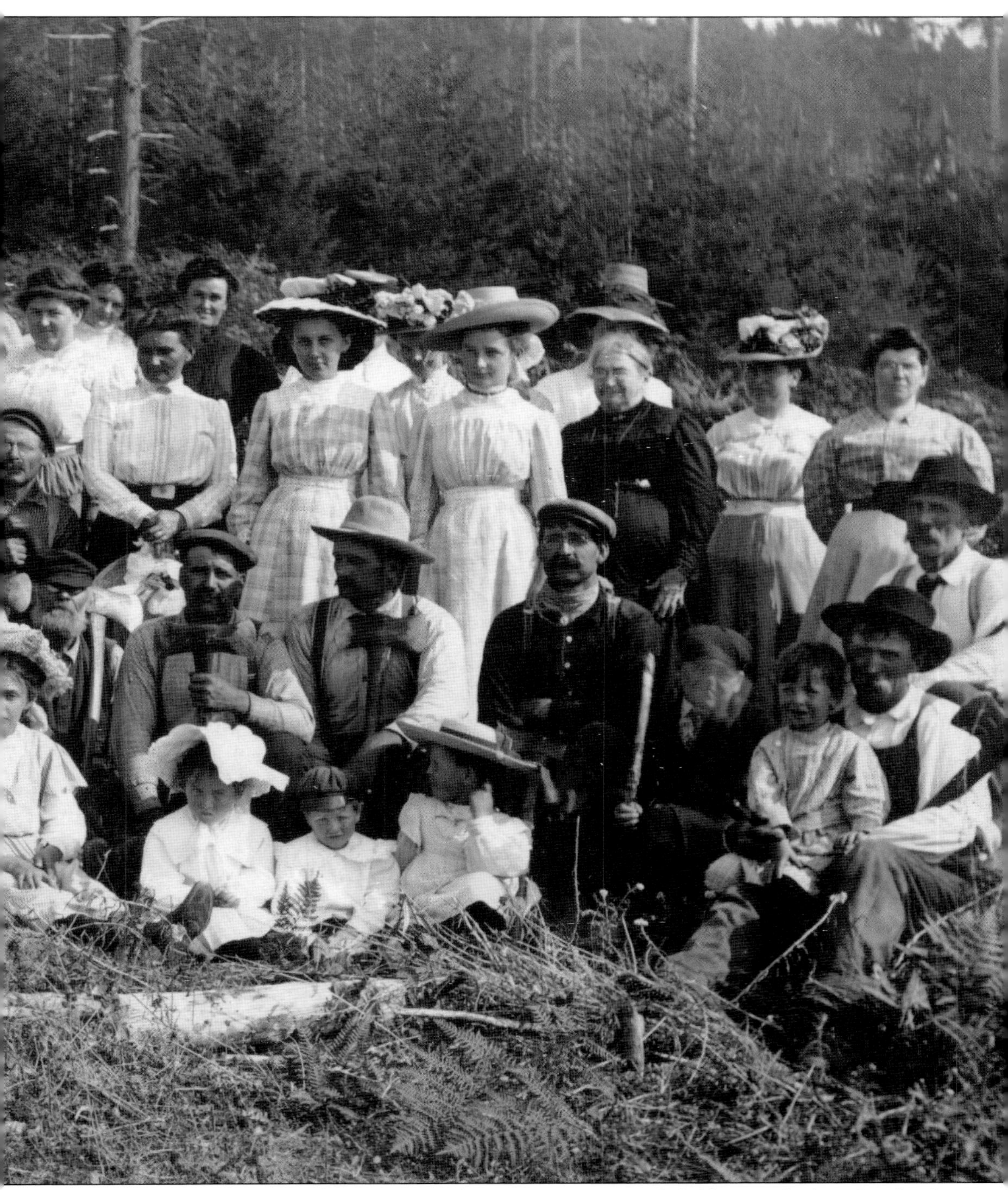

tradition of tackling difficult projects together. Men, women, and children worked to clear land on Fisherman Bay Road, described as "where Washington House used to have their office" and "where later Mrs. Pickering had a telephone office." Ellen Pierce sits in the center. An old-timer commented, "Pity we couldn't have a picture of the food that was served!"

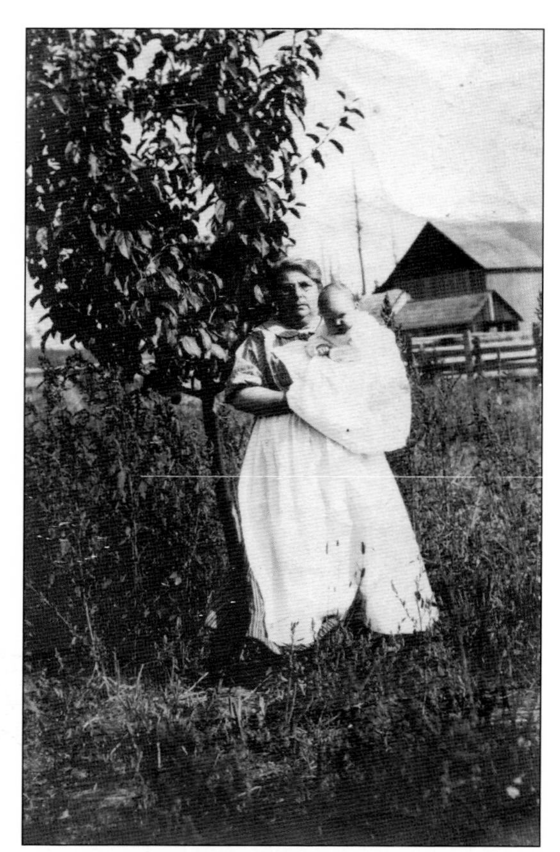

Geneva Roberts was a midwife who delivered Thelma Wilson on September 25, 1905. Obtaining medical care on the island was difficult. James Leonard Davis completed two years of medical school and served as a doctor to help ailing neighbors. Later Dr. U. C. Bates boated over from Charles Island (then known as Bates Island) to provide care. Incorporated in 1971, the Catherine Washburn Memorial Association created, owns, and operates the Lopez Island Medical Clinic.

After the Lopez Village School closed, the building housed a restaurant and later the Lopez Island Fire Department. Marguerite Goodrow recalls that in the old days, everyone responded to fight fires together. In 1976, the department built a new station next door, and the school was converted to library use and moved. The department now has four stations on the island, providing both fire and emergency medical services.

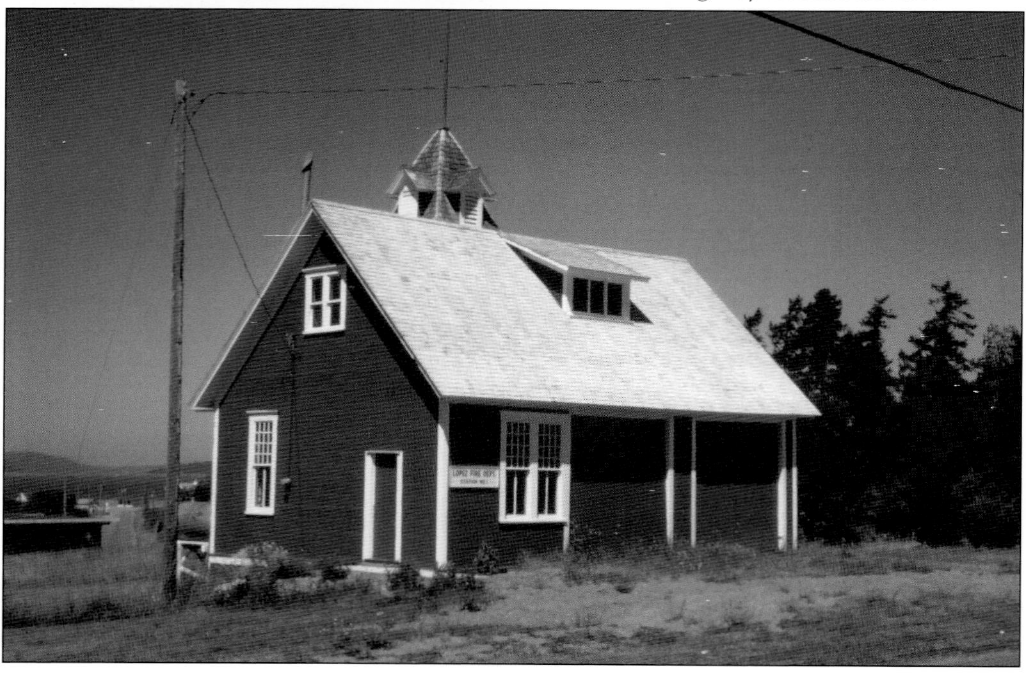

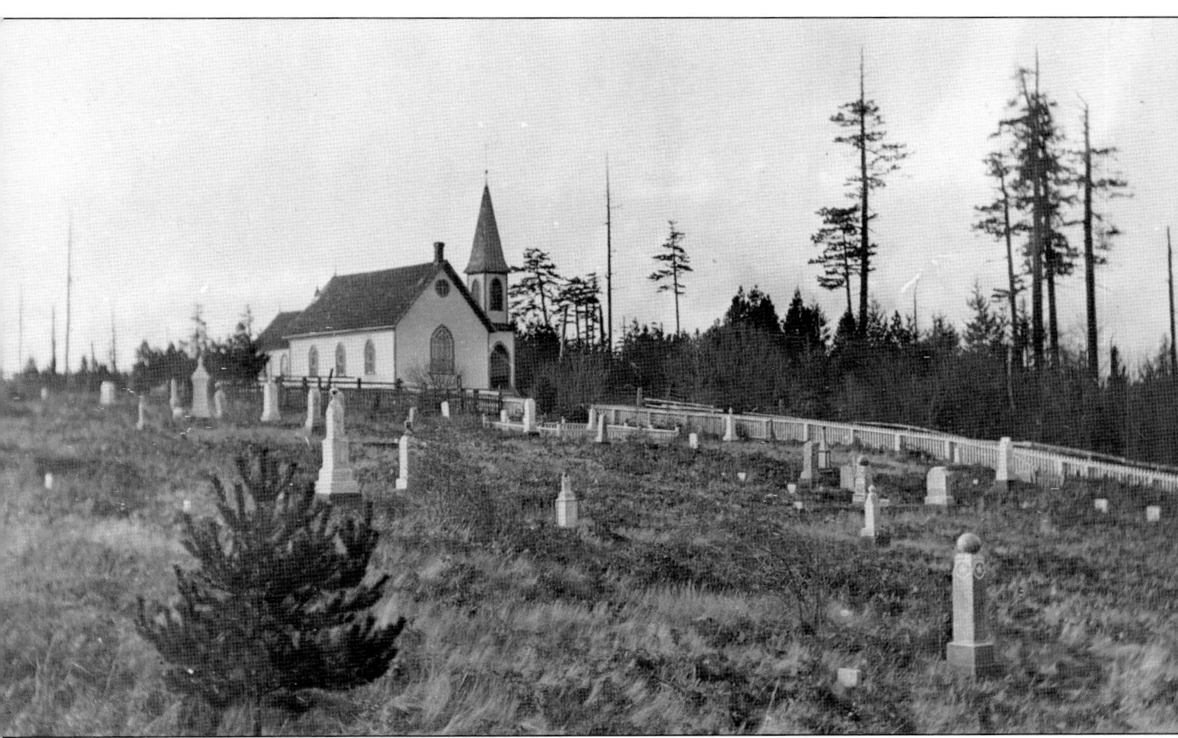

Beloved Center Church was built by volunteers over two years starting in 1887 on land donated by the W. T. Graham family. William Graham and James Cousins Sr. built the foundation; Dan Barlow brought lumber on the *Henrietta*, which was owned by his father, Arthur "Billy" Barlow; and James Buchanan and Charles Kent built the structure. William Lampard plastered, and Carl Cary and his son Harry painted. A parsonage was built at Richardson in 1903, but ministers did not last long. The parsonage was later sold during the Depression for $123. A favorite 1930s minister was Rev. W. W. Goodrow. People said when Goodrow married a couple, they stayed married. By the 1940s, services were held in the village, and Center Church fell into disrepair. In 1965, the Lopez Cemetery Association acquired the church, and in the 1980s, Nicki Giard and Barbara Pickering created the *Lopez Island Cookbook* to support restoration. Today the church again serves the community for services, weddings, funerals, and other events.

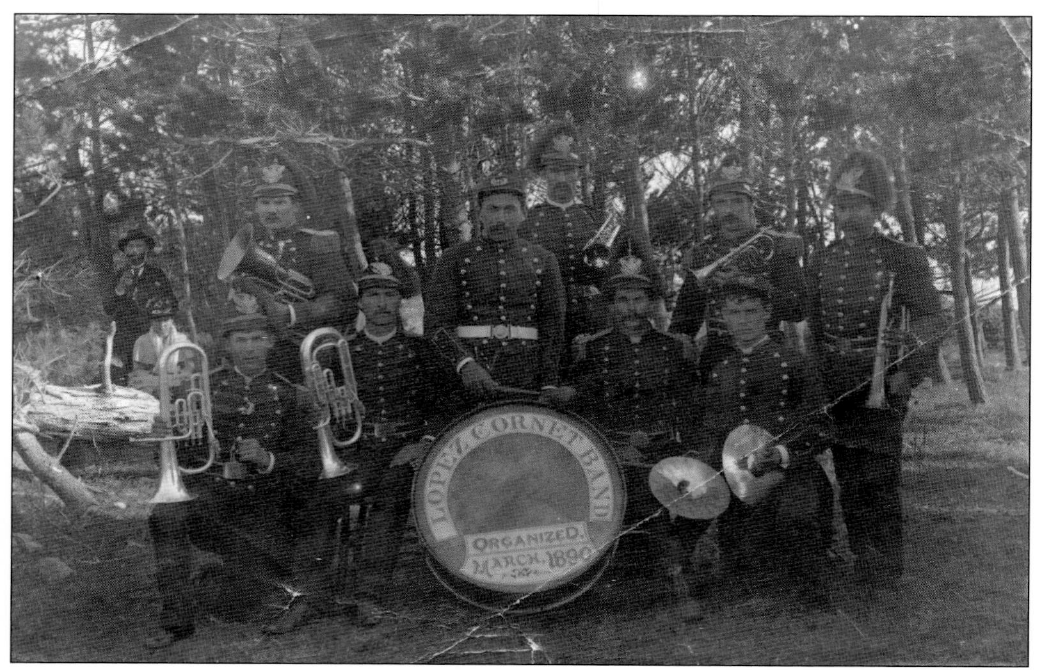

When the Lopez Cornet Band formed on March 3, 1890, only one member had any musical training. By March 10, band members acquired four instruments, and by May 1, they performed for the first time at a May Day picnic. Band members from left to right are (first row) George Cary, Joe Thornton, Charles Phelps, and Charles Wood; (second row) Dick Sumner, Millard Hutchinson (son of Hiram E. Hutchinson), Harry Cary, Sam Britt, and Robert Hummel. An 1891 newspaper article praised island newcomer Phelps as a man of "fine musical abilities," who was "cheerfully contributing his talents" to help his fellow musicians. Band members and baseball players mingled during regular weekday evening games, as shown in this *c.* 1900 photograph. The article reported, "Experts in the manly science" of baseball and the Lopez Cornet Band met regularly for "practice, recreation and business."

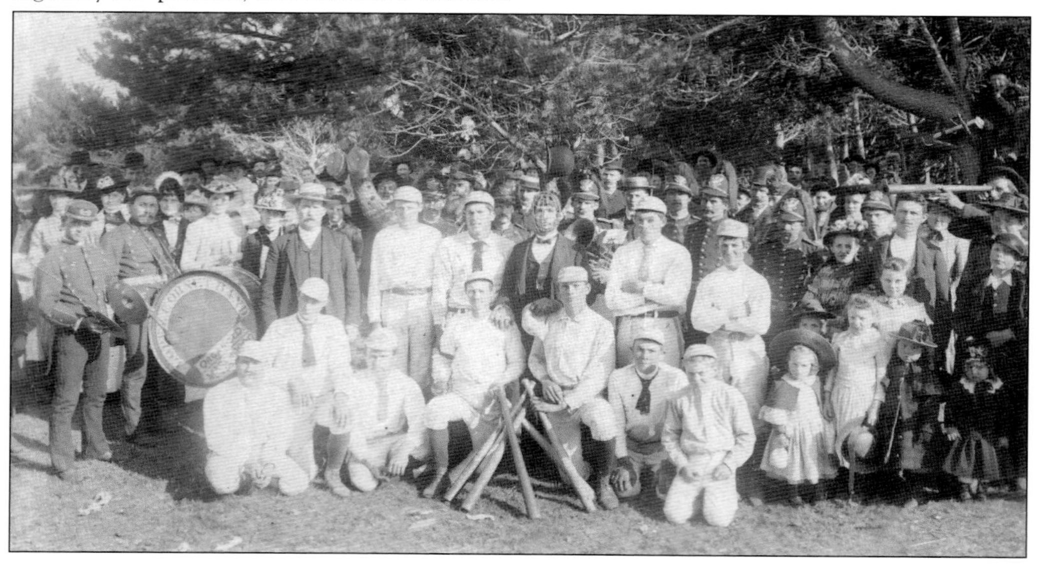

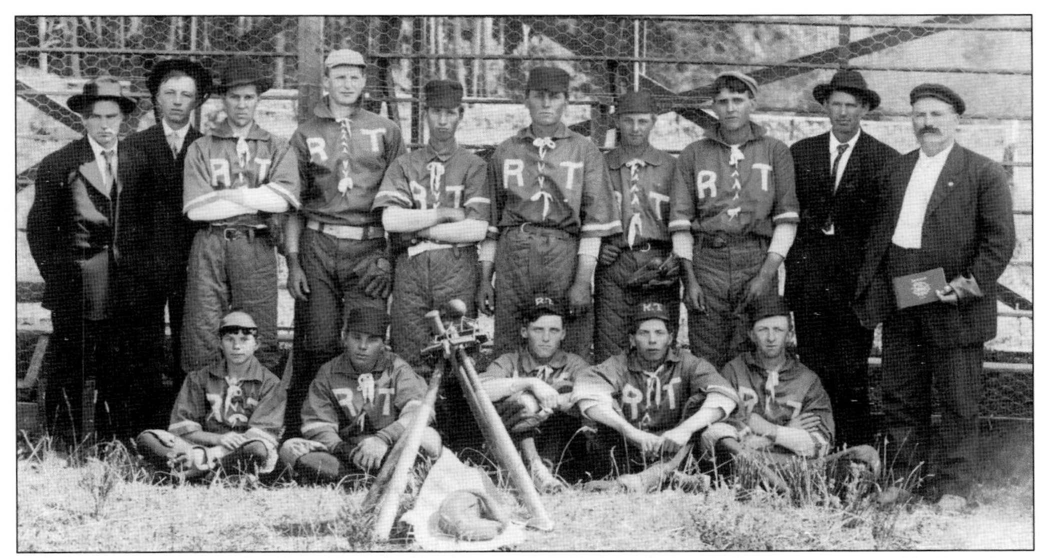

The Richardson Tigers played baseball at the airfield located above the parsonage at Richardson, one of seven island ball fields, about 1910. Team members from left to right are (first row) Herbie Ringerbaugh, Philip Range, Sam Wilson Jr., Leo Towell, and Claud Graham; (second row) Jim Blowers, Howard Graham, Sam Taylor, unidentified, Ab Graham, Robert Burt, Lyall Graham, Emory Raymond, Ed Blowers, and Wally Bolton.

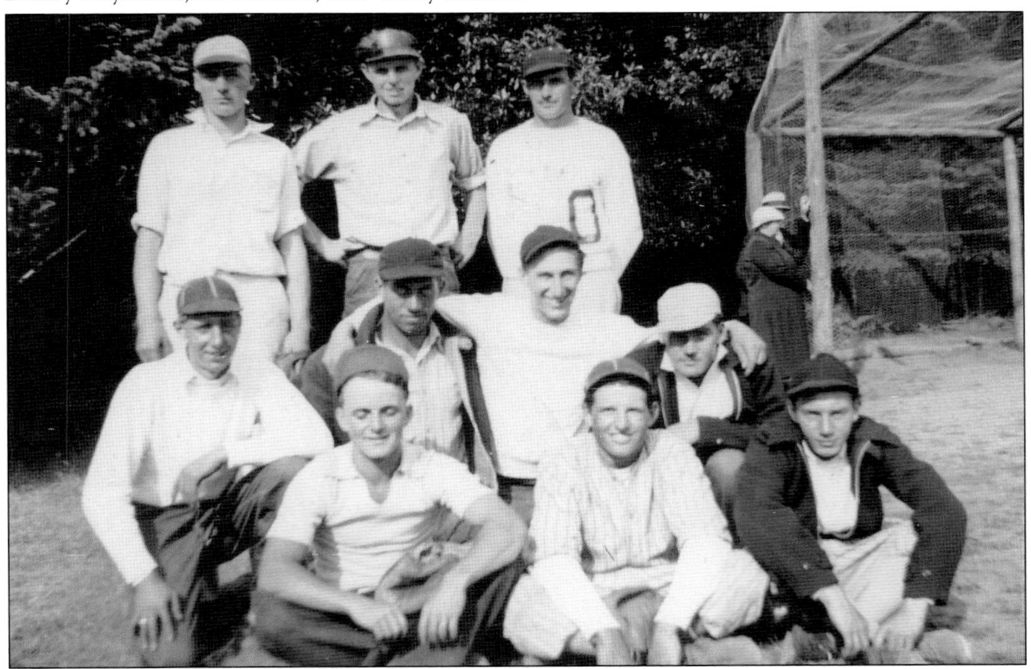

A good year for the Lopez Island baseball team was 1935, when they won the county championship on Orcas Island 5-4. Winning team members from left to right are (first row) Garner Wilson, Phil Hastin, and Woody Evans; (second row) Gene Bosch, Edgar Goodwill, T. J. Blake, and Homer Evans; (third row) Melvin McCauley, Dick Pickering Sr., and Duane Goodrow. Teacher Ira Beham and an unidentified woman stand at the backstop.

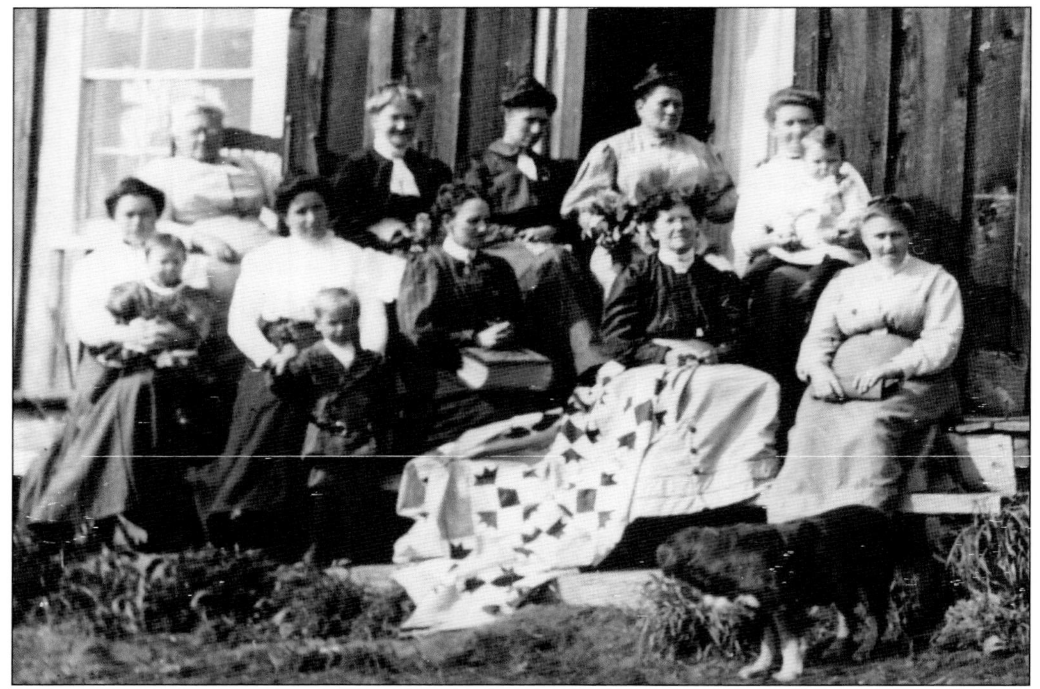

Quilting bees helped create beautiful and functional works of art that often became special gifts. Gathered together from left to right are (first row) Sarah (McNallie) McCauley (holding Myrtle McCauley), Lottie Hodgson (holding Norman Hodgson Jr. in front of her), Emma Oliver, unidentified, and Elizabeth McNallie; (second row) unidentified, Mary Graham, unidentified, Isabella Bloor, and Barbara McCauley (holding Sam McCauley). Signature quilts, signed by the quilt makers, first appeared in the 1840s in Baltimore, Maryland. They declined in popularity after the Civil War and then had a resurgence in the newly settled Western states after the 1880s. The quilt shown here was made for Mary Jane Eaton in 1911 for her 44th birthday. It was signed by 25 women and donated to the museum by Mary Jane Fagerholm-Reece and her family in honor of the Eaton, Brown, and Fagerholm families.

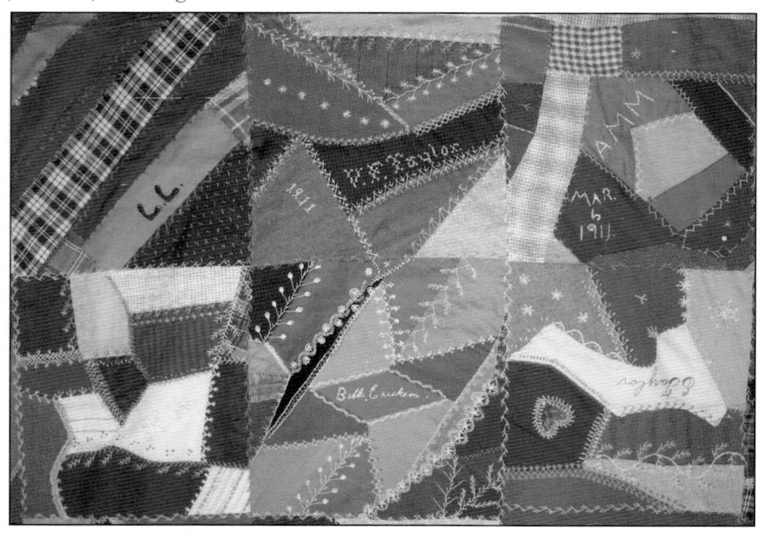

Hunting helped islanders gather a vital food source, but by the time this photograph was taken, game bird hunting for sport had become popular. Sam Wilson Jr., shown here with his dog, killed two birds, including a ring-necked pheasant. Ring-necked pheasants were imported from China between 1881 and 1884 and proved to be prolific reproducers, providing hunters with a colorful bounty.

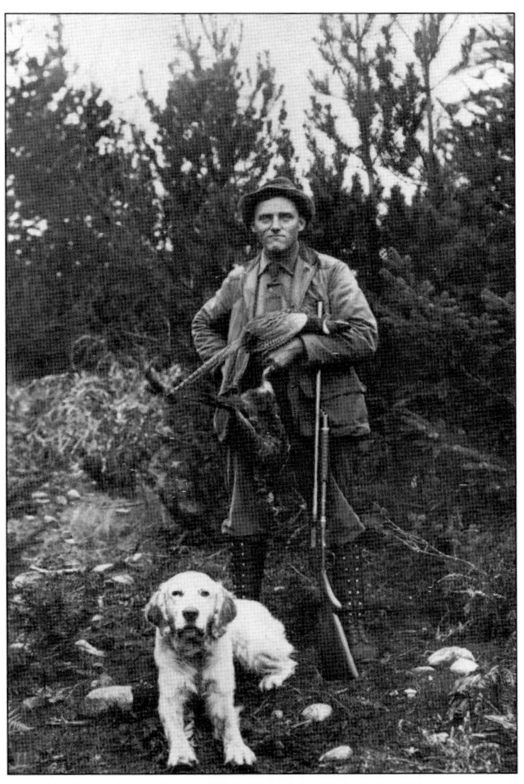

The Knights of the Maccabees is a national fraternal benefit society formed after the Civil War to provide insurance to deceased members' families. Lopez Island had its own branch of the organization, shown here about 1906. From left to right are (first row) Johnny Graham, Tom King, John Cousins, Norman P. "N. P." Hodgson, and Erv Eaton; (second row) unidentified, Nick Davidson, Robert Cousins, Amoe Carr, Joe Cousins, and Ab Graham.

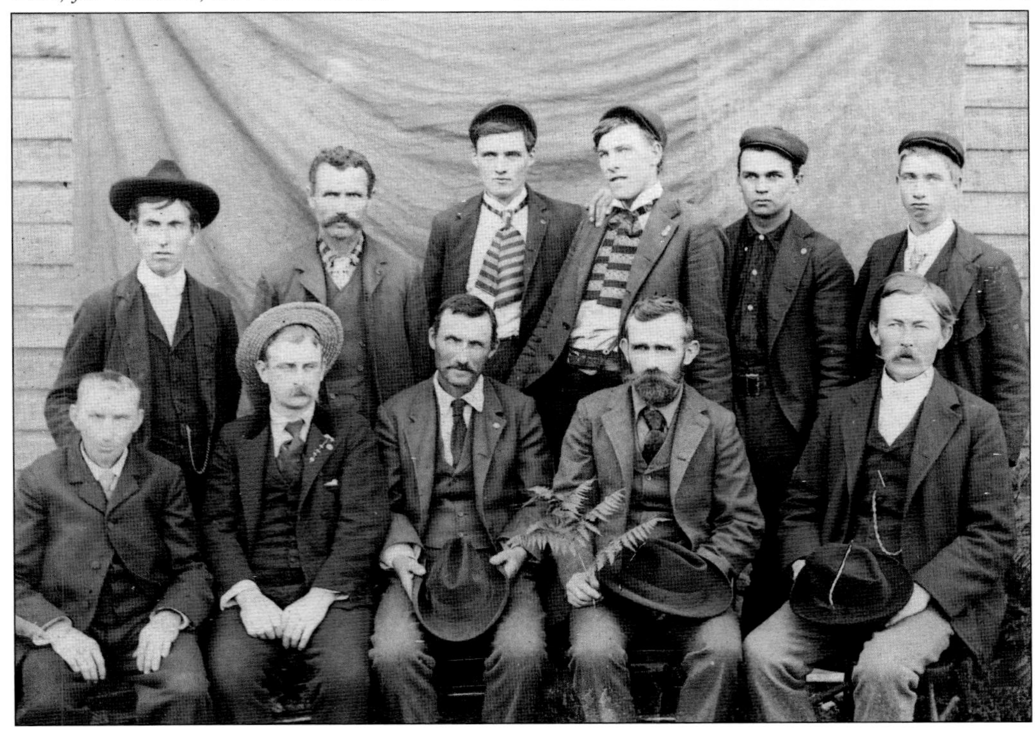

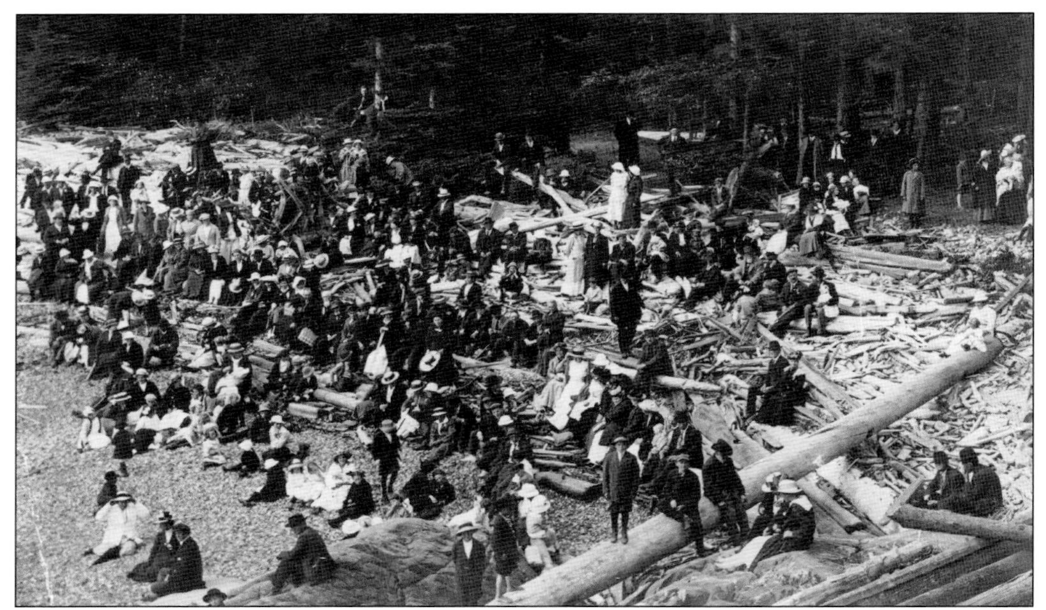

Pioneer picnics were an enjoyable way for descendents of island homesteaders and early-20th-century settlers to gather annually to share fun and historical stories. Formed by Isabella Bloor, the Pioneer Association held its first picnic in 1915 or 1916 on Bloor's Beach. Donning their Sunday best, picnicgoers started a tradition that has survived to this day.

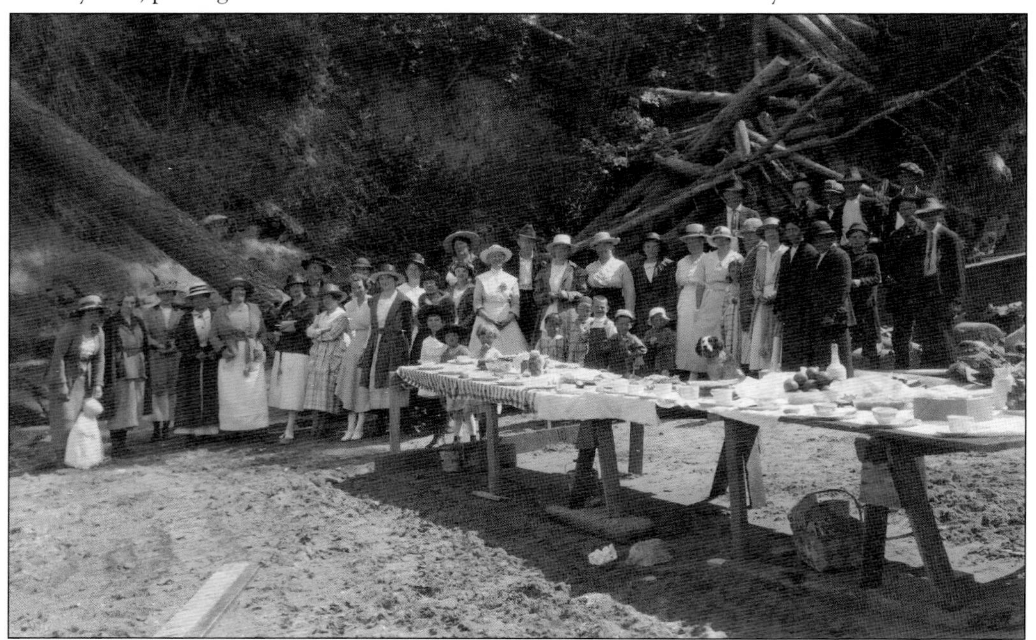

Beach picnics and potlucks bring islanders of all ages together for socializing and camaraderie. Families represented at Mary Farnsworth's birthday party include Carr, Weir, Higgins, Eaton, Stratford, de Gez, Bridges, Carsley, Hastin, Fagerholm, Branum, Gallanger, Larrabee, Leison, Farnsworth, Engle, Buchanan, Tralnes, Nielsen, Sperry, MacLeod, Noyd, Sheen, Chadwick, and Bergen. Farnsworth stands in the center, wearing a white dress and a brimmed hat.

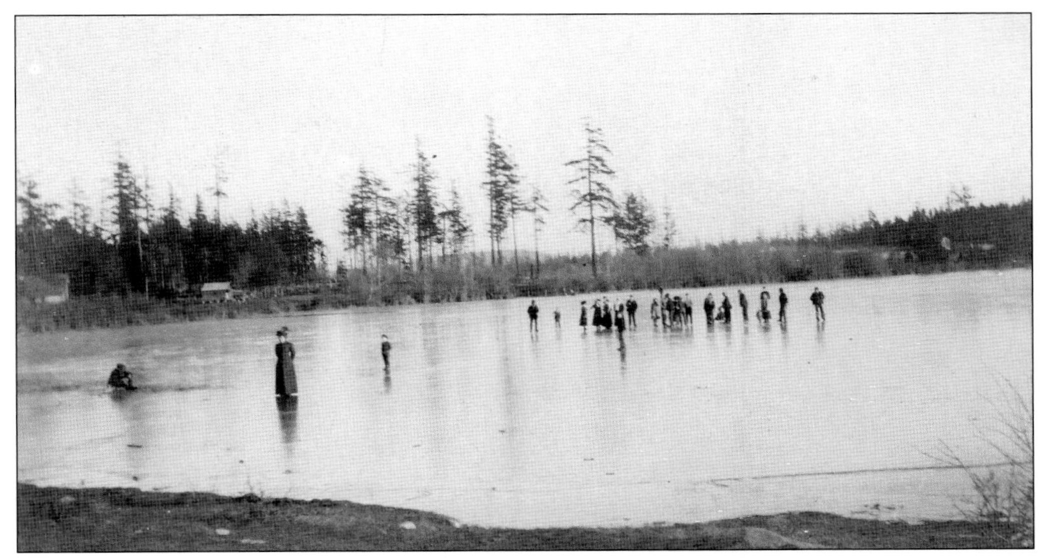

Ice-skating is a rare treat, as today Hummel Lake rarely freezes in the winter. Old-timers told Lopez historian Gertrude Boede that they used to skate on Hummel Lake quite often but were unable to date this picture. Donald Fagerholm described Hummel Lake as the island's main recreational area in the 1930s, with summer swimming and winter skating. Children enjoyed a sand beach and separate dressing bathhouses for boys and girls.

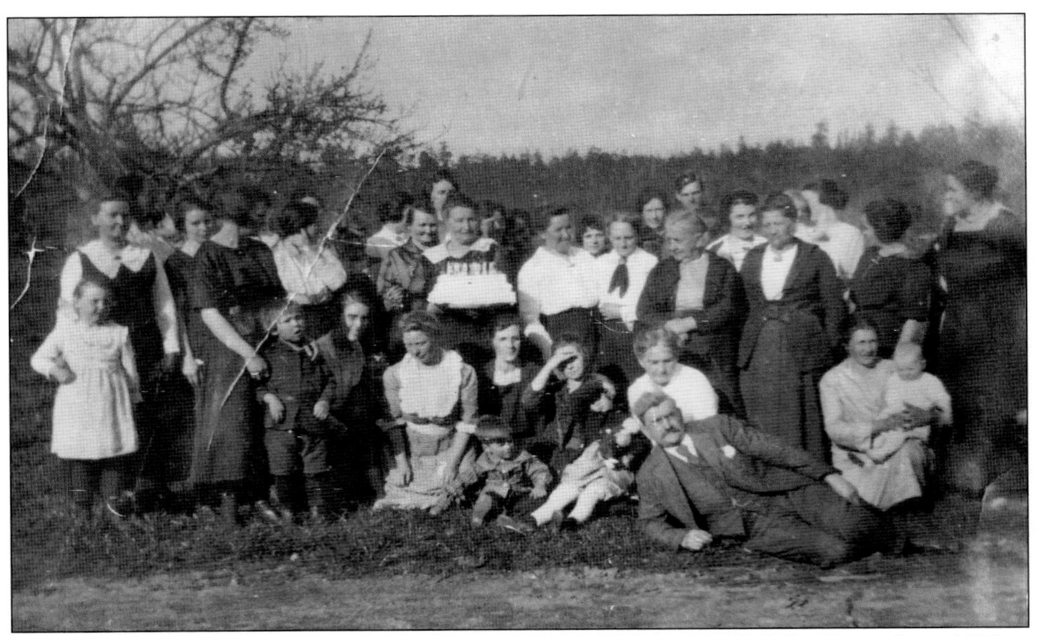

Sanna Tralnes, holding the cake, started the Birthday Club on her 50th birthday about 1922 to help people in need. For years, each club member contributed as many pennies as her age, and the money helped families who were "hard up." Club members also sewed clothes and made layettes for young mothers. Joining the celebration is Marguerite McCauley, the child on the left.

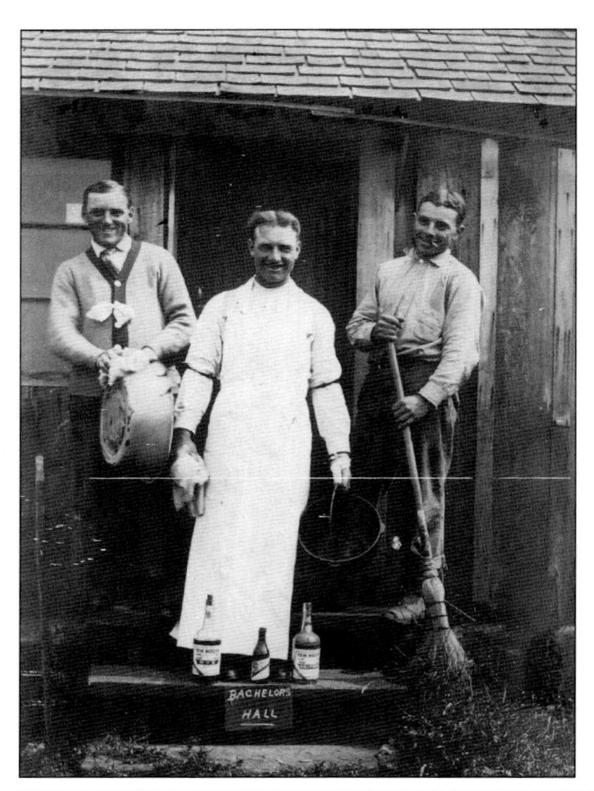

Humorous photographs made into postcards were sent to friends with a quick note. From left to right, Sam Wilson Jr., cousin George Wilson, and Philip Range stand in front of "Bachelor's Hall," with liquor bottles at their feet. Sam sent the card to Cora Standley of Richardson, saying, "I am going to keep my promise and send you one of these beautiful pictures. Ha! Ha!"

Dozens of houses and buildings have been moved from one location to another on the island, including the McCauley farmhouse, the Ender house, the Burt farmhouse, and the Lopez Village School. This photograph shows the Wilson blacksmith shop being moved on property now known as the Kring farm.

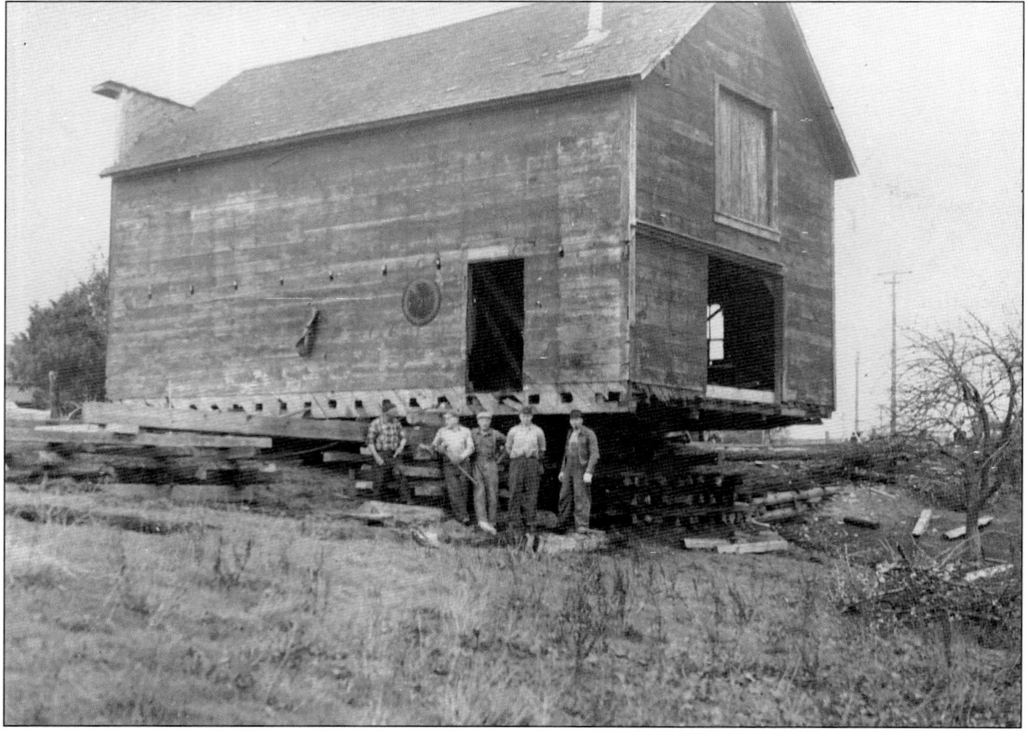

Shown here in 1912, Lydia Richey exemplifies the island's love of music. She graduated from Mills College in San Francisco and married Seth T. Richey, son of George and Sarah Richey. A fine musician, Lydia taught piano, mandolin, guitar, violin, and banjo to her many students. She is fondly remembered for her contributions to the days when all of Lopez's music was homegrown.

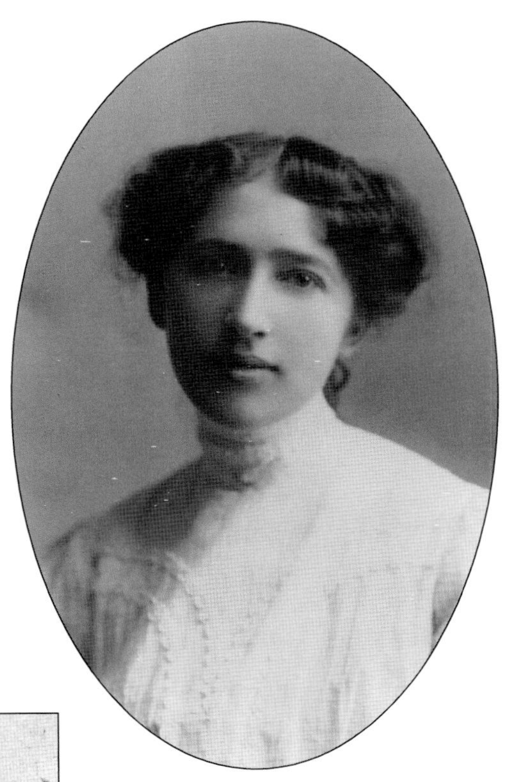

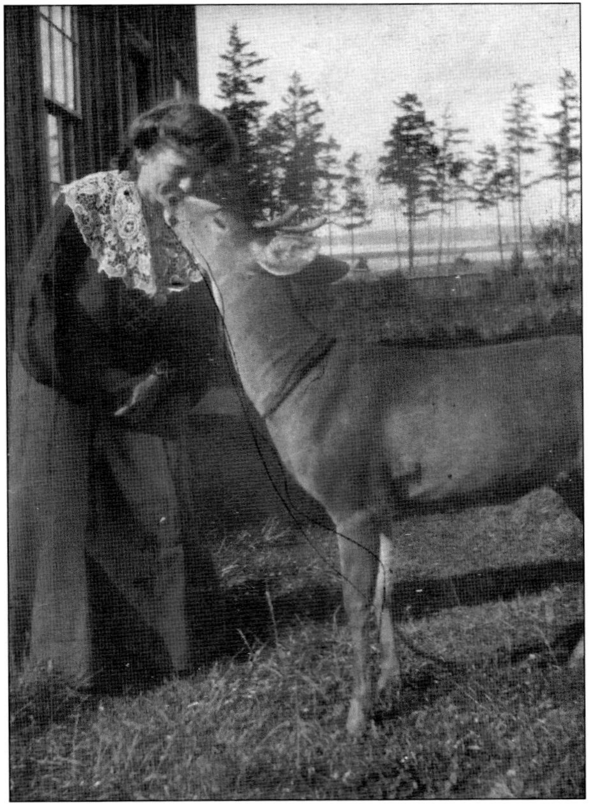

Lopezians love animals, often choosing a special name for every animal on the farm. Here, Stella Wood Blake nuzzles a deer, having earned its trust. Marguerite Goodrow told the story of her pet deer Johnny, who drank water alongside her father's dog named Jock. Goodrow tied a little bell around Johnny's neck to protect him, and for years, Johnny came out of the nearby woods when she called his name.

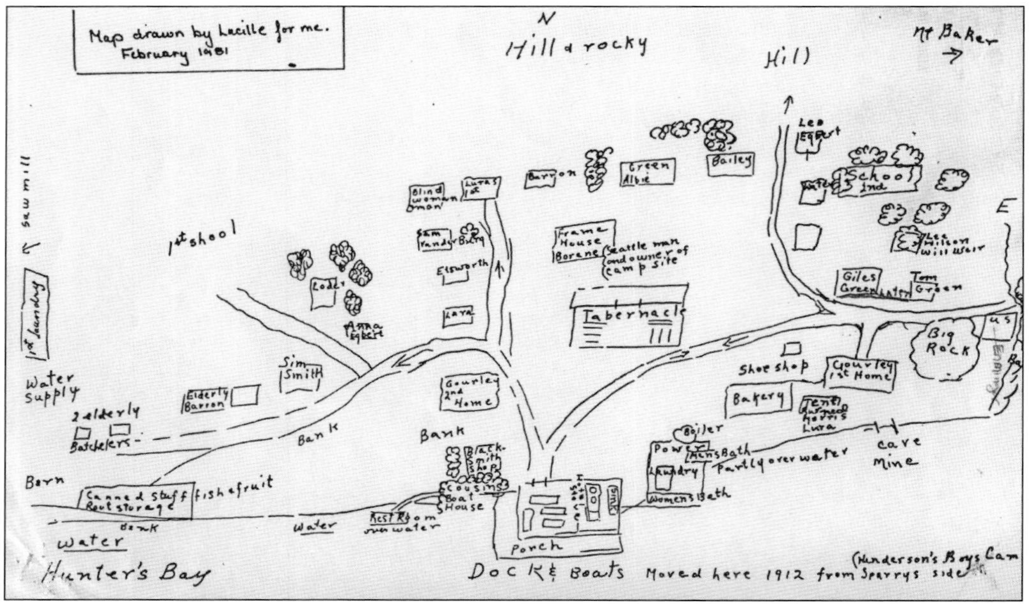

In 1907, Thomas Gourley created a Seattle religious movement seeking a utopian brotherhood that shared resources. Unwelcome in Seattle, Gourley moved his followers to Sperry Peninsula and later to Hunter Bay, where they built a dining hall, bakery, cobbler's shop, barn, dock, school, and houses, some of which are shown on this map. The colony unraveled by 1920, when followers lost faith in Gourley's leadership and the community disbanded.

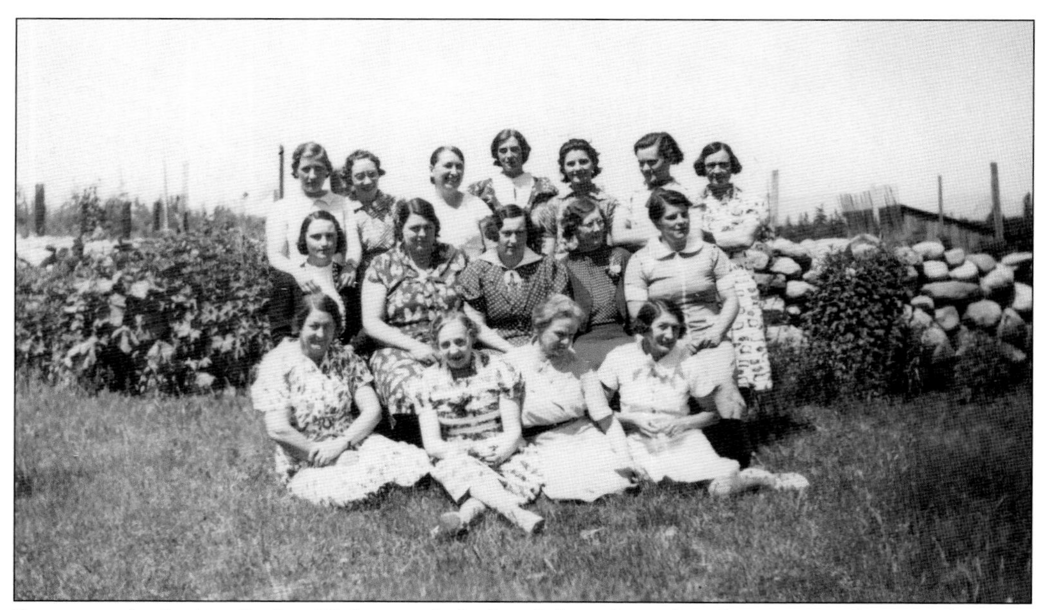

For years, the Ladies Bridge Club provided a break from busy days farming, working, and raising families. Club members in this 1935 photograph from left to right are (front row) Ellie McCauley, Charlotte de Gez, Stella Blake, and Meta Carr; (second row) Ethel Fagerholm, Nora Fagerholm, Lavinia Erb, Harriet Kilpatrick, and Etolin Gallanger; (third row) Hazel Lundy, Ethel Carr, Dorothy Fagerholm, Mabel Cary, Grace Pickering, Cora Austin, and Anna Hodgson.

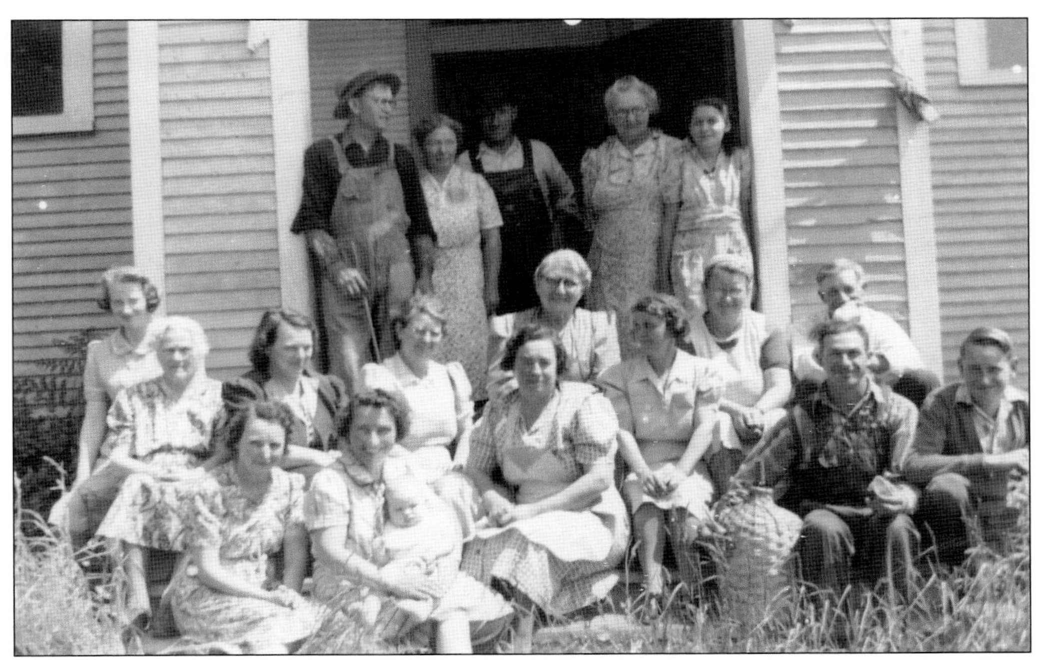

In 1941, the government furnished cotton bales, and people made mattresses together at Mud Bay School. Shown from left to right are (first row) Mae Burt, Violet Norman, Phyllis Hastin, Vera Lowery, Sadie Coffelt, Kenneth Hume, and Art Norman; (second row) Evelyn Tralnes, Maggie Grumwold, Eva Gorsage, Helen Hastin, Doris Gugelman, Anna Braun, and Lowell Lovejoy; (third row) Walter and Minerva Lampard, Jens Branum, Sara Tralnes, and Louella Hume.

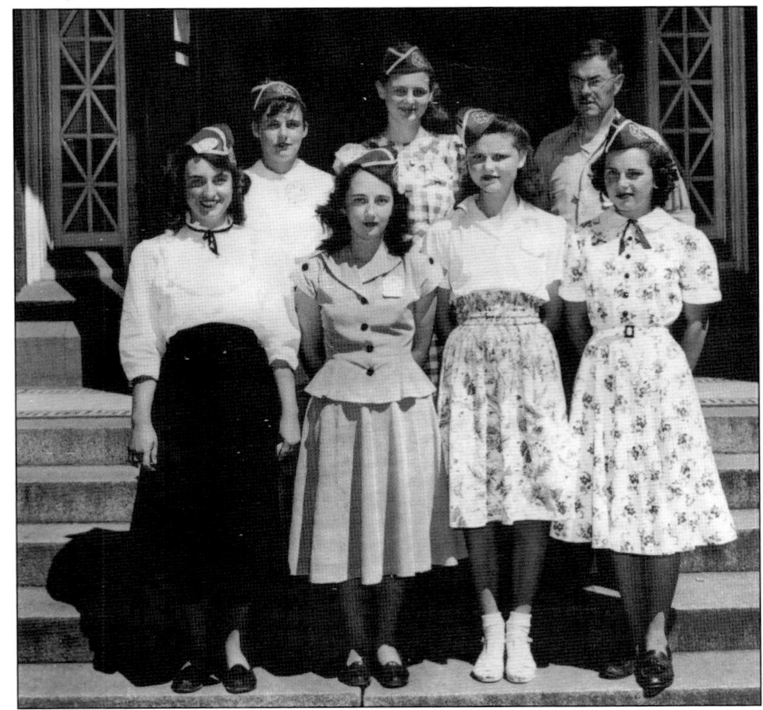

Helping young people learn valuable skills, 4-H has played an important role in island life. Attending a 4-H conference in Pullman from left to right are (first row) Vivian Lowery, Melba Fagerholm, Jean Lindholm, and unidentified; (second row) unidentified, Eleanor Boede, and Mr. Baker (the county 4-H agent). For many years, Pierre Franklin led Lopez 4-H groups, teaching animal husbandry.

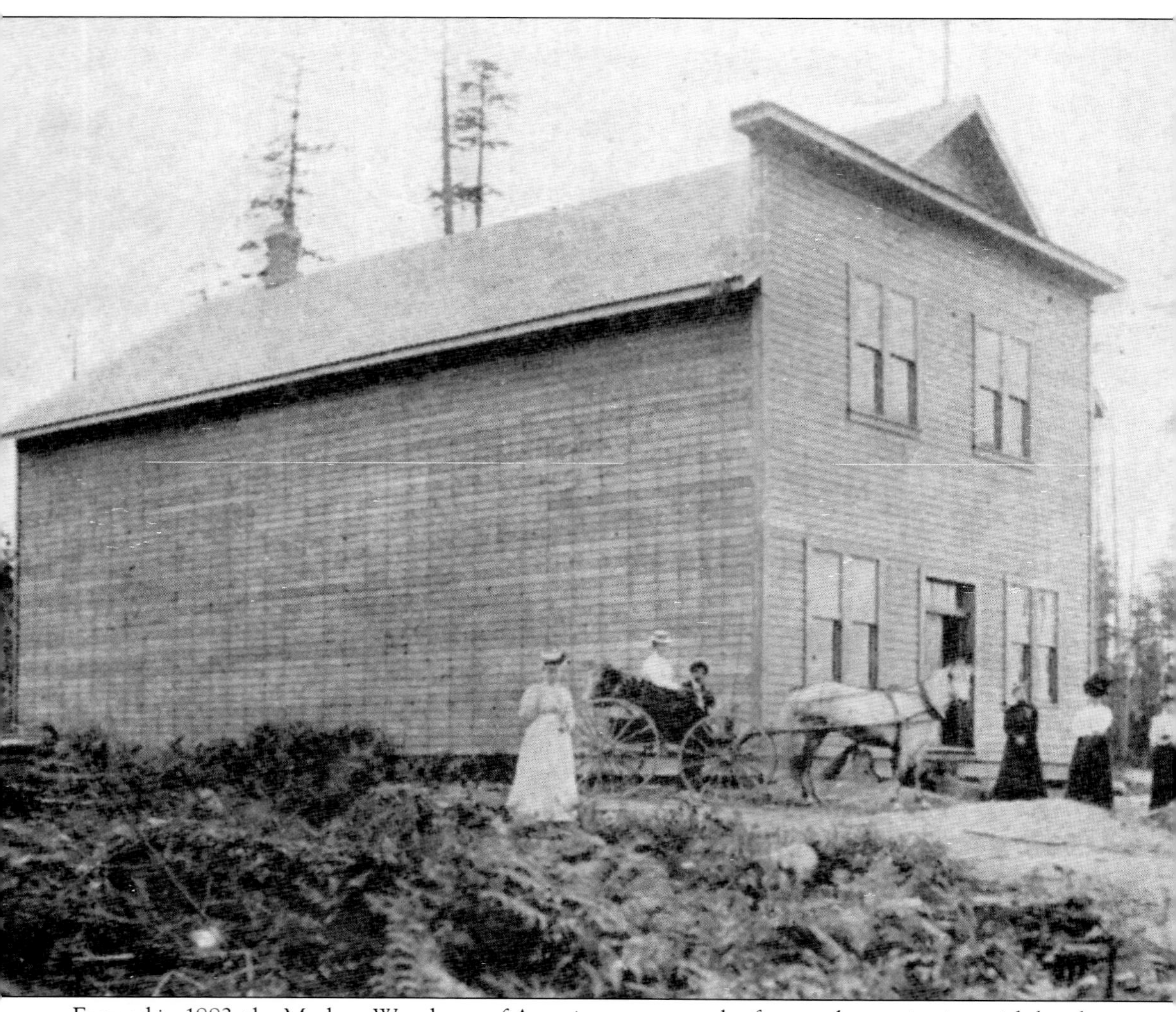

Formed in 1883, the Modern Woodmen of America was a popular fraternal organization with local chapters called camps. The Lopez Island Camp was chartered in 1898. Among the original 11 members were brothers Joe and William Gallanger, Thomas Blake, Thomas Bell, Robert Hummel, and J. C. Warner. The group decided to build a meeting hall, and George Orcutt donated half an acre of land. The building was completed in 1900 and hosted Woodmen meetings for many years, including those of the Royal Neighbors of America, the women's charitable auxiliary. During the Great Depression, the Woodmen sold the building to the Lopez Commercial Club. In the 1950s, the hall was sold to the American Legion for $1 and named the Hoey-Kjargaard American Legion Hall for Alan Hoey and Harald Kjargaard, who died in World War II. The Legion became a favorite place for community dances, auctions, parties, senior lunches, and a Halloween haunted house. In 2003, Lopez Senior Services acquired the hall, and the volunteer group Friends of Woodmen Hall performed needed improvements and restored its original name, Woodmen Hall.

Four

Learning Together

Early islanders prized education and worked together to found schools for the island's children. James and Amelia Davis spent half of all farming proceeds on books and magazines, taught their own children, then circulated materials to other families as an informal lending library.

The Lopez community formed four school districts, one each at Port Stanley, Lopez Village, Mud Bay, and Center. Although the State of Washington permitted local residents to form school districts, the cost of building and maintaining schoolhouses, paying teachers' salaries, and buying books and materials were paid by each local district. In 1893, the Barefoot Schoolboy Law passed, which made the state responsible to pay for education, but decades later, many island schools still had to buy their own materials through district levies or do without.

In 1936, Lopez voters approved consolidation of the four districts into one, and by 1941, the new school on Center Road opened, with the luxury of indoor plumbing, running water, electric lights, and central heat. Louis Washburn moved to Lopez in 1942, was hired to run the district in 1943, and shortly thereafter, Lopez students completed 12th grade on the island for the first time.

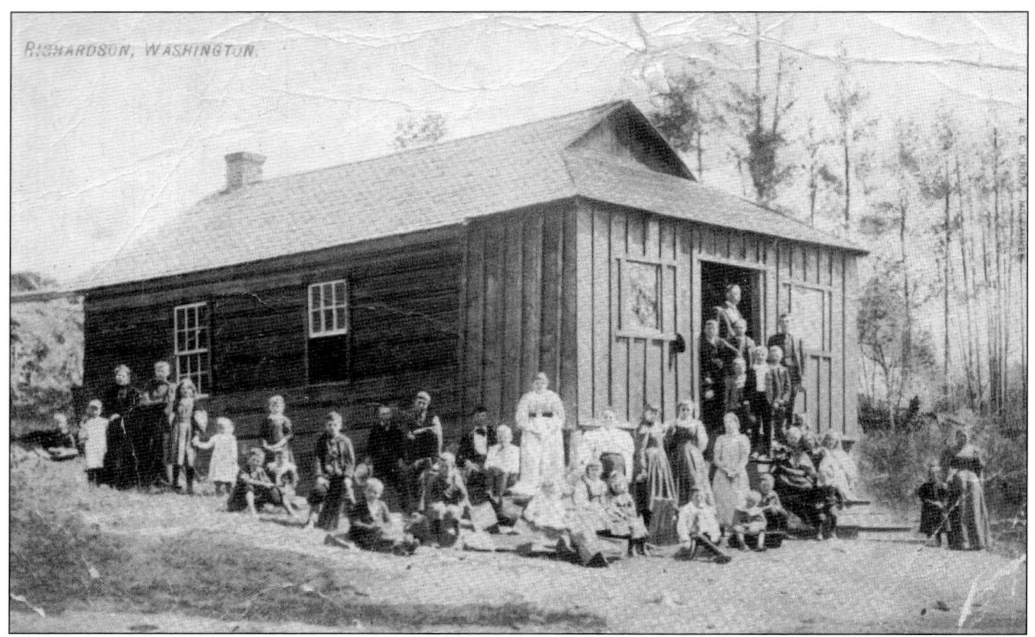

The first school district on the island was created about 1873, but south-end classes were held in private homes until the log cabin Center School was built in 1882, located at the intersection of Center and Richardson Roads. Children who have been identified in the 1901 photograph (above) with teacher William E. Clark are George Hastin, Laura Cousins, Isobel Cousins, Robert Cousins, Joe Cousins, Hazel Wilson, Wallace Burt, Bob Wilson, Percy Towell, Grace Wilson, and Gertie Towell. Around 1884, the district built a second log cabin school at Mud Bay, alternating use of the two schools. Standing in front of the old Mud Bay log schoolhouse, from left to right, are John Osgoodby, Philip Fagerholm, Charlie Anderson, Walter Anderson, and Victor Anderson. The last day of school in the old log cabin Center School was in January 1903.

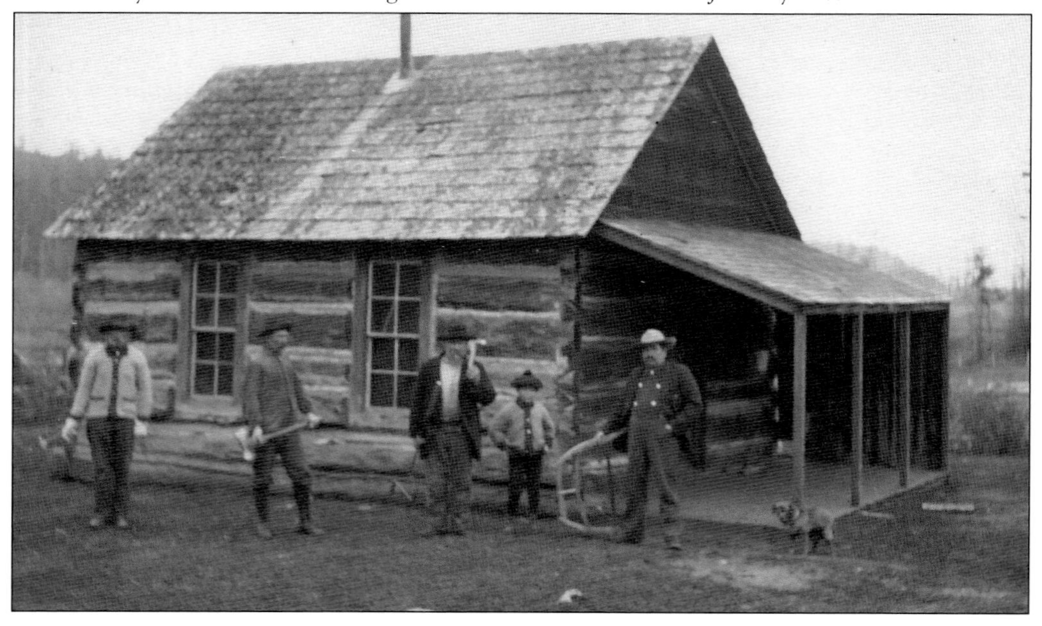

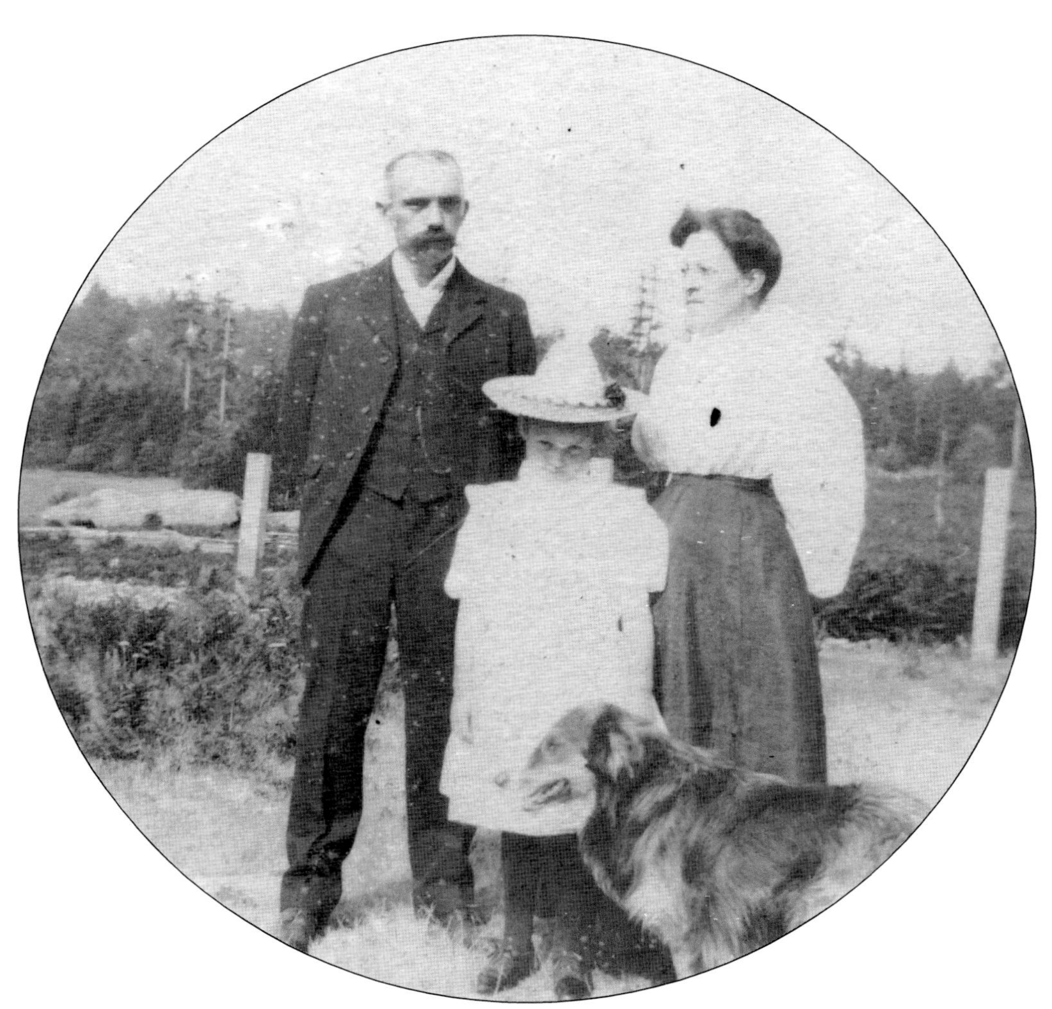

One of Lopez's early teachers was L. W. Tucker. A teacher at the log cabin Center School, Tucker is pictured here with his wife and daughter, Mabel. Early schools had no grades, and students were expected to become proficient in reading, writing, and arithmetic in the three months school was in session each year. In addition to instructing the students, teachers often also had to perform daily chores, such as starting fires in the woodstoves and lighting lamp wicks before the children arrived. If a teacher chose not to perform such tasks, the responsibility fell onto a school board member, and the teacher's pay was reduced accordingly. Teachers often earned meager sums and then paid some of their earnings back into the community for room and board with Lopez families. This photograph of the Tucker family was made into a postcard and sent, "with love to Mrs. Graham."

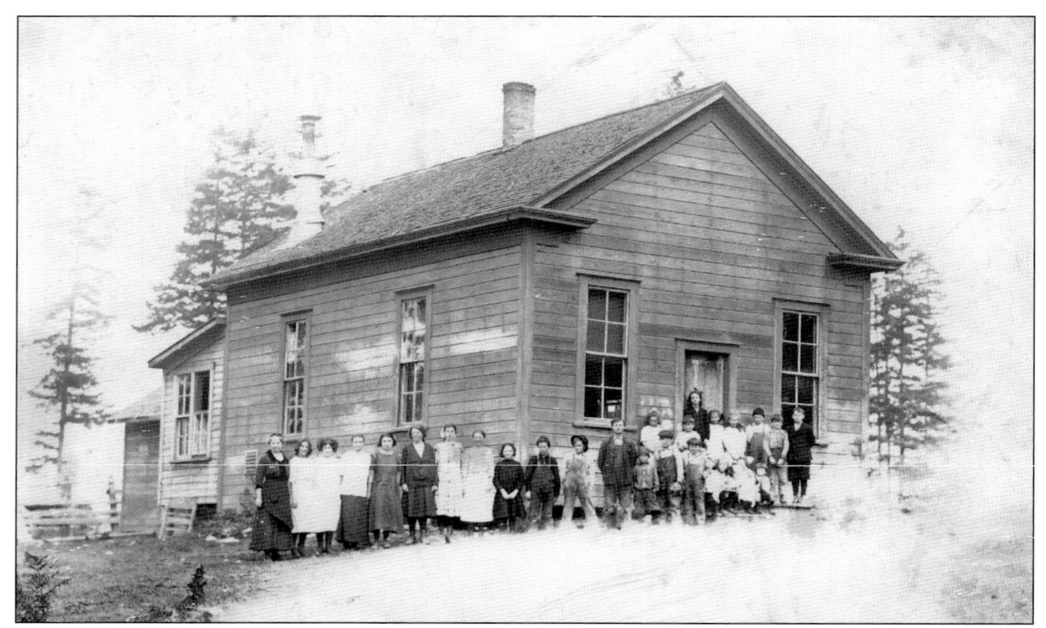

The Port Stanley School District built its first school, a rough log cabin, about 1876. The building has long since disappeared, and no known photograph of it exists. Pictured here, a second Port Stanley School was built about 1888. The third Port Stanley School was donated to the Lopez Island Historical Society and Museum. A photograph can be found on page 126.

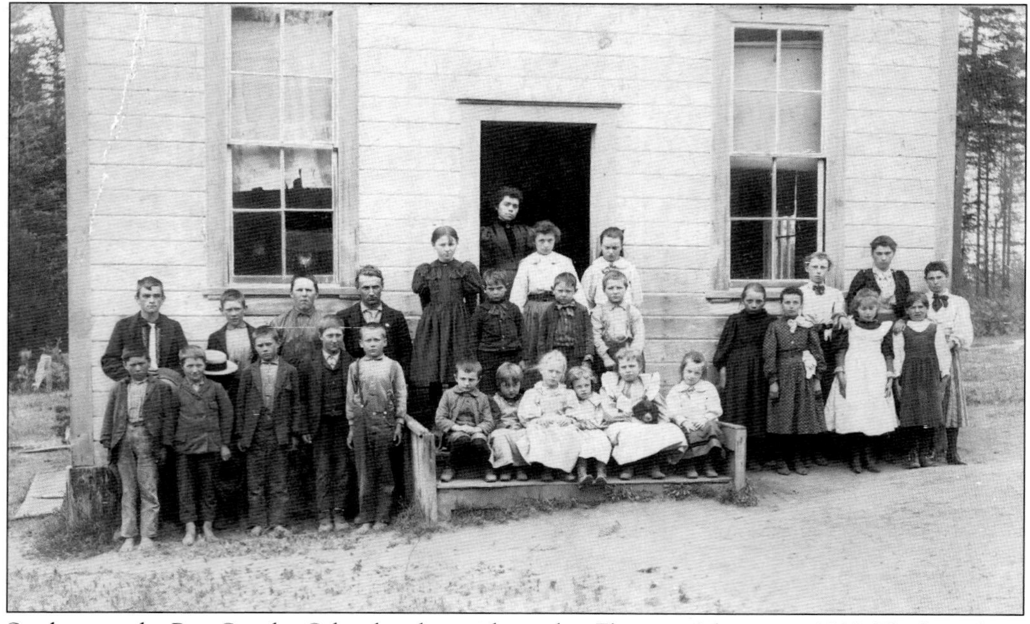

Students at the Port Stanley School gather with teacher Florence Johnson in 1897. The boys from left to right are (first row) Willie Carle, Chester Coffelt, Fred Cochran, Enoch Coffelt, and Ollie Cochran; (second row) Homer Troxell, Andrew Deffenbach, Seth Richey, and Joe Biggs. Other students are Eva Snyder, Dora Butler, Nettie Hummel, Roy Snider, Viola Coffelt, Agnes Duffy, Viva Erb, Lily Blake, Florence McMurray, Fay McMurray, Dora Winton, and Laura Hackwell.

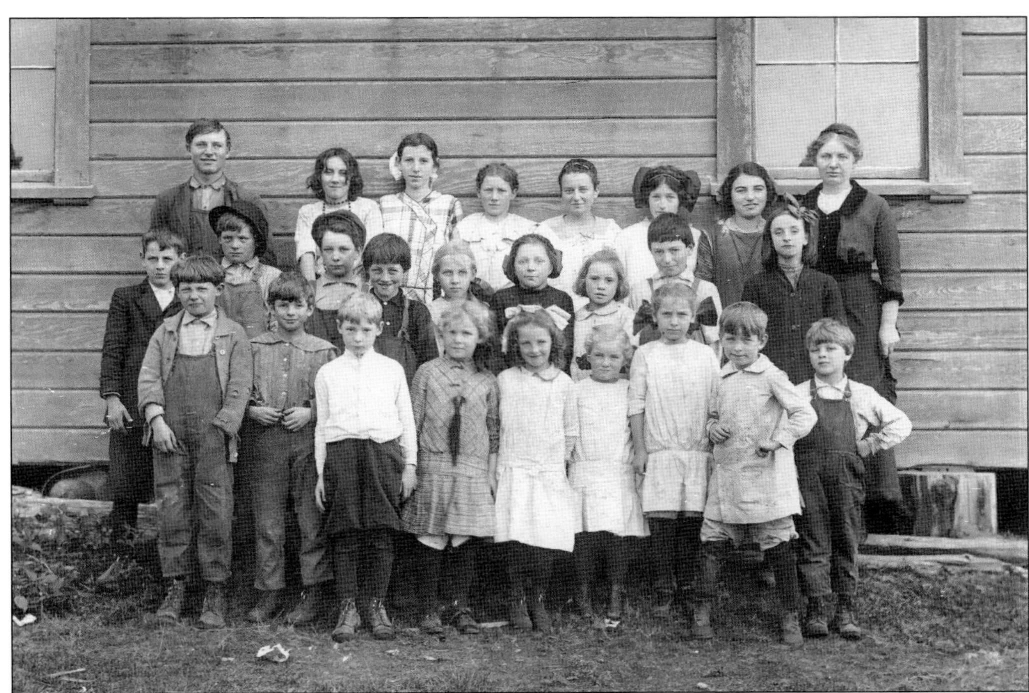

Port Stanley School students from left to right are (first row) Wakefield Strafford, Elmer Gawley, Frank Christian, Dottie Christian, Evelyn Burt, Wilma ?, Dorothy Kilpatrick, Frank Kilpatrick, and Clifford Gawley; (second row) Richard Bell, Henry Erb, Edward Ringler, Clarence Burt, Florence Christian, Elva Ringler, Margaret LeMaister, ? Mitchell, and Martha Gawley; (third row) Wyatt Coffelt, Myrtle Gallanger, Alice Bell, Harriett Gallanger, Amy Gallanger, Mary Hudson, Effie Davis, and teacher Mary Erb.

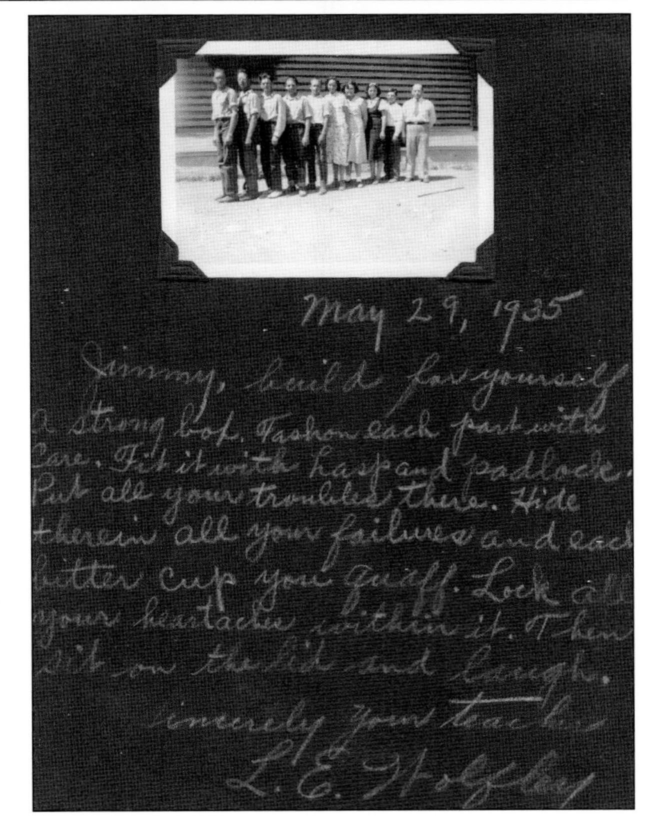

May 29, 1935

Jimmy, build for yourself
a strong box. Fashion each part with
care. Fit it with hasp and padlock.
Put all your troubles there. Hide
therein all your failures and each
bitter cup you quaff. Lock all
your heartaches within it. Then
sit on the lid and laugh.

Sincerely your teacher
L. E. Wolfley

In 1935, Port Stanley School teacher L. E. Wolfley wrote poems to students, such as this one to Jimmy: "Build for yourself a strong box, fashion each part with care. Fit it with hasp and padlock. Put all your troubles there. Hide therein all your failures and each bitter cup you quaff. Lock all your heartaches within it. Then sit on the lid and laugh."

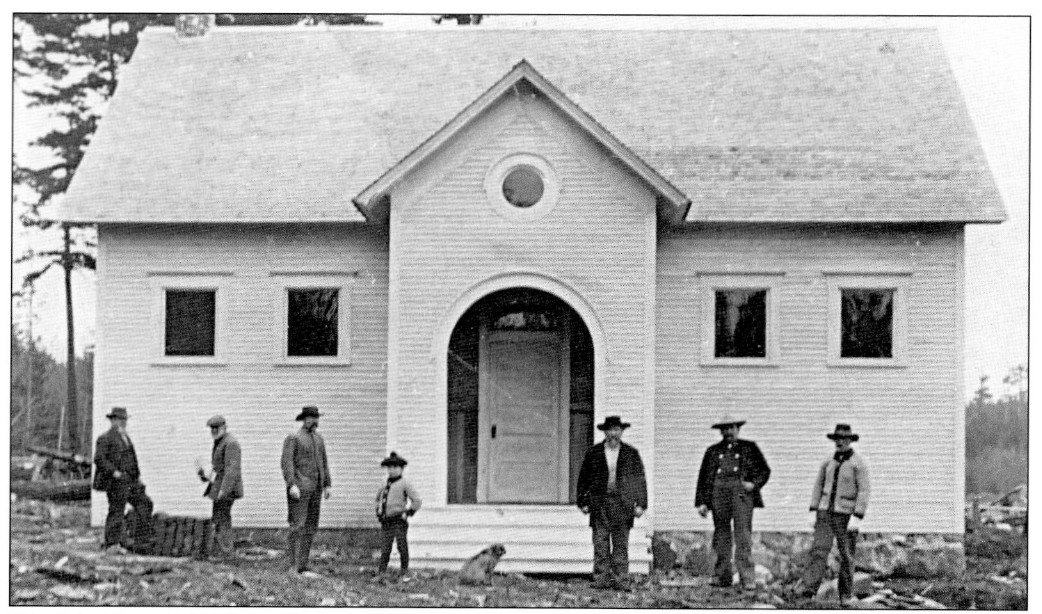

The Mud Bay School was built in 1909 and replaced the original Mud Bay log school. Standing from left to right are Joe Burt (builder), Henry L. Dikeman, unidentified, Walter Anderson, Charlie Anderson, Victor Anderson, and possibly Ervin Eaton. Interestingly, they wear the same outfits in the lower photograph on page 70. Perhaps photographs of the old school and new school were taken the same day. The school still stands at the corner of Mud Bay and Aleck Bay Roads.

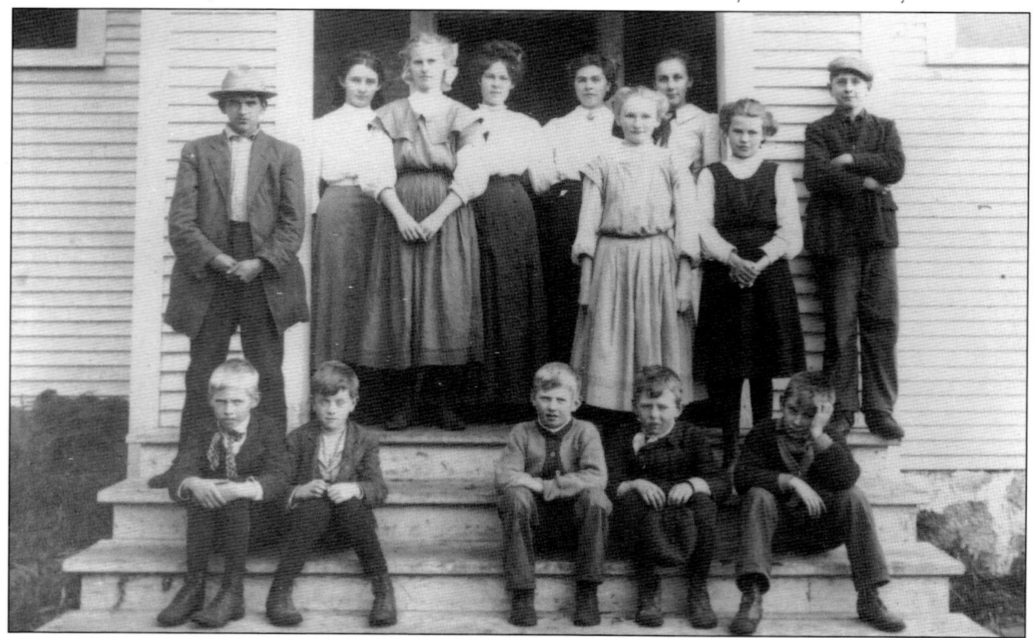

Students and teacher posing in front of the Mud Bay School from left to right are (first row) Sig Schruder, ? Pusey, Richard Pusey, Walter Anderson, and Albert Fagerholm; (second row) George Chadwick, Nina Eaton, Alma Norman, teacher Cora Scribner, Margaret Range, Jennie Fagerholm, Florence Eaton Fagerholm, Jennie Albertson (Schruder), and Merell Range.

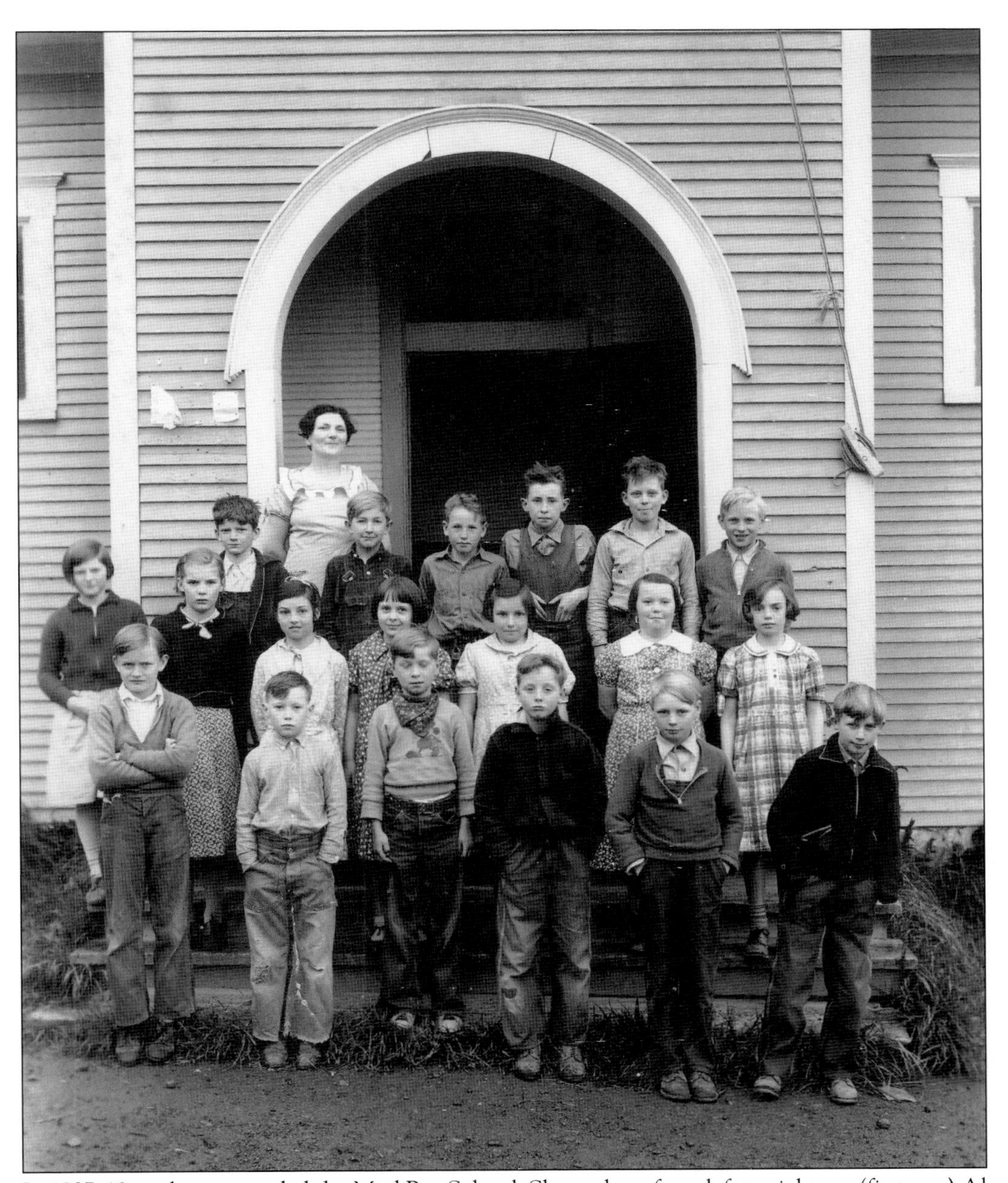

In 1937, 19 students attended the Mud Bay School. Shown here from left to right are (first row) Al Lovejoy, Dale Dwight, Bruce Kilpatrick, Billy Bosch, Darold Harmon, and Billy Gaddis; (second row) Donna Graham, Esther Schroeder, Charlotte Orcutt, Lanita Davies, Pat Lynn, Eileen Dwight, and Joan MacLeod; (third row) Louie Schruder, Duane Weeks, Ed Norman, George Higgins, Billy Burt, Pete Nielsen, and teacher Lillian Engle. Ona Jean (Gallanger) Goodrow remembers that the students nicknamed it "Islandale School" because they thought the name *Mud Bay* did not sound very clean. The school served a dual community purpose, opening on Sundays for services led by Rev. W. W. Goodrow. Many students lived off island to complete high school, where they worked to cover their room and board while staying with other families, until Lopez school districts consolidated and the new school was built on Center Road.

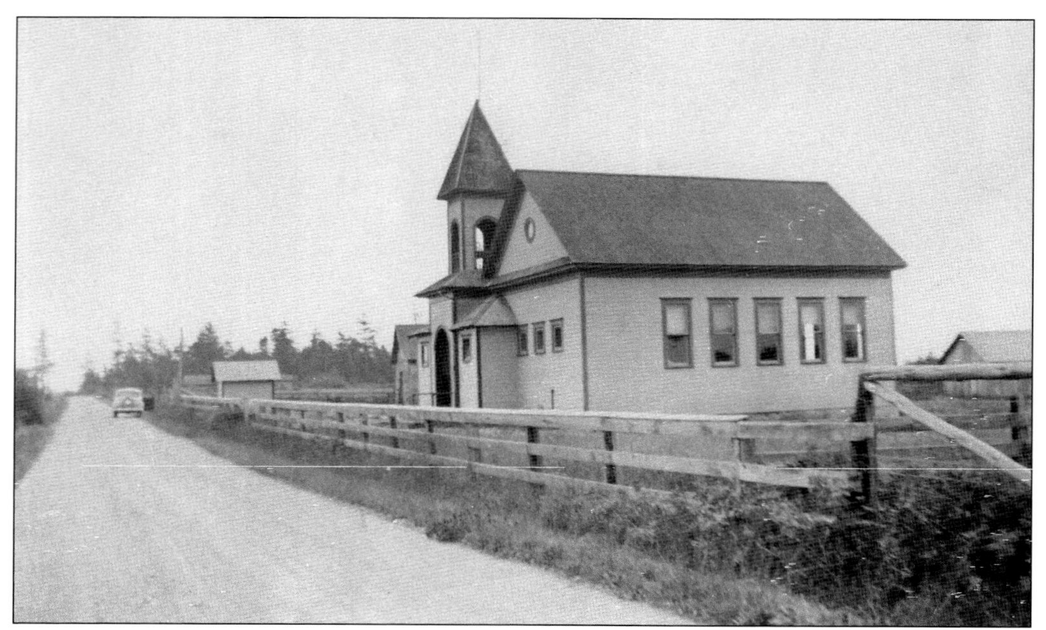

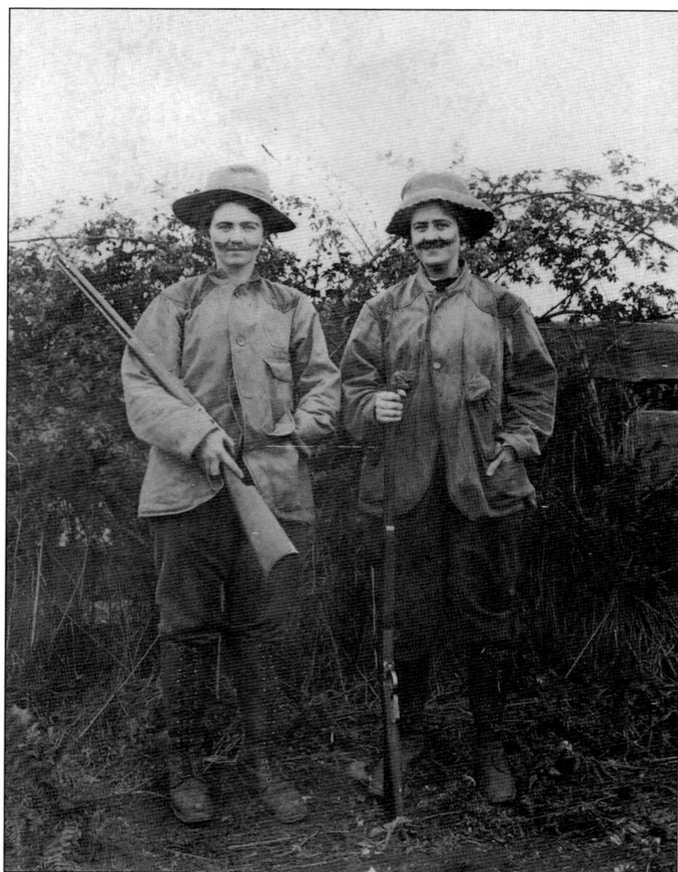

The Center School was built around 1900 on Richardson Road and served schoolchildren until the districts were consolidated in 1941. Later the building became the Grange Hall and is still in active use today. The cupola shown here on the front of the building was later removed because it leaked. Florence Allen and Louise Wakefield taught at Center School around 1905.

Cora Standley Graham and Gladys or Florence Guard, a Center School teacher, are dressed up as hunters holding guns and wearing fake mustaches in this humorous postcard. Teaching was one of few acceptable jobs for single women in those days, and typically, if a woman married, she had to forfeit the job. On the back of the postcard, Graham wrote, "I would rather be a boy any day then a girl."

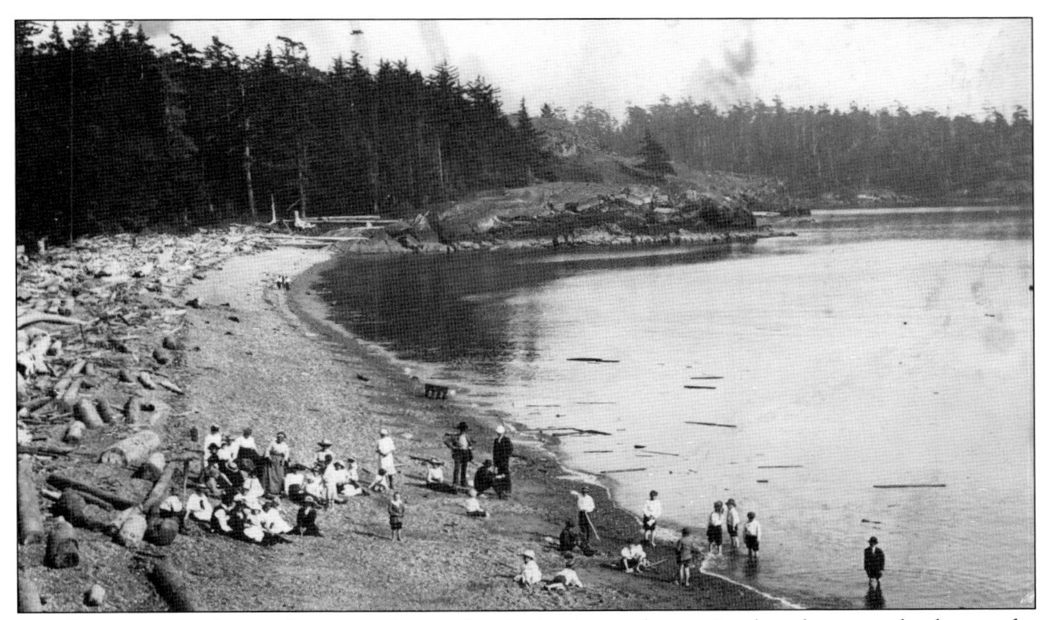

Beaches provide the perfect spot for a school picnic, as shown in the photograph above of a Center School gathering on Bloor's Beach around 1910. Historian Gertude Boede remembered being at the picnic but could not identify herself in the photograph. By 1939, Center School's population had grown substantially. Shown below from left to right are (first row) Herbert Reece, Luverne Weeks, Margaret Hodgson, Shirley Forest, Melba Fagerholm, Elaine Gorsegnor, Norraine Orcutt, Zoe Blake, and Zarna Buffum; (second row) Gene Higgins, Jean Jensen, Gerald Davies, Lawrence Schruder, Donald Erb, Robert Burt, Harry Burt, Hannah Jensen, and Vivian Lowery; (third row) Eileen Bell, Carol Anderson, Fern Burt, Ruth Wilson, Dan Wilson, Irwin Hoffman, Michael Schruder, Carroll Weeks, and Robert Orcutt; (fourth row) Clarence Schruder, Floyd Dwight, Milton Buffum, Ray Lampard, Ralph Orcutt, and Burton Graham.

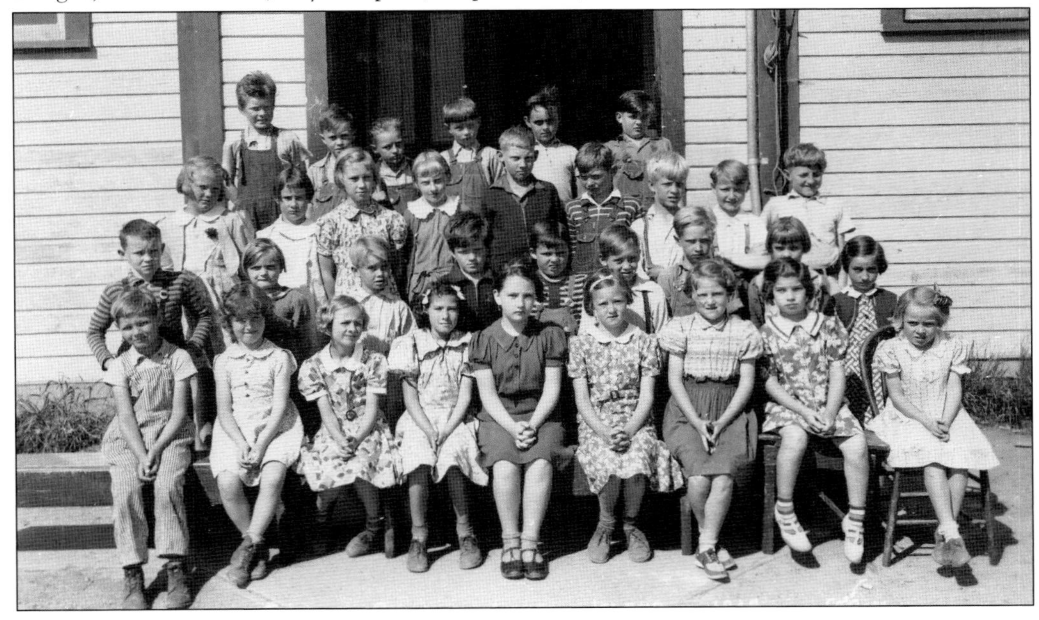

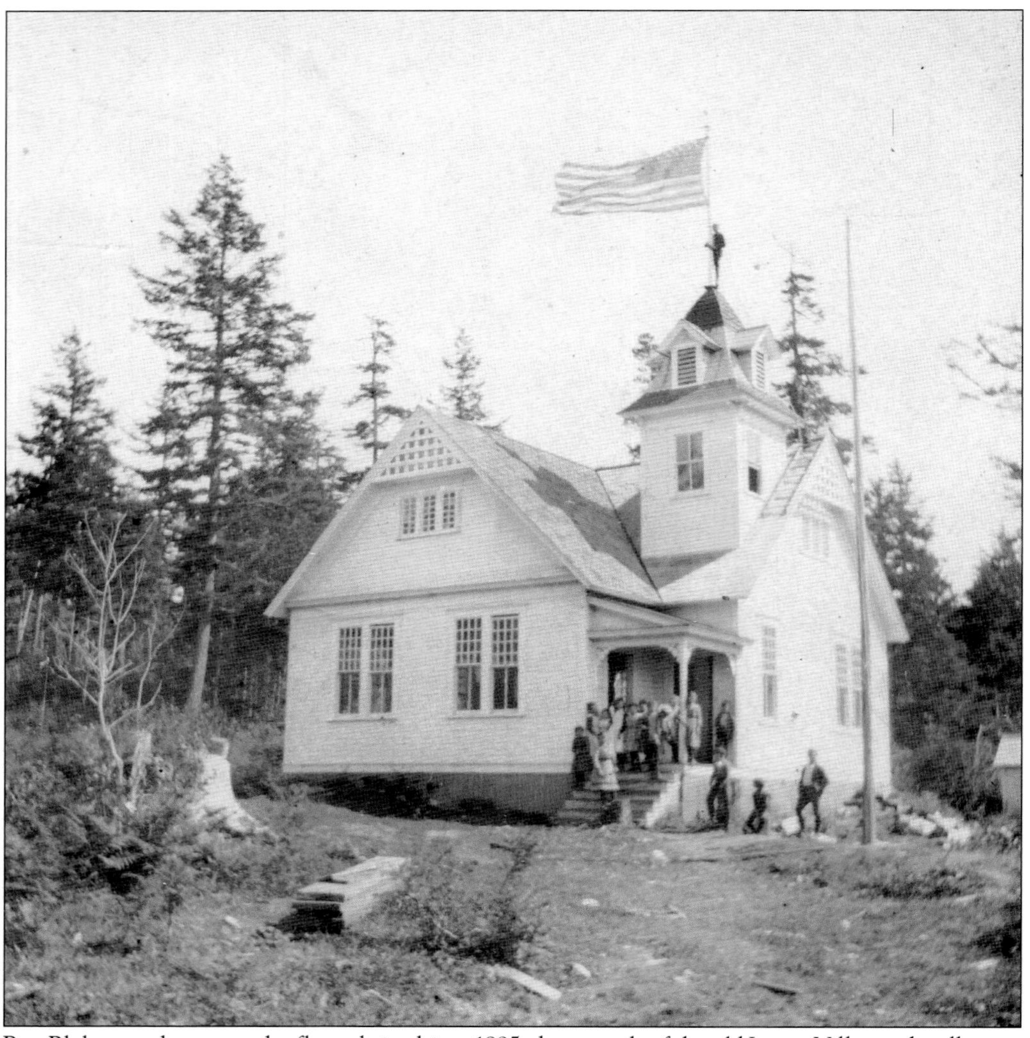

Roy Blake stands next to the flagpole in this *c.* 1895 photograph of the old Lopez Village schoolhouse. An 1894 newspaper article announced that the schooner *Port Admiral* was in port, with the lumber aboard for the new school at Lopez. By August 1894, the newspaper reported, "Our schoolhouse is well underway." The little red schoolhouse was built by Newton Jones, Jim Farnsworth, and perhaps Charles Cantine. A 1901 article reports that the school opened on Monday, May 20, with 32 pupils enrolled. The teacher was Miss Leonard. Other early teachers were Mrs. Nichols, Miss Kimple, Miss Cheaver, Sicily MacDougal, Ethel French, and Elsie Timmerman.

Twenty high school students and their teacher stand on the school steps in 1935. From left to right are (first row) Imogene Richey, Alys Blake, Norma Wilson, teacher Ira Beham, Grace Kilpatrick, Edna Gallanger, and Arthur Coffelt; (second row) Albert McCauley, unidentified, Erwin Fagerholm, Howard Brown, Philip Petersen, Robert Roberts, and Irving Buchanan; (third row) Sterling Douglas, Reggie Pickering, Ben Wood, Bernard Davies, Elbert "Bud" Hastin, Lawrence Coffelt, and unidentified.

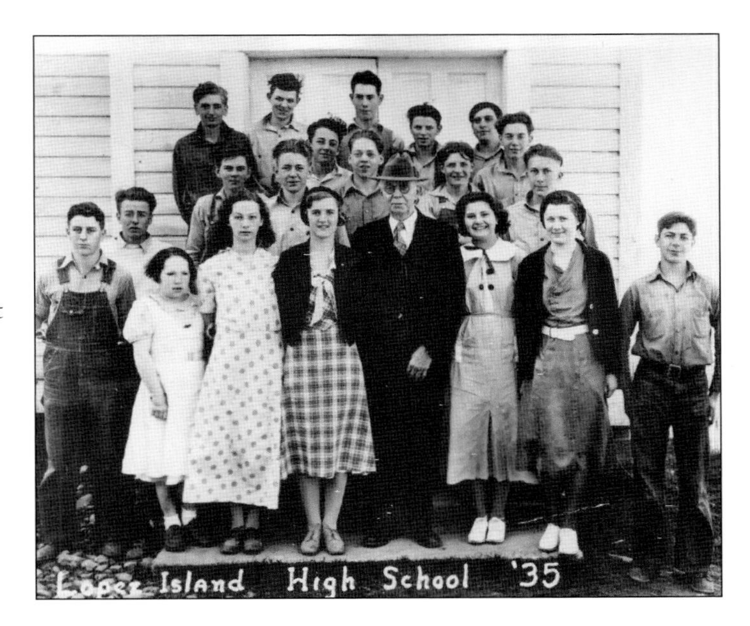

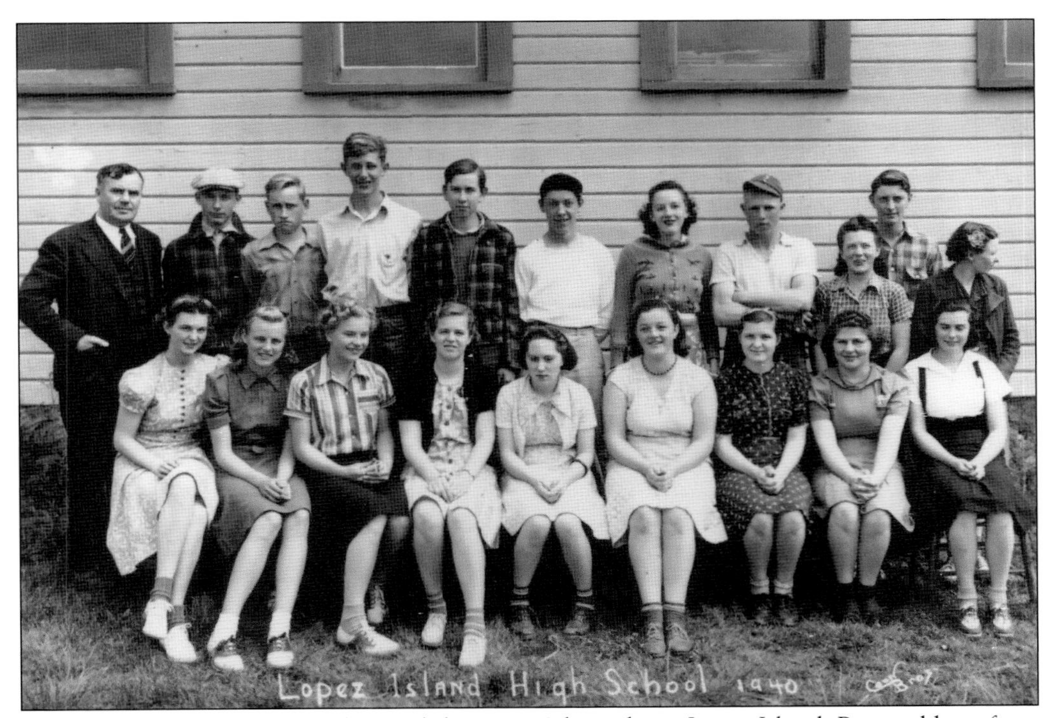

By 1940, students could complete 11th but not 12th grade on Lopez Island. Pictured here from left to right are (first row) Esther Tralnes, Marjorie McCauley, Johanna Nielsen, Jean Tralnes, Adele Richey, Alberta Peterson, Maxine Roberts, Alma Coffelt, and Mary MacLeod; (second row) teacher John Hill, Charles Lampard, Arthur Norman, Eldon Weeks, Donald Fagerholm, Arthur Kilpatrick, Mary Lovejoy, Garner McCauley, Ona Jean Gallanger, Aubrey Whitcom, and Burnell Burt.

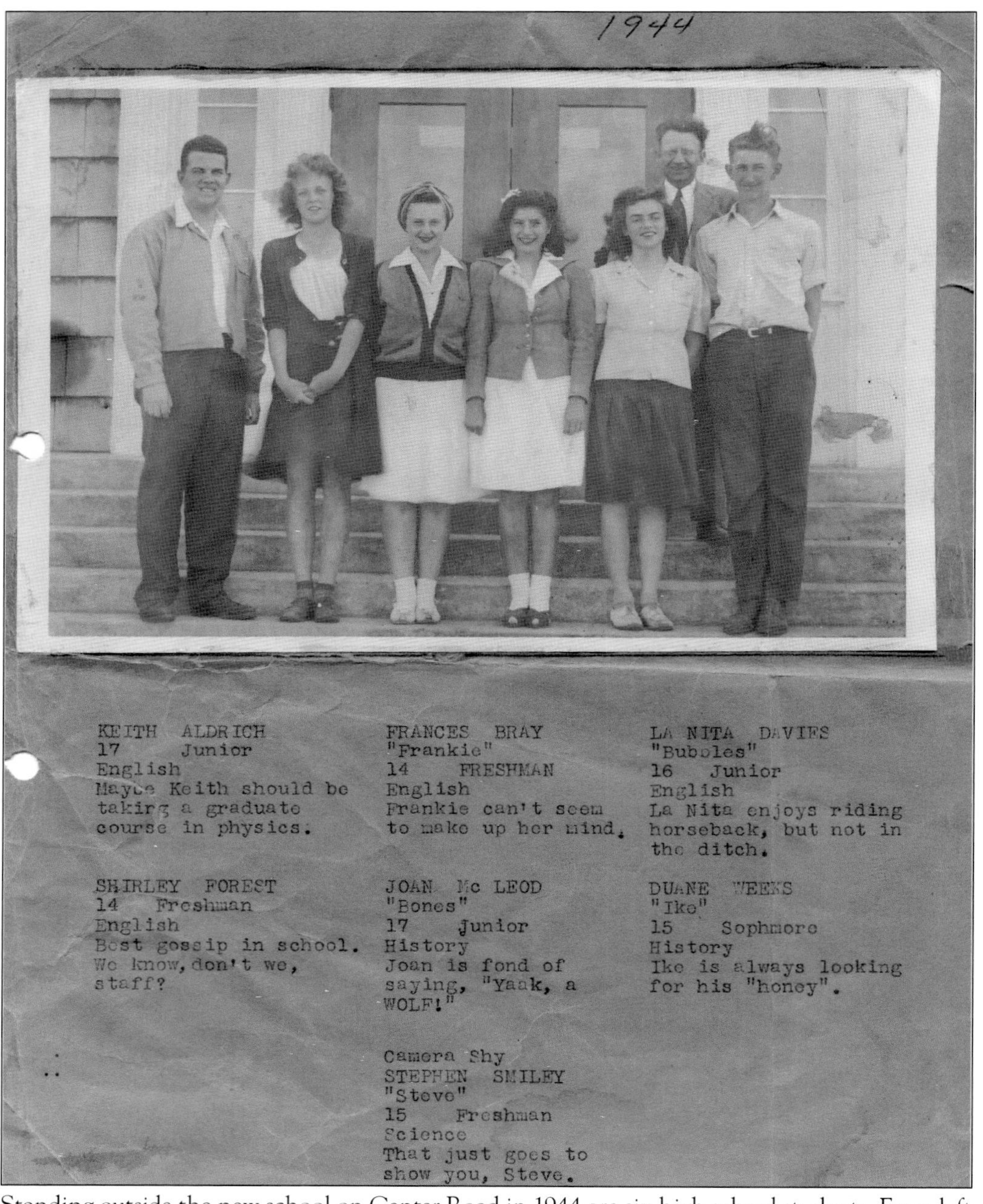

Standing outside the new school on Center Road in 1944 are six high school students. From left to right are Keith Aldrich, Shirley Forest, Frances Bray, Joan MacLeod, LaNita Davies, and Duane Weeks. The yearbook descriptions gently poke fun. They say, "Keith Aldrich, 17, junior, Maybe Keith should be taking a graduate course in physics; Shirley Forest, 14, freshman, Best gossip in school; Frances Bray, 14, freshman, Frankie can't seem to make up her mind; Joan MacLeod, 17, junior, Joan is fond of saying, 'Yaak, a WOLF!'; LaNita Davies, 16, junior, LaNita enjoys riding horseback, but not in the ditch; Duane Weeks, 15, sophomore, "Ike" is always looking for his honey." Today Weeks, a great-grandson of Amelia Davis, safeguards Lopez history, including preserving his great-grandmother's diary.

Five

Husbandry and Harvest

Writers from the late 19th through mid-20th centuries used superlatives to describe Lopez Island farming. The "best," the "finest," the "most suitable," "most favored," and "most excellent" describe the prosperous, well-kept farms Lopezians established and nurtured.

Many early Lopez farmers came from the Midwest, principally Iowa, but others were the sons and daughters of Irish farmers who fled the potato famine. On Lopez they found fertile soil, relatively flat land, and a favorable climate. In 1909, a Lopezian wrote, "A cool, even temperature will never fail to return a superior crop to the husbandman . . . Year after year, as faithfully as the tides roll and the sun shines, we get an abundant crop of perfect fruit."

Dairying was also profitable, and by 1908, the island had its own creamery and shipped 1,500 pounds of butter a month to Seattle, Bellingham, and Anacortes. By 1930, there were 134 farms on the island, and Lopez shipped 15,000 pounds of cream and large quantities of eggs, poultry, fruit, and other products.

In 1964, writer David Richardson noted Lopez's 500 inhabitants lived much the same way as their pioneer fathers and grandfathers had: "Now, as then," he wrote, "the best way to make a living on Lopez is to wrest it from the soil, or from the sea."

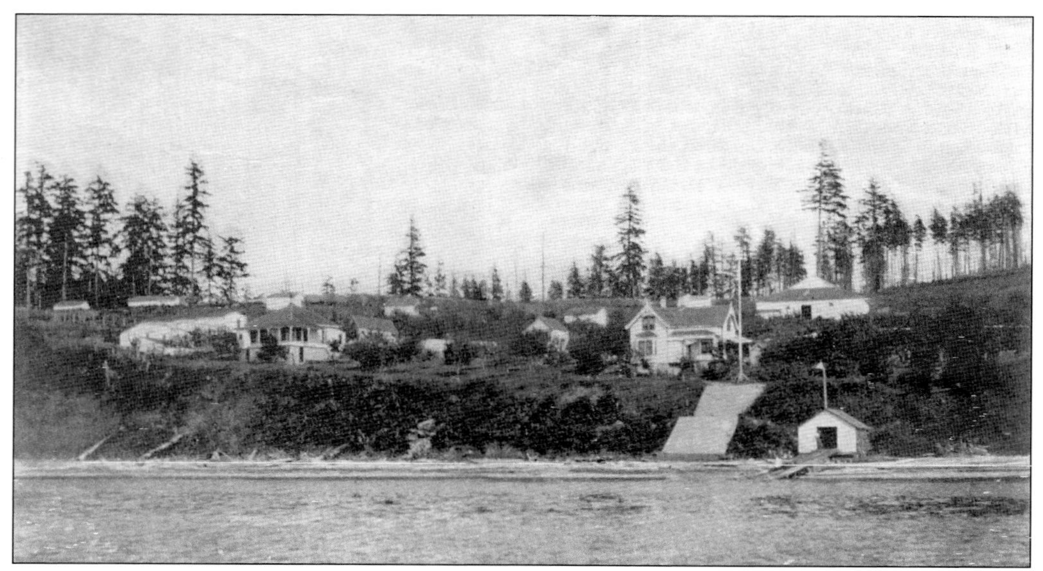

Located 2 miles north of Lopez village, the 800-acre Gem Farm had 500 prolific fruit trees, up to 1,000 chickens, and a herd of prize Jersey cows. Judge I. J. Lichtenberg moved from New York City to Seattle, became King County's first superior court judge, and then retired to Lopez Island to start Gem Farm in 1897. His son Ben later became the proprietor. No trace of the farm exists today.

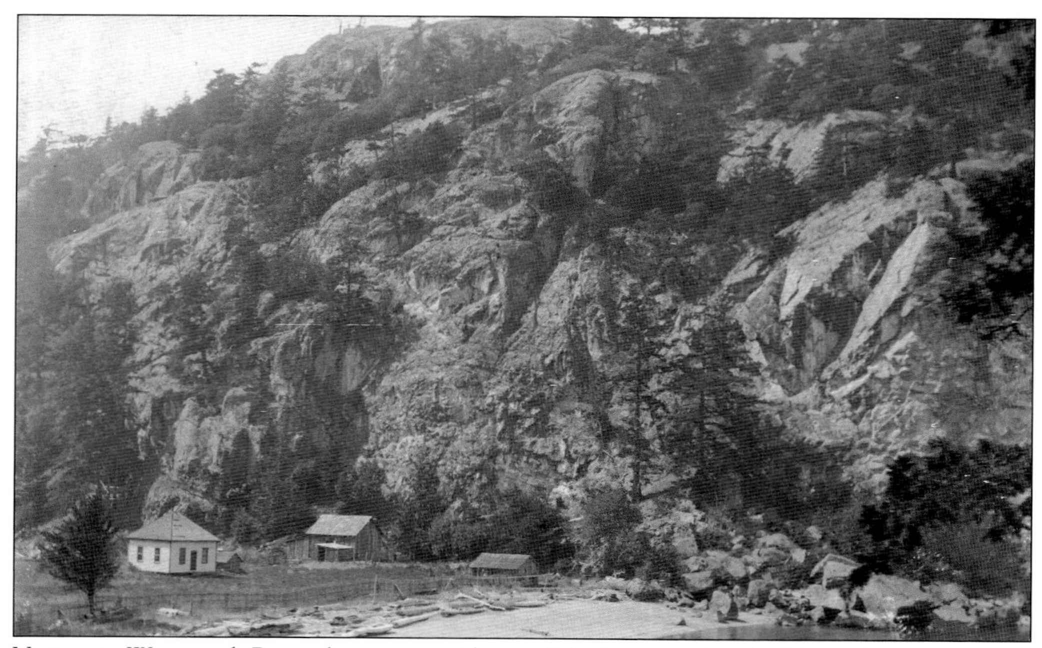

Visitors to Watmough Bay today see no evidence of the house and outbuildings that once graced the shoreline and were owned by Mr. Mork (pronounced *Merk*). Mork kept a cow, made butter, and sold it at Richardson store. The hill was known as Mork's Mountain until people started to call it Chadwick Hill. Early shoreline farms relied on the sea for transportation.

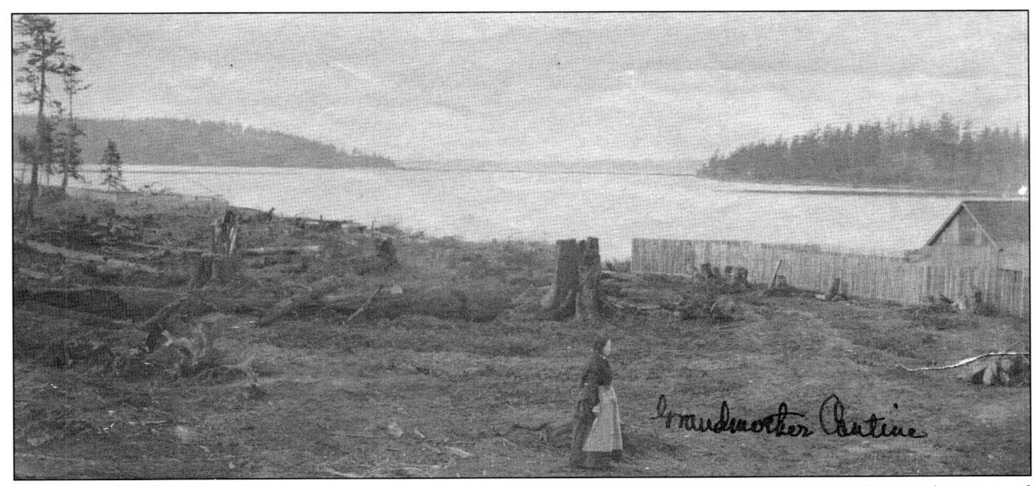

About 1893, Charles Cantine moved to Lopez Island with his wife and mother, shown here, and cleared a "dense labyrinth of trees," south of the current transfer station. Cantine planted an orchard of 1,200 fruit trees, and in 1900, he shipped 300 boxes of apples, 1,000 pounds of cherries, 1,500 pounds of prunes, and 40 cases of strawberries to market. Cantine helped build the Lopez Congregational Church.

Cash Paid out

9 Dys stump puller	27.00
9 " (Wood) helper	9.00
13½ " Wright. Hauling stumps & plowing	27.00
1 " Wood cleaning stumps	1 00
1 " Hasting " "	1.00
Apple & other Trees	29.50
Frgt & Same	6.00
Help setting Trees	5 00
Taxes on your land	3.16
	108.66
	54.22
	162.88

My work on your land & board acct-

2½ day Pulling stumps with horse & chain	5.00
9 Dys Self & horse pul stumps	20.25
4 " " Horse & waggon picking up stumps	8.00
2½ dys setting Trees	3.12
Boarding men	
Bird 9 dys, Wood 10 ", Wright 13 ", Other 5 " — 37 dys, 30¢ per day	11.10
	3.70
Boarding Wrights Team 13½ dys 50¢ per day	6.75
	54.22
	3.70
	57.92
	9.00
	66.92

Rec'd from You

Oct	25.00
Dec	50.00
Jan	52.00
Feb	55 00
Mar	30 00
"	30 00
	242 00

Paid Warren 4.00
" 55 5 0

66.92
108.66
175.58

Crop acct

Sowing oats & peas	
Harrowing in same	3.00
Planting potatoes	5.02
Picking up roots	
Cash 3½ days	4.55
Self Horse 3½	5.25
For Seed peas & oats	4.50
8 sacks potatoes	2.50

Following the financial panic of 1893, Cantine bought 600 apple trees for $42 (or 7¢ each) for his new orchard. Cantine kept a detailed record of expenditures spent to clear land and plant trees, as shown here. A letter writer, Cantine regularly corresponded with his son Ed, and in 1896, he wrote, "Between weather and bugs and democracy, the farmer has a rocky time of it."

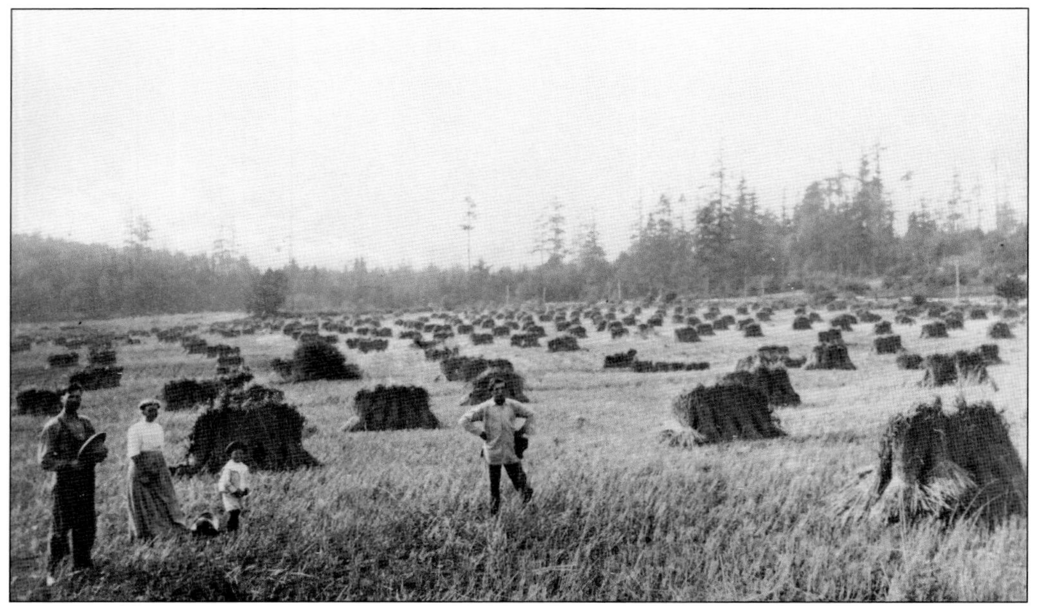

Sam McCauley stands in front of neatly piled stacks of grain with his son and daughter-in-law, Jim and Barbara McCauley. Sam and his wife, Jane, had seven sons and moved west from Ontario, Canada, to San Juan Island. When the McCauley boys did not like San Juan, the family moved to Lopez Island to join Jane's brother James Buchanan and Jim and Barbara, who had already made Lopez home.

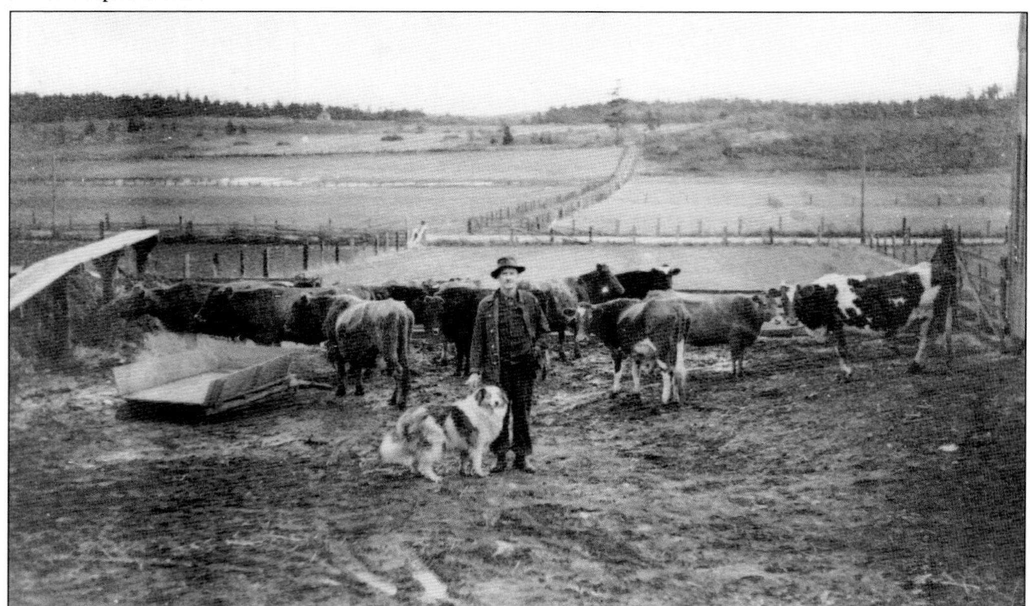

Jim McCauley and his dog Jock stand at the McCauley farm near his dairy herd. McCauley's daughter Marguerite Goodrow recalls that cream was picked up by the San Juan Dairy Association and West Coast Creamery. After threshing, grain was ground for the cattle and excess was sent for sale from Richardson. Everybody helped each other. Goodrow said if people had extra potatoes, they shared them.

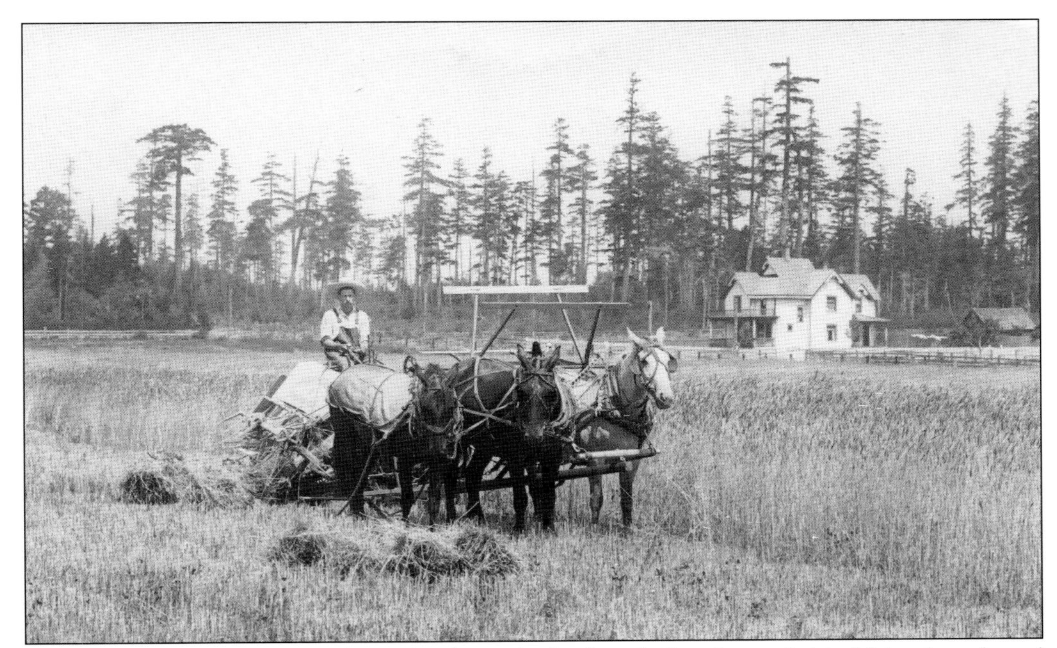

Wallace Burt sits on a horse-drawn binder with the Joseph Burt house behind him. Joseph and John Burt, together with their brother Peter and his son Robert, built the "house of seven gables." John designed the house, which included a library, a reception hall, four bedrooms, and a laundry chute between floors. The house later passed to Otto Kjargaard and was moved to its present location on Airport Road in 1979.

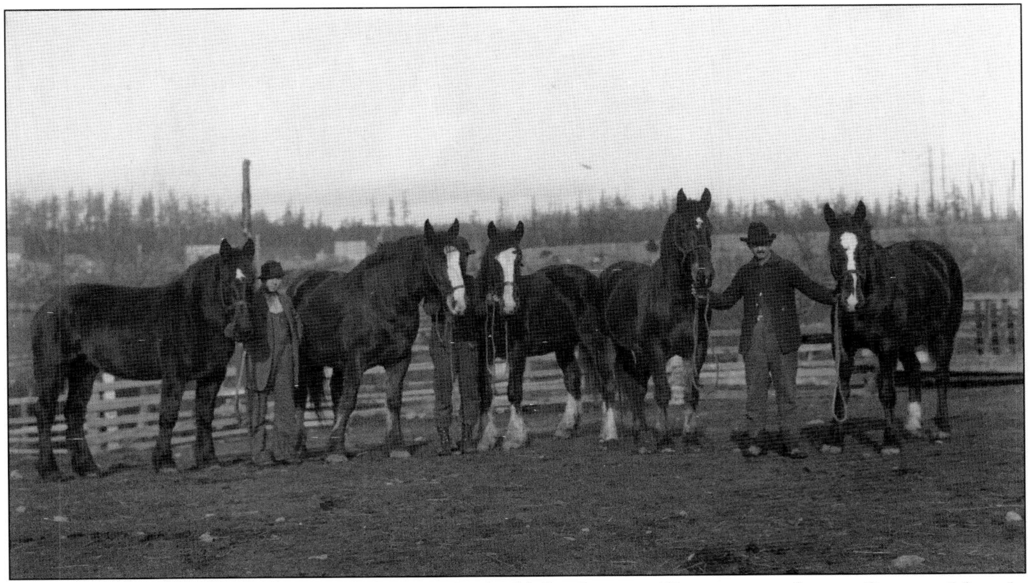

Bill Burt, Henry Bartlett, and Sam McCauley hold five horses. Horses served an indispensable role in farming, from pulling the plow or binder to transporting people, crops, cream, grain, or fruit to the docks, where steamers picked them up to be sold in mainland markets. Horsemanship was a skill prized by islanders whose livelihoods depended on these utilitarian, well-loved partners.

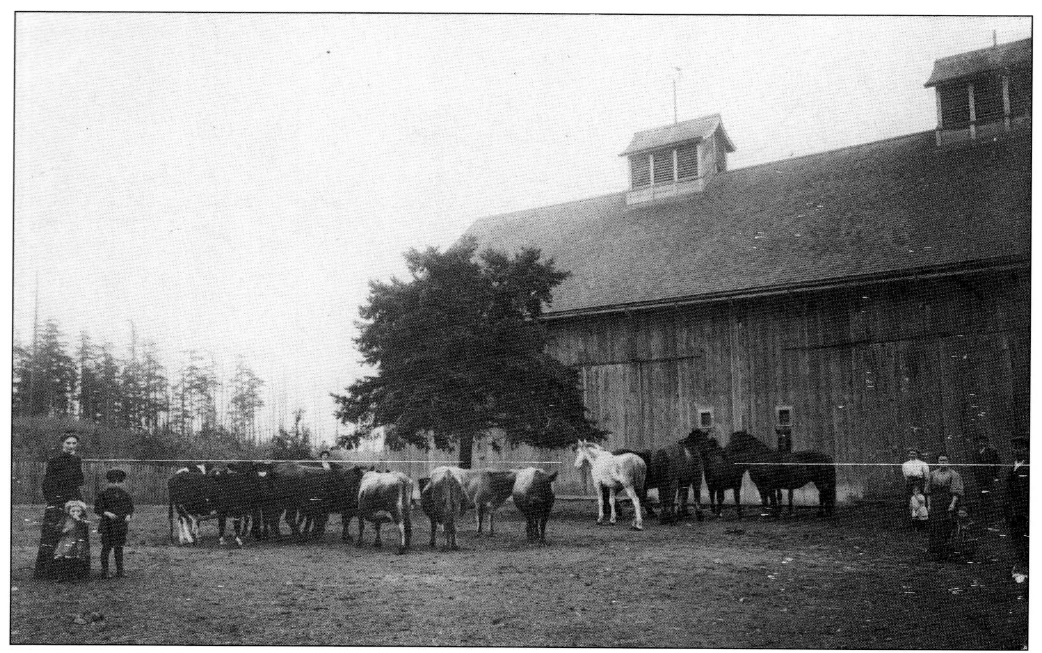

Horses and cows gather in front of Lyman Weeks's barn on Channel Road. Standing from left to right are Henrietta Blake Weeks, Ellis Weeks, and Lincoln Weeks. The people on the right are not identified. After Hiram E. Hutchinson died, his sister Irene developed Lopez Village. Lyman Weeks, wanting to leave the "crowded" village, moved to the 160-acre homestead in 1880, and in 1890, the Novotny brothers built the barn. The farm later belonged to George Gallanger.

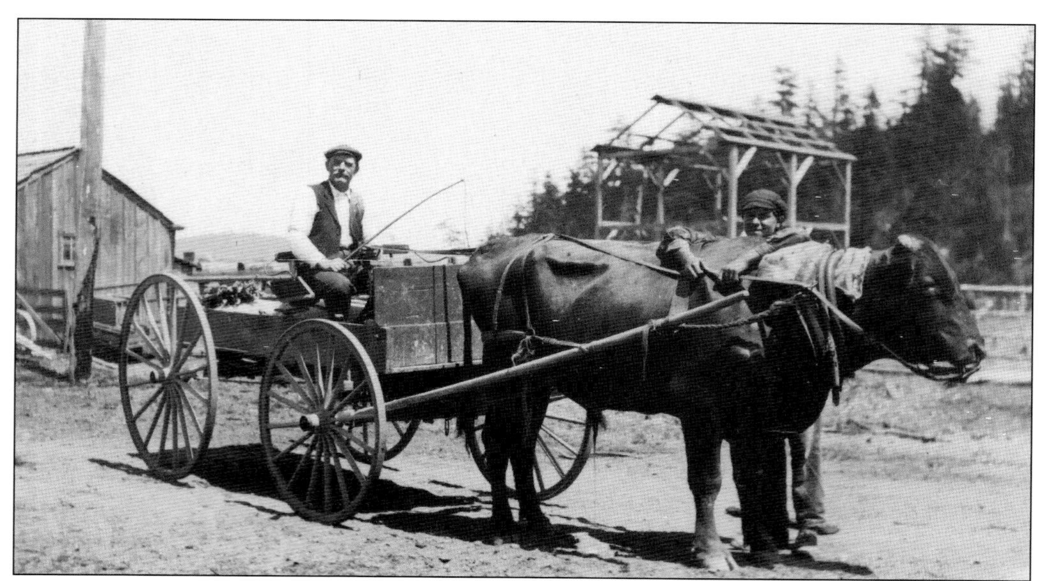

Tom Bell sits in the buggy seat and holds the reins of an ox-drawn wagon, and Stephen Orcutt stands with his arms resting on his ox's back. Bell was born in Scotland and arrived on Lopez Island about 1893. Orcutt came to Lopez as a child in 1899. Oxen were a powerful, gentle alternative to horses with the strength to pull out a tree stump or transport heavy grain sacks.

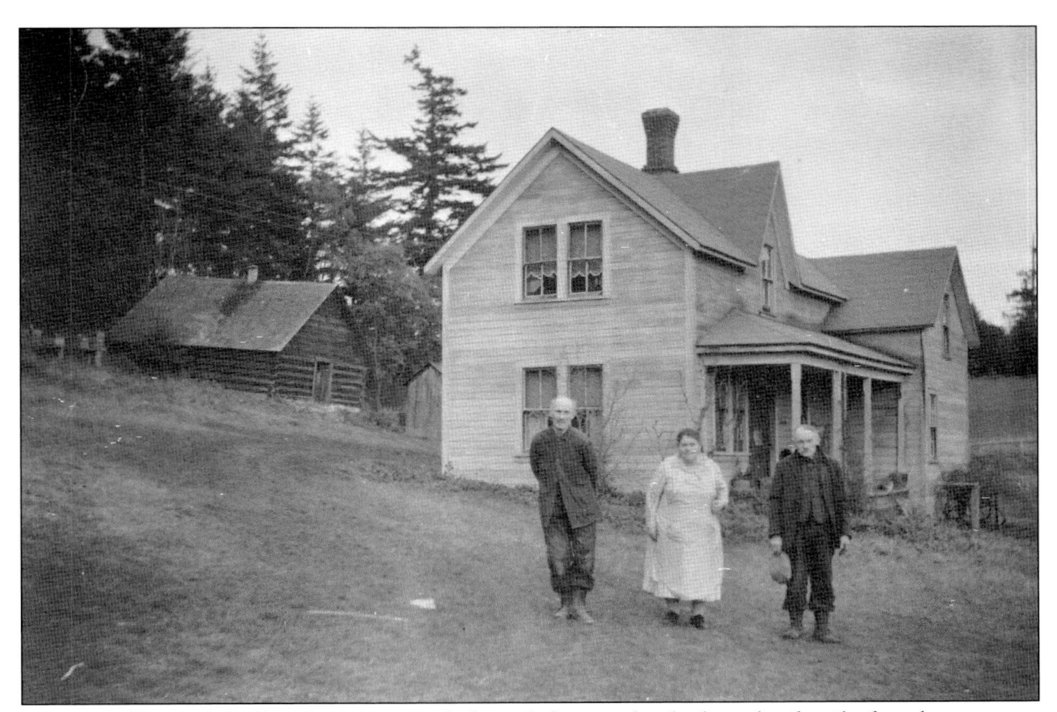

Jimmie, Ella, and Willie Cousins stand, from left to right, before the family farmhouse near Hunter Bay. Their father, James, hired Jasper and John Coffelt to build a small family home, and the house was moved to its present location and enlarged. The farm produced fruit, grain, and cattle. Ella taught school on Lopez Island from 1883 to 1891. Willie and Jimmie were bachelors and continued to farm together after their parents died.

1940
April 10 Fine day
I hauled rocks for the ditch all
day Lee Wilson laid the rocks in
the ditch all day Roy Wilson helped me
haul rocks in the afternoon.
Mrs Schruder and Son Myer visited
us in the afternoon. Fifty seven
years ago today we left San Fran
cisco. for Port Townsend. There was
Father and Mother and Ella. James
and myself. and Uncle William
Heron. Robert Carr and doughter
Mary Jane. Henry Cuyle his wife and
four children three boys and a girl
His brother in law George First
and wife. and two other men, an
Irishman named Tom King and an
English-man named Bill Waters
they were both going to Seattle. The
Cuyles were going to ~~Osceola~~ Osceola
King co Wash Henry Cuyle died
in 1905
April 11 Warm Spring day I hauled
rocks with Baldy and Dan Roy
Wilson hauled rocks with Barney
His father Lee Wilson laid the rocks in ditch

Willie Cousins kept a detailed diary that recorded daily Lopez farm life. In this 1940 excerpt, he records hauling rocks that day, as well as a memory of all the people he traveled with 57 years earlier when he and his family left San Francisco for Port Townsend and eventually Lopez. In another entry in 1948, Willie wrote, "I hoed Canada thistles. I hoed out 3,800 today."

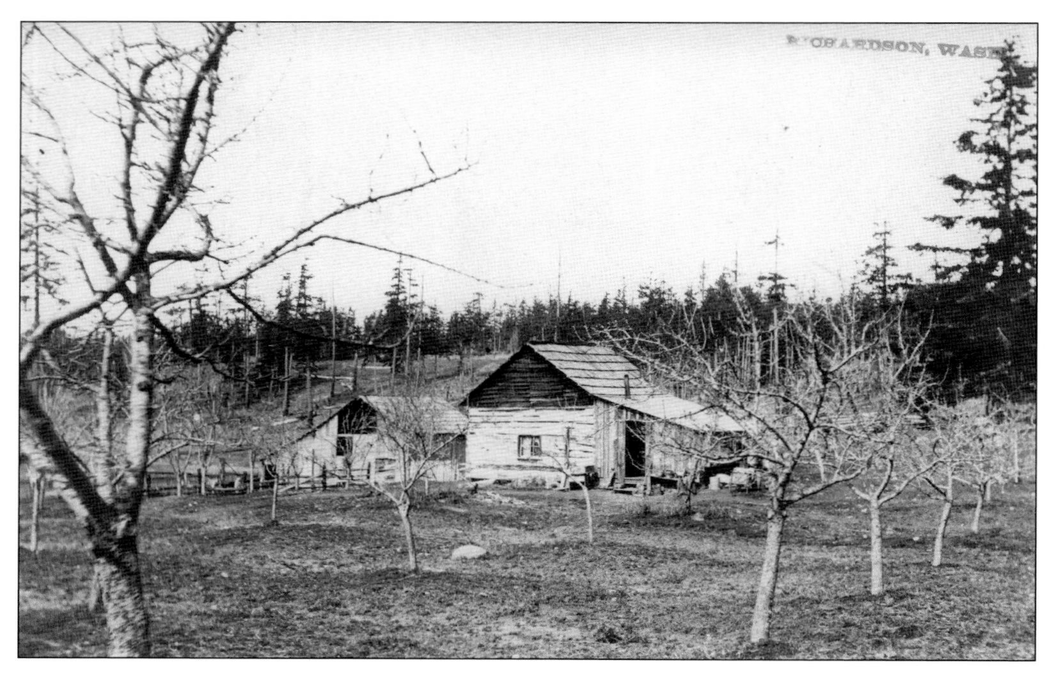

Born in County Cork, Ireland, Bartholomew (Bat) Clancy came to Lopez in 1883 as a boy of 14 to help his aunt Ellen Clancy and uncle John Bartlett on their farm in the Center Valley. Bat later had his own farm with a farmhouse, barn, and orchard at the north end of Mud Bay Road, shown above. He raised and owned dozens of horses and a flock of sheep and is seen below standing with his bull Nye. He is credited with bringing with him the yellow rose that grows along Mud Bay Road just south of Center Road when he moved to Lopez from Ireland. He remained a bachelor and died in 1931.

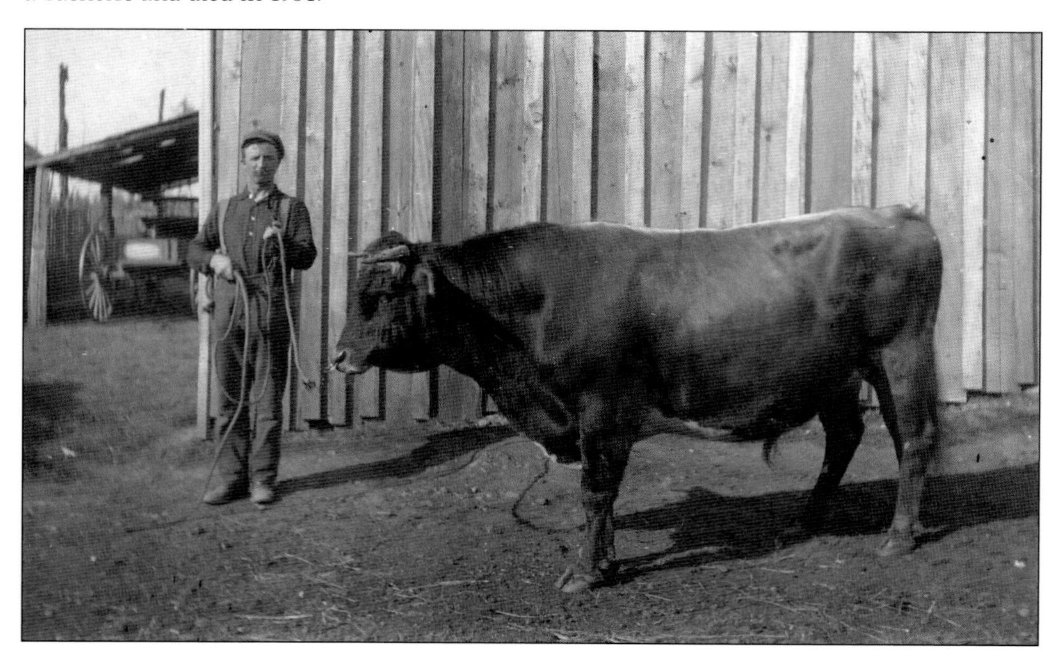

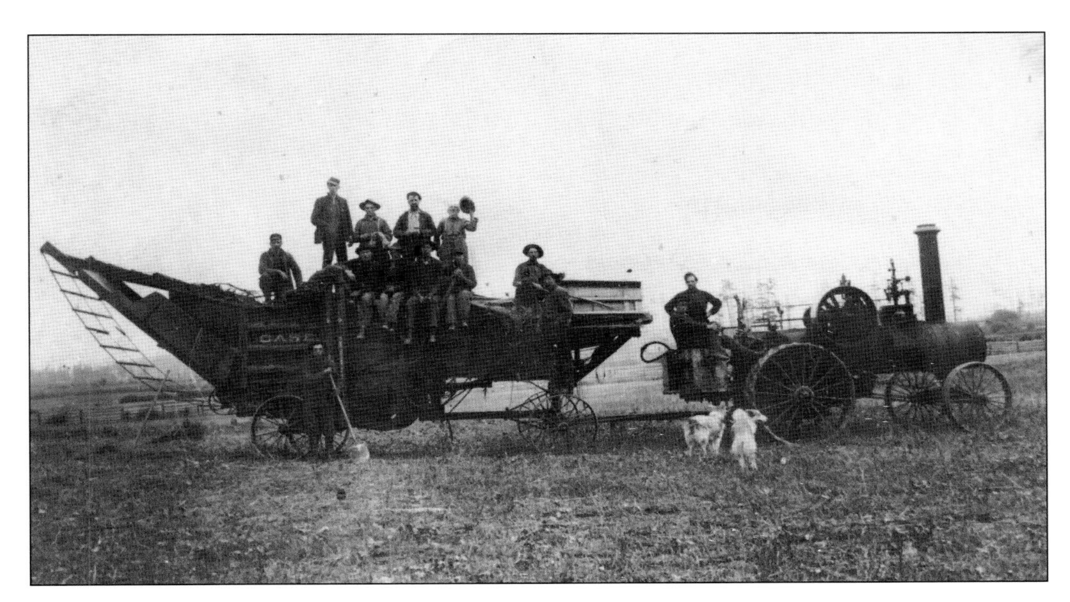

Threshing machines remove grain from the chaff, or straw. John Bartlett brought the first threshing machine to Lopez in 1876. Farmers worked together moving from farm to farm to get all the grain harvested. In the 1910 photograph above, Bartlett waves his hat, while James H. Buchanan is on the tractor. The threshing crew pitched bundles into the threshing machine, got wood and water for the steam engine, and hauled away the freshly threshed grain. Women helped and often cooked for the crew. Below, threshing crew members from left to right are (first row) Jim Buchanan, Bat Clancy, Corrine Buchanan, Ed Sumner, Percy Towell, perhaps Leo Towell, Frank Stevens, Lou Bolton, perhaps Bill Burt, unidentified, unidentified, Tom or Charlie McCauley, unidentified, and Ellen Bartlett; (second row) Jennie Buchanan, Norman Wilson, Lyle Visgar, unidentified, Sam Wilson, and Bartlett.

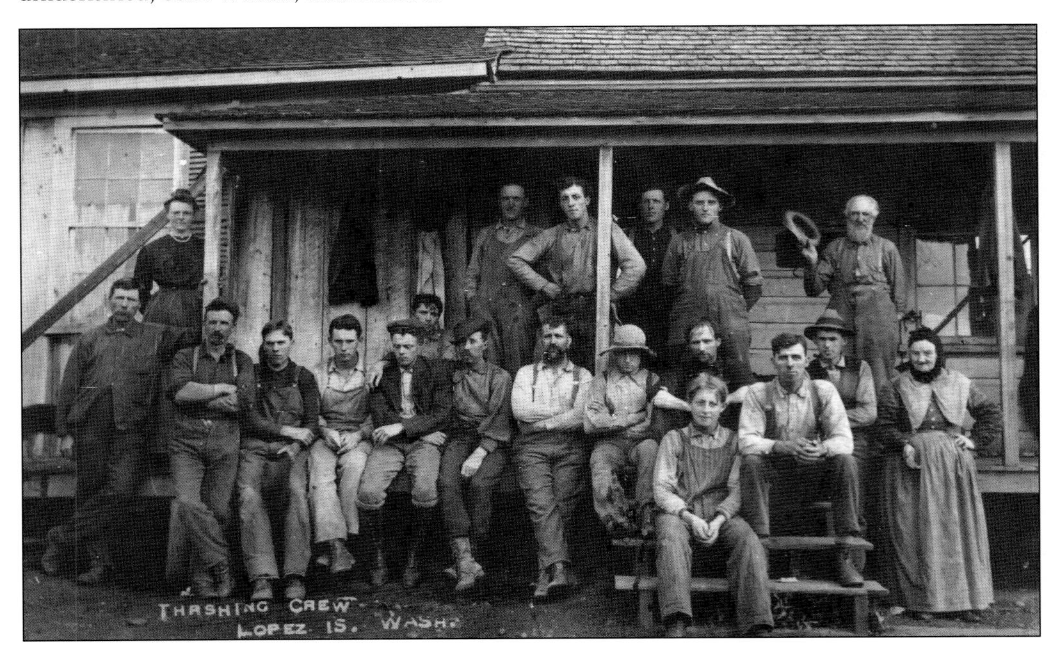

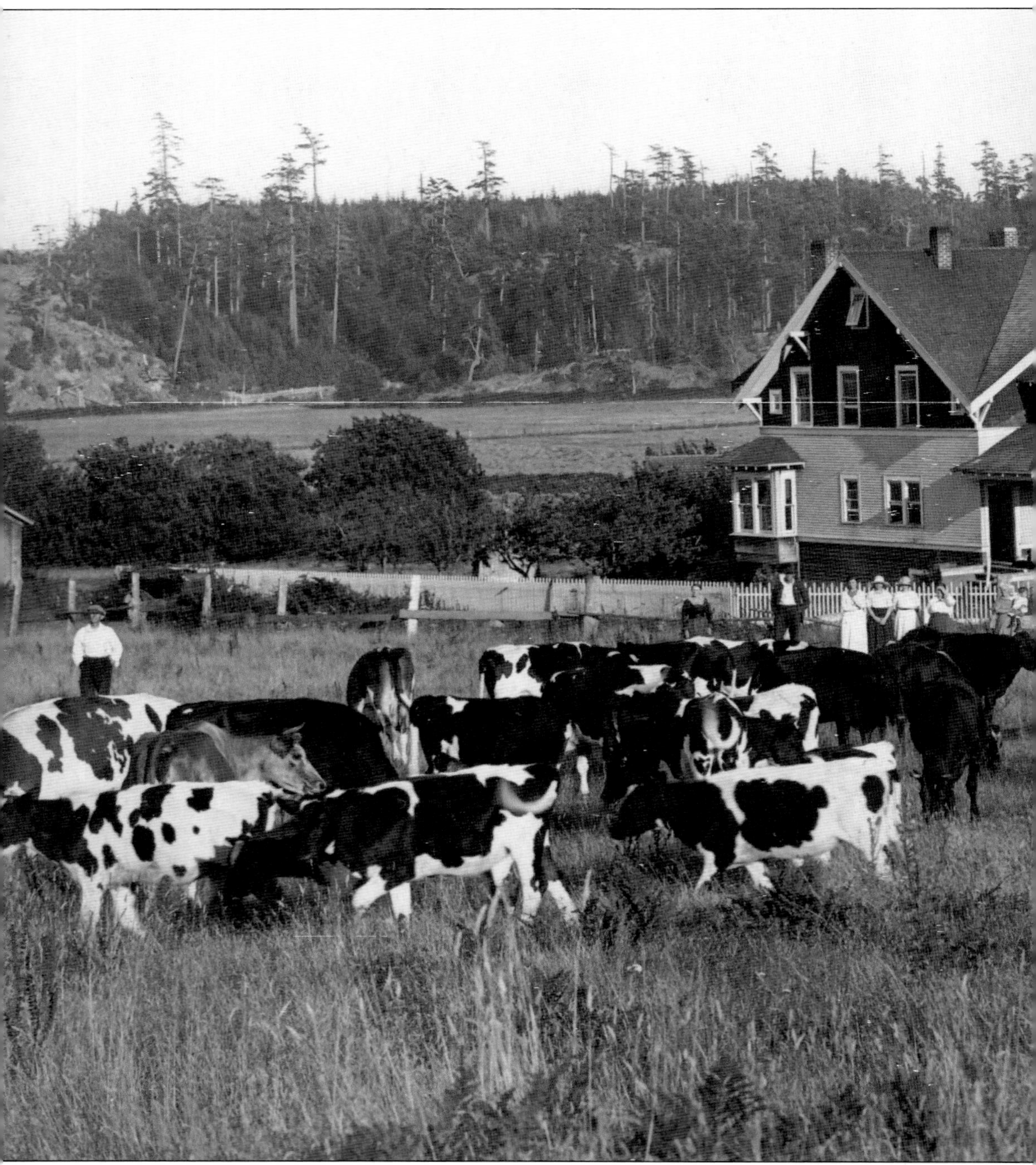

The above photograph captured the third house on James and Amelia Davis's property, known as the Davis Ranch, around 1921. The Davis family raised cattle, sheep, pigs, chickens, and horses, as well as fruit, berries, potatoes, vegetables, hay, and grains. Farming produced enough to supply the family with a little to spare, but fishing was the family's primary income source. Family legend says that their son James Ernest Davis earned enough money from one year's successful fish trap to build the house. Amelia carded, spun, knitted, dyed wool, made clothes for the family, and

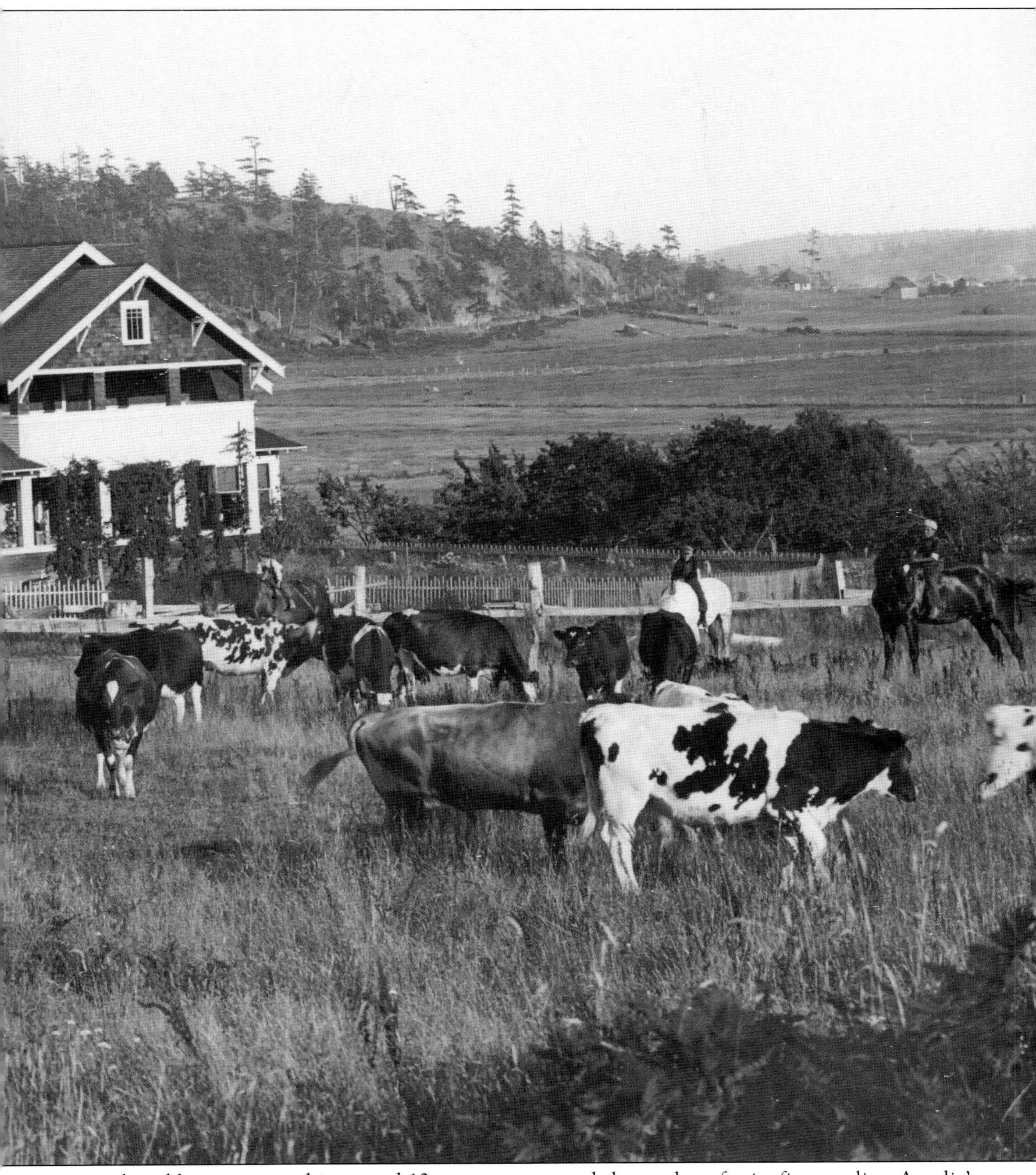

produced butter so good it earned 10¢ more per pound than others for its fine quality. Amelia's great-grandson Duane Weeks identified family members in the photograph. From left to right are Russell, Arthetta, James Ernest, Lenore (without hat), Bernice, unidentified, and unidentified. James Ernest's wife, Maybelle Troxell Davis, stands below the steps holding their youngest child, Gaza Lorraine Davis. Noel, Leonard, and Hilliard are on horseback.

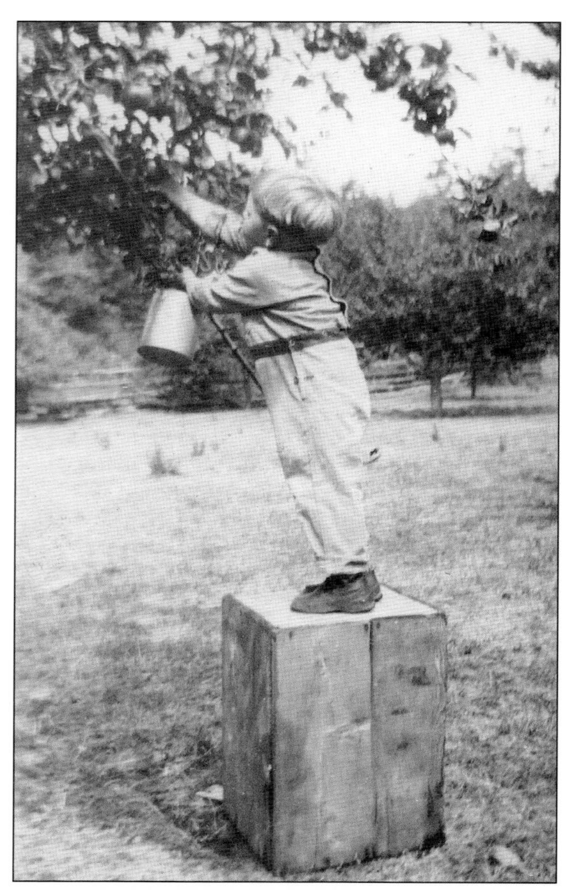

Donald Fagerholm stands on a fruit box picking apples at his grandparents' Mary Jane and Erwin Eaton's farm. Fagerholm was born at the MacKaye Harbor fish camp and later lived in the village. He moved to Friday Harbor to finish high school, where he worked in a dairy for room and board. He joined the air force during World War II.

Avery and Bob Wilson, wearing identical hats and jackets, hold a horse and a colt named Ginger. The photograph was taken about 1910 at the Wilson barn. The boys' parents were Samuel Wilson and Mary Eliza Gallanger. Island children did not often get special treats such as ice cream, as it was not generally available, but ice cream did arrive by boat for special occasions, including holidays.

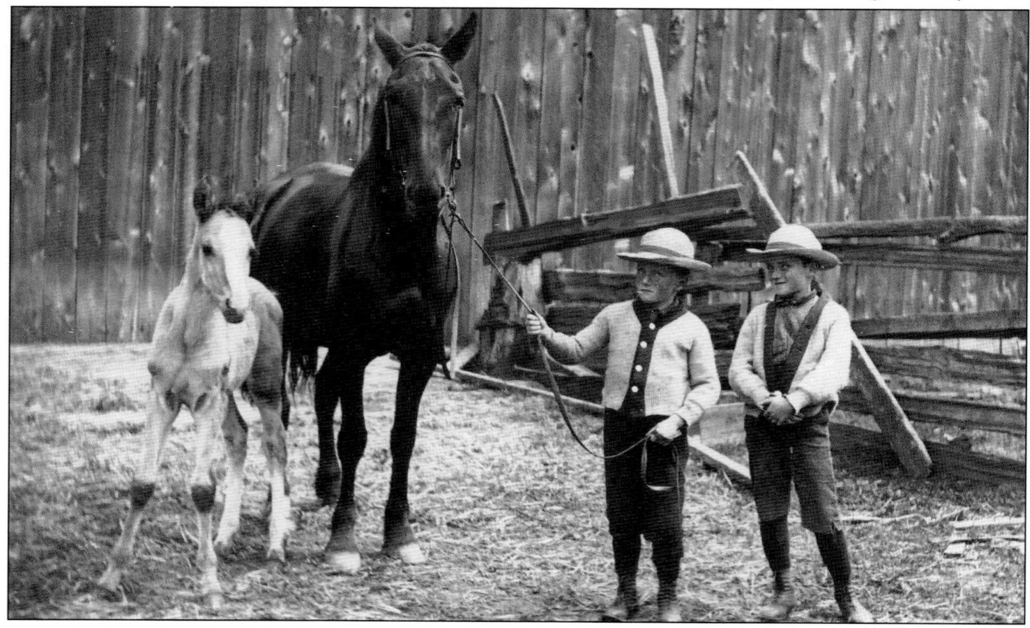

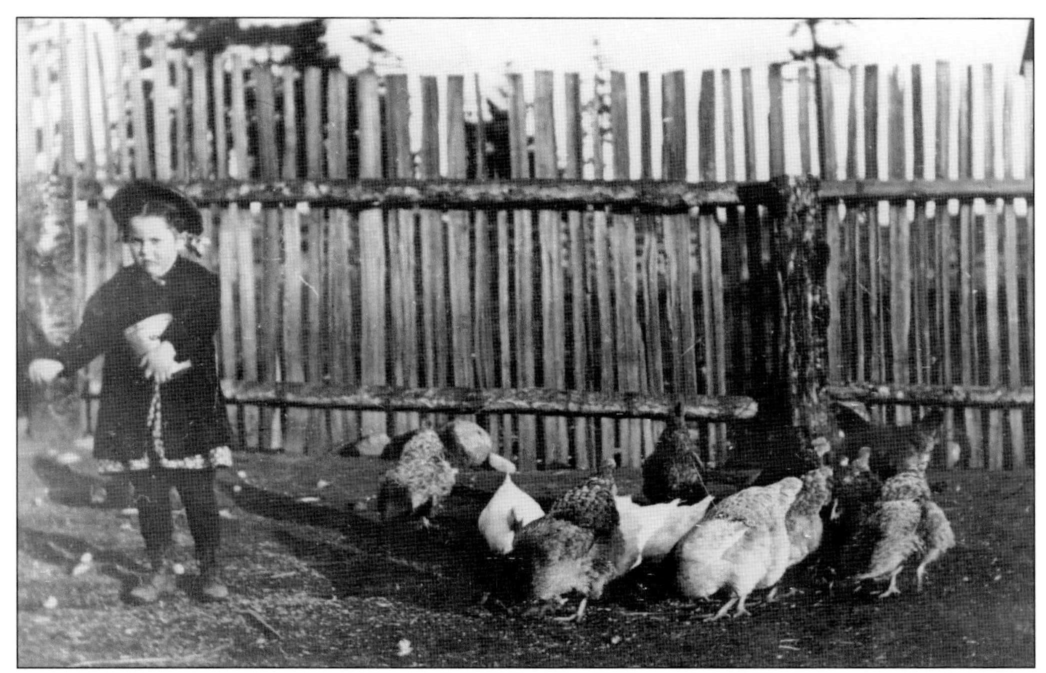

Zella Wilson feeds the family chickens from a tin can. Born in 1907, Zella was the daughter of William Wilson and Gladys Taylor. Children often helped on the farm by doing daily chores, feeding chickens, or gathering eggs. Saturday night was typically bath night, and parents brought the boiler pan to the stove to heat water. Zella married Ernest Froberg and eventually moved to Bellingham.

Here one of the Davies's children, probably Bernard, holds the reins of two very strong, trustworthy draft horses named Babe and Bettie at the family's Dill Road farmhouse. Gerald Davies remembers, "Our father worked very hard plowing the fields, planting and harvesting crops with a team of horses." The family had a large garden, milked about 12 cows, raised and slaughtered their own meat, and raised chickens for eggs.

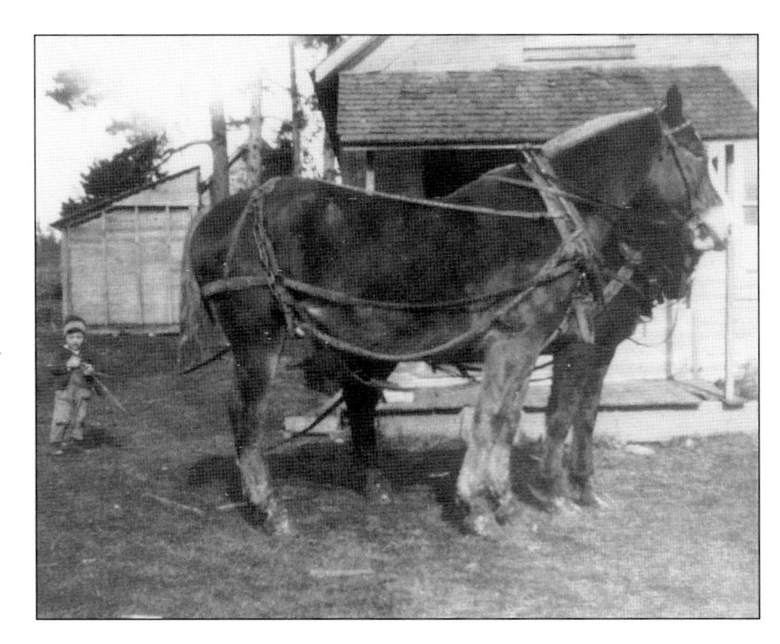

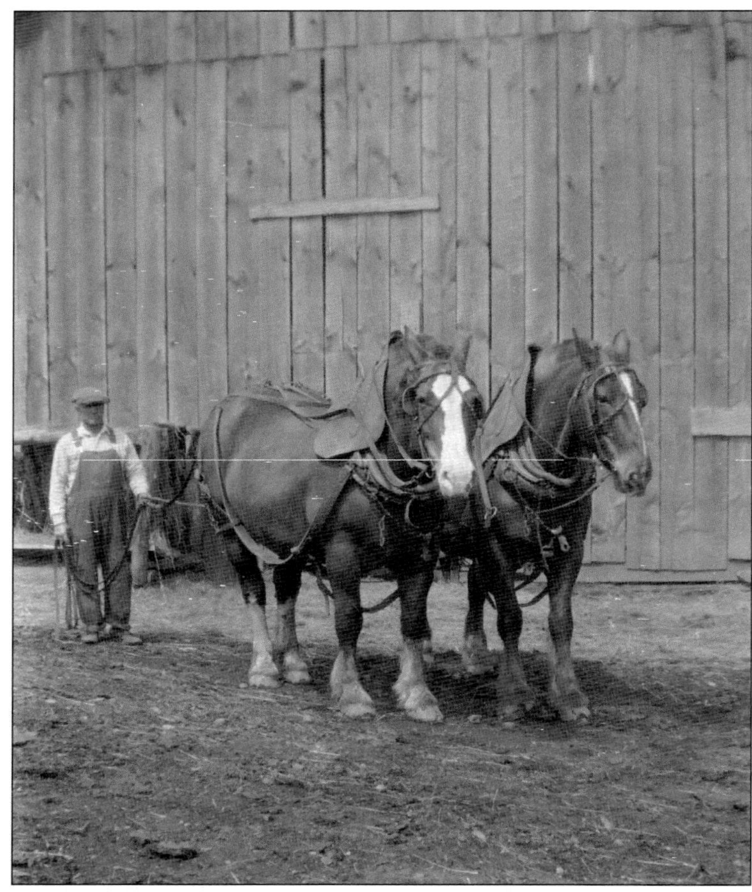

The photograph at left depicts George Wilson and a team of horses outside William Graham's barn at Richardson. Wilson rented the place from Graham before Graham sold it to his stepson N. P. Hodgson. The photograph below shows the barns and silos after the farm was sold to Hodgson. Hodgson had a herd of purebred, registered Guernsey cows, and these buildings represent a typical dairy farm, with the creamery to the right. In the 1930s, Lopez was known as the "Guernsey Island." By the 1980s, the silos were gone and the barn converted to a home and caretaker's apartment.

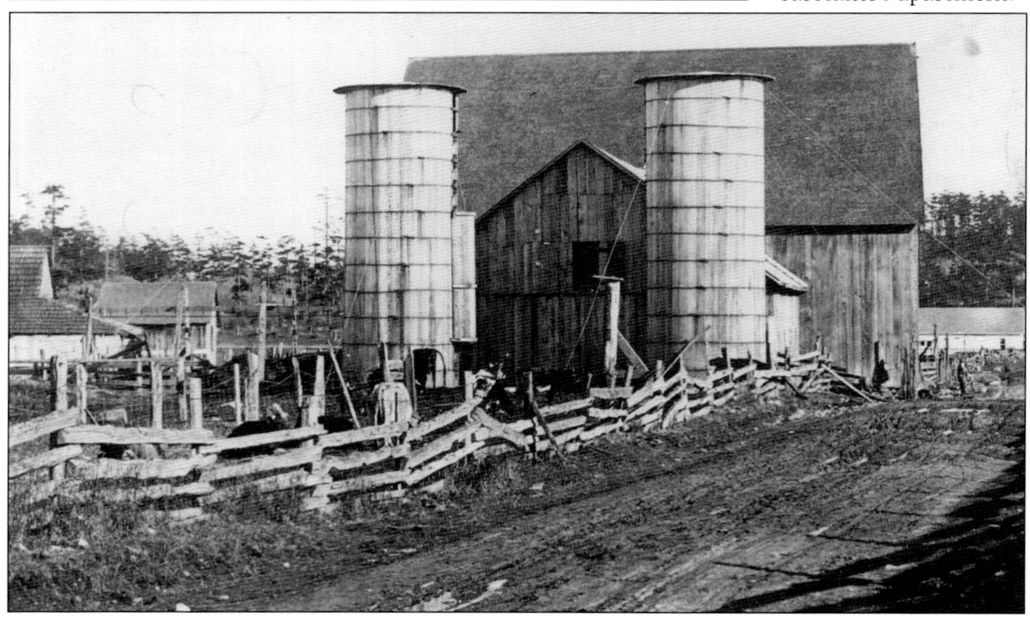

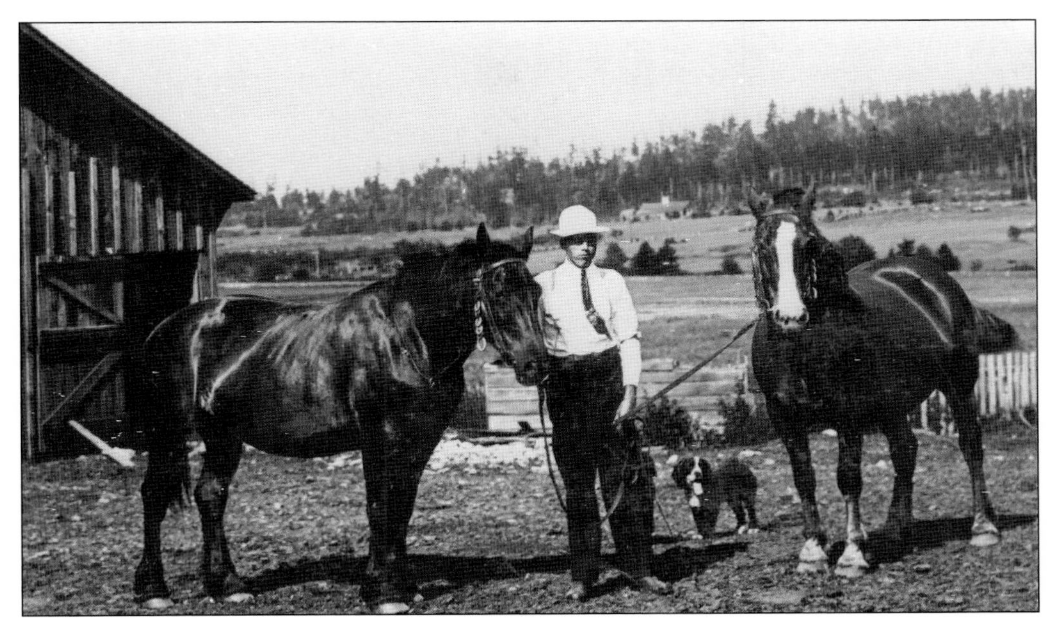

Geordie McCauley, in a shirt and tie, stands with horses. He was one of seven sons of Jane and Sam McCauley and the twin brother of Matthew Edmond "Eddie" McCauley. When asked what she liked best about life on Lopez, one old-timer said, "It's the greatest place to raise your kids." Geordie married and raised a large family with his wife, Ruth.

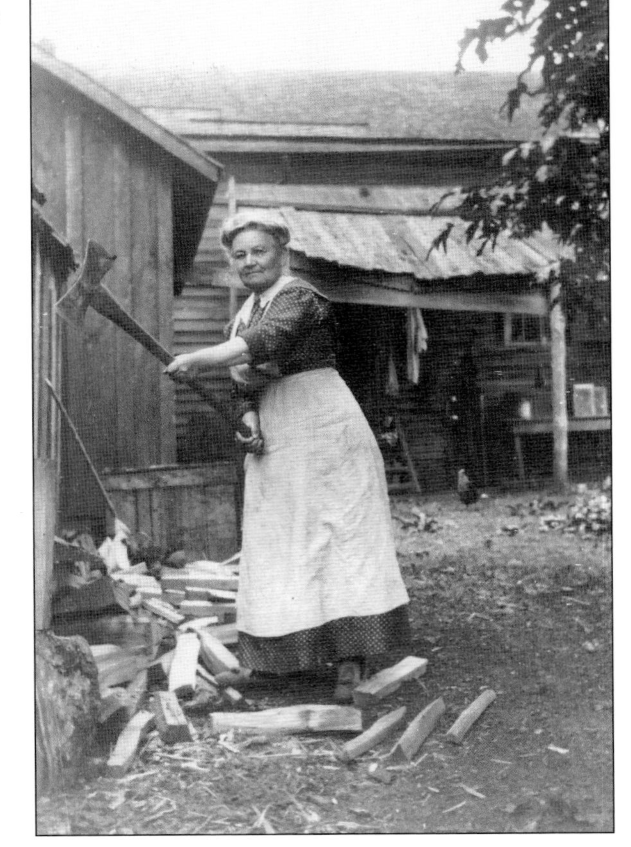

Maria Hackwell splits wood on her place near Sperry Peninsula. The third of eight daughters born to Charles and Mary Brown, Maria was married to James (John) Hackwell and John Osgoodby, who each passed away, and finally Ben Korman. She had two children with James (John) Hackwell, Laura and James, who are buried next to her in the Lopez Union Cemetery.

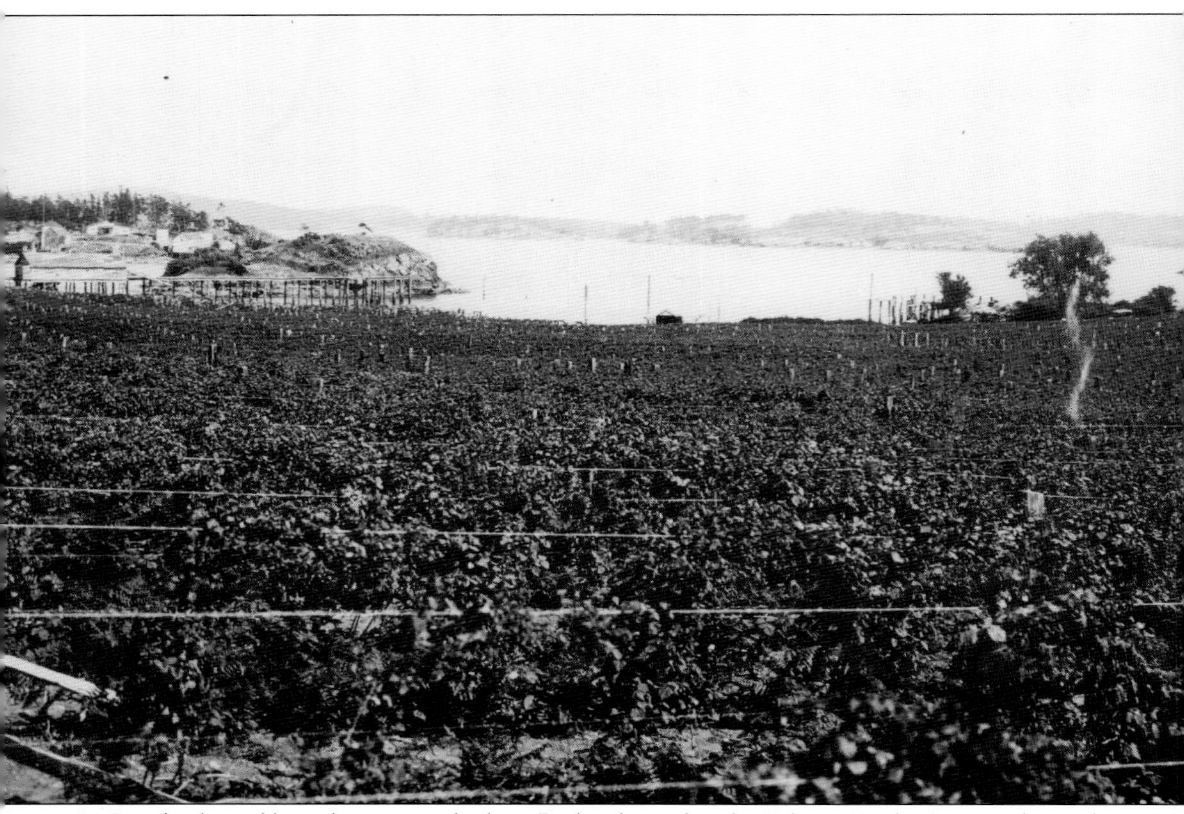

Ira Lundy planted loganberries overlooking Richardson after the Salmon Banks Cannery burned down in 1922. The berry patch gave employment to many former cannery workers, as well as other islanders. This 1923 view looks toward Richardson and shows the first Richardson store just above the Hidden Inlet Cannery before the new one was built in the late 1920s out over the water. The pilings in the photograph may be the remnants of the Salmon Banks Cannery. The first year Marguerite McCauley Goodrow picked berries at Lundy's loganberry patch, she was seven years old. She remembers that regular pickers were paid 18¢ per flat crate, and each crate contained 12 boxes. People who only picked occasionally received 15¢ per flat. Goodrow was an 18¢-per-flat picker, made $25 in her first year, and picked every summer thereafter.

Six

When Fish Was King

Reefnetting, a fishing technique originated by Native Americans, has been practiced in Lopez waters for perhaps thousands of years. Historian John Goekler writes that Iceberg Point, Flat Point, and the mouth of Fisherman Bay were home to Native American fish gears of the Samish Tribe on southern Lopez Island and the Lummi Tribe on northwest Lopez Island.

After the introduction of steam-powered pile drivers, settlers combined a Native American invention based on weir fishing with techniques from Scandinavia, New England, and the Canadian Maritime provinces to create a new method of fishing known as fish traps.

Pile drivers drove posts up to 150 feet long into the sea bed, and the traps were hung with wire and nets to intercept salmon on their return to spawning grounds. Reefnetting declined, and the traps dominated Lopez fishing from 1894 through 1934, "when fish was king," the focus of this chapter.

Many factors combined to end the fish trap era. The Great Depression, competition with purse seine boats, the public's distaste for perceived packing company monopolies, and alarm over fish run declines spurred voter passage of Initiative 77 in 1934, outlawing the traps. After that, fishing, whether by reefnetting, purse seining, or gillnetting, still remained a principal source of income and sustenance for island families for many years.

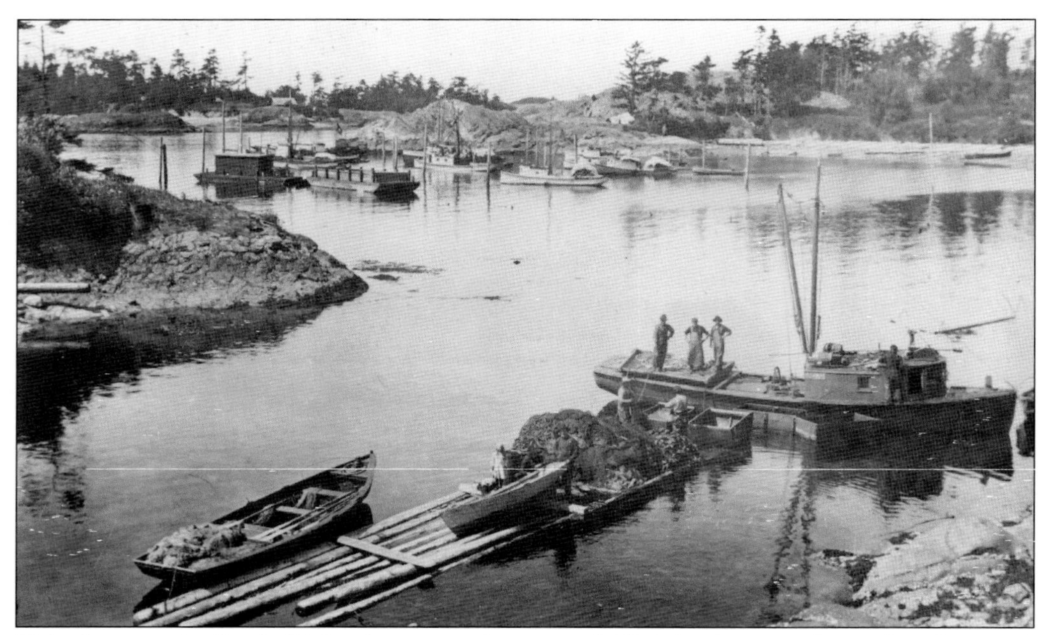

This photograph of early Richardson was taken around 1900. Looking southwest from Lovejoy's Point, a fish crew camping tent is seen in the background. The Hodgson-Graham Cannery, also known as the Salmon Banks Cannery, and the Hidden Inlet Cannery had not yet been built. Trap fishing off Lopez Island started in 1894. One trap was near Fisherman Bay and the other was on Long Island, southwest of Richardson.

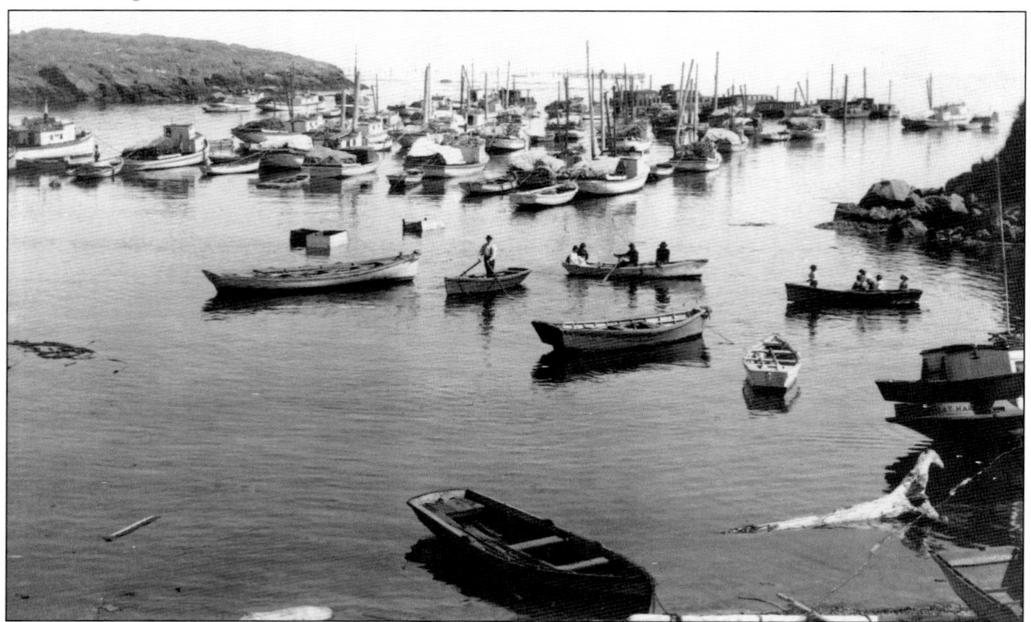

Fish traps are visible in the background, as purse seiners tie up in Aleck Bay. Purse seine men fished for five days straight, tied up in the harbor at night, and then went home from Friday afternoon to Sunday afternoon for the "closed season." As many as 275 seiners tied up at Richardson at one time. Purse seiners and fish traps competed for the same fish, and resentments sometimes arose.

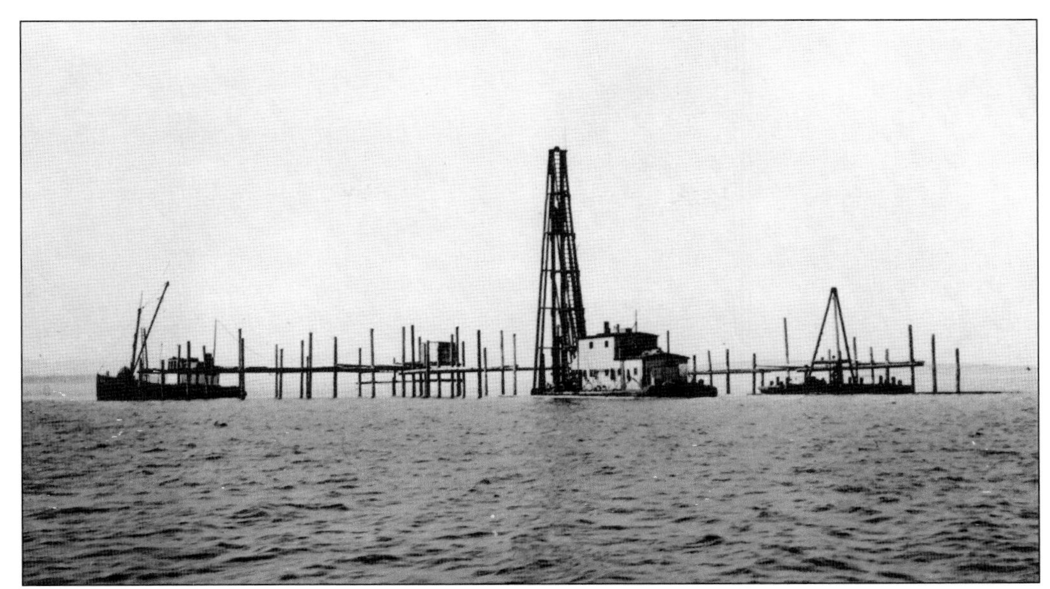

The boat *Mercury* drives the fish trap. To construct a trap, pile drivers drove logs up to 150 feet long into the seafloor about 10 feet apart. Tarred nets and later galvanized chicken wire were hung from water surface to seafloor. A long lead directed fish toward the trap and then into ever smaller enclosures where they were caught in the final chamber called the spiller.

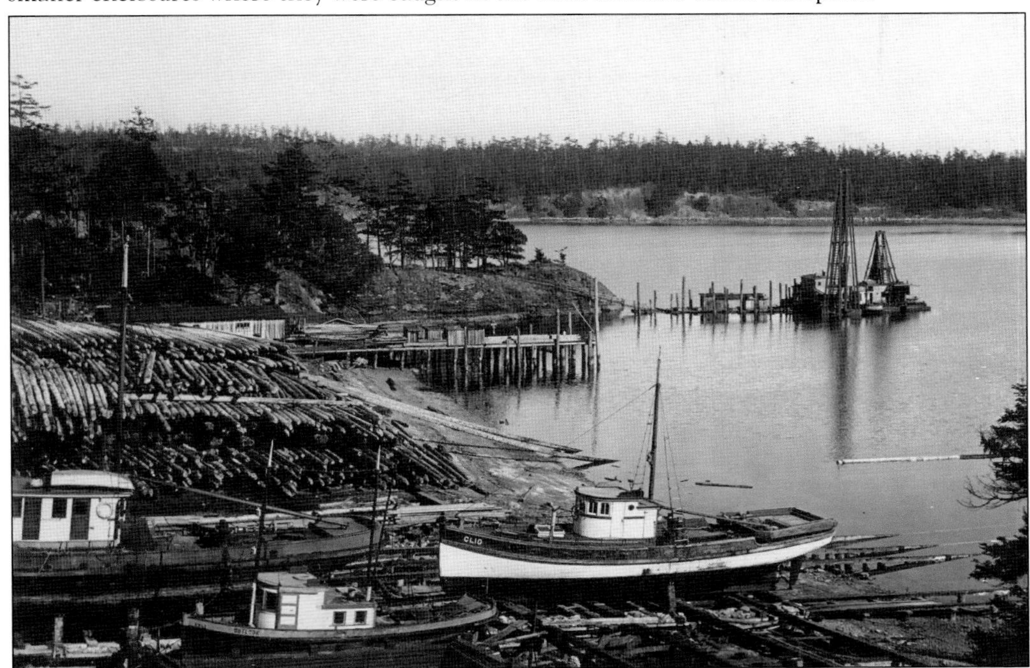

Logs are stockpiled at MacKaye Harbor ready for fish trap construction, as pile drivers and pullers sit at the dock. Surveying and pile driving began in early spring. The fishing season lasted through October, and traps were dismantled and towed home in the fall. Puget Sound once had 400 traps. In the teeming Salmon Banks off San Juan Island, traps were stacked so close together they "looked like a forest."

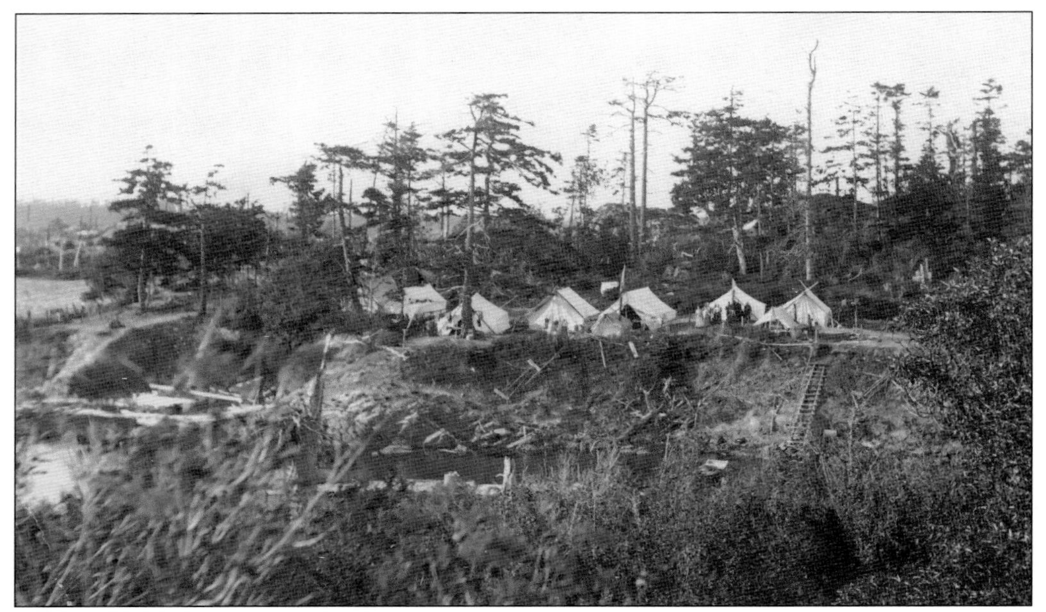

Fishing crews slept in tents and huts along the shore, like those shown here at Lovejoy Point. A 1901 article reported more than 400 men fished at Richardson that year, and one purse seiner hauled so many fish it could not lift the net. The 1901 catch was estimated at over one million fish, not including the thousands dumped back into the sea when no market for them was found.

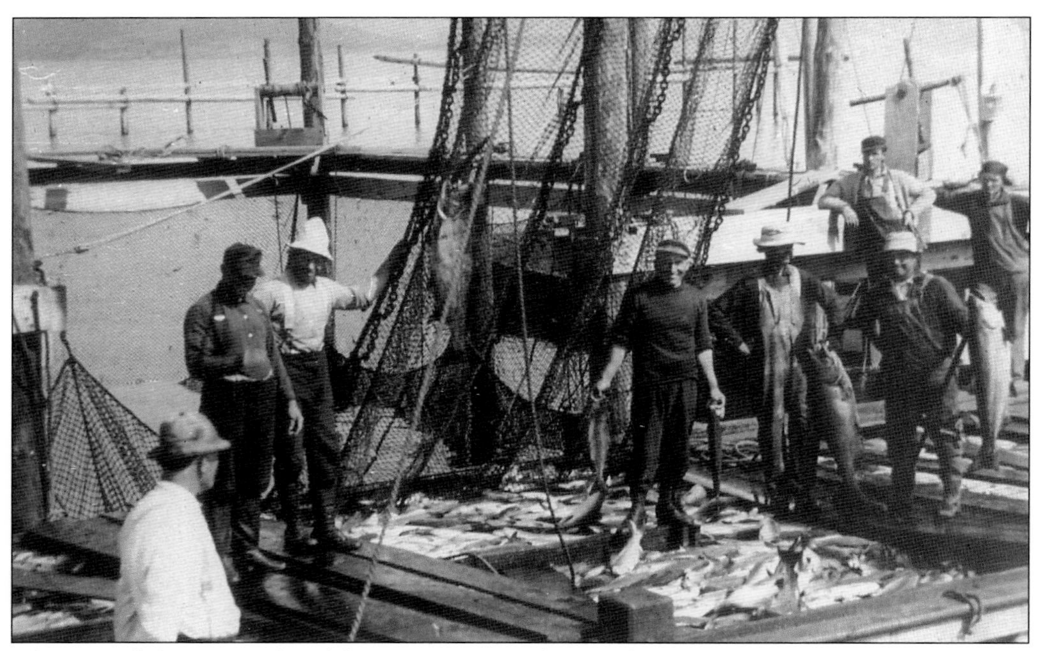

John Troxell, known as the "fish trap man," stands in a white shirt and hat on the Long Island trap while fish are being "lifted," or harvested, by a steam brailer. Commonly a lift yielded 15,000 fish, but Troxell's Long Island trap once caught 40,000 in two days. Legend says fish were so packed into the spiller that crewmen could have walked on them.

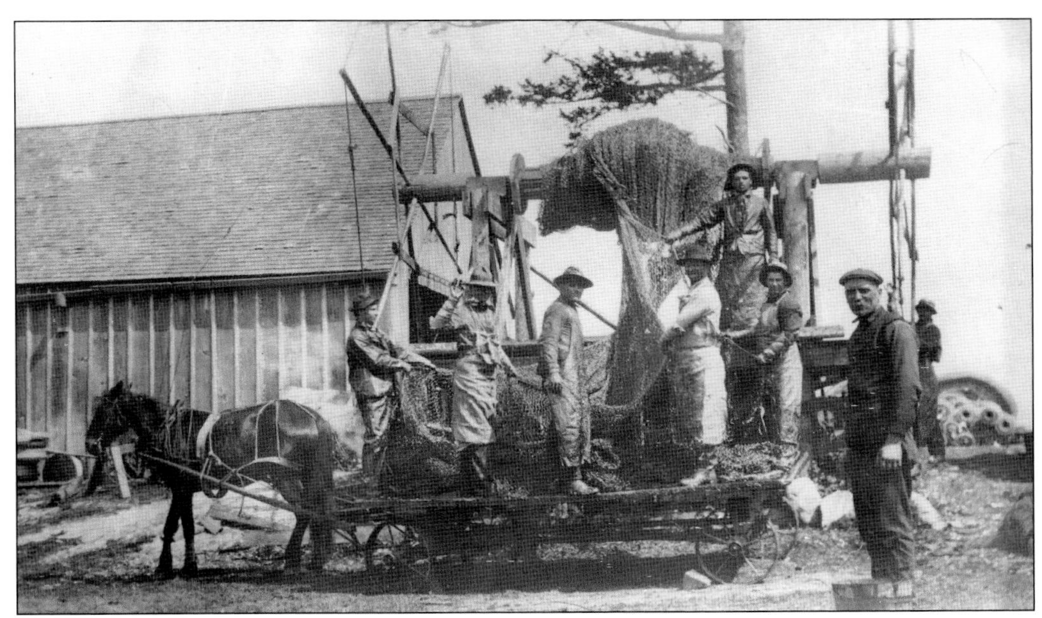

By 1897, the Oceanic Canning Company opened near Richardson. In early fish trap days, cotton webbing was coated with tar to protect it from the saltwater, and then the nets were held down by heavy weights once underwater. Tarring the nets at Oceanic from left to right are Nick Davidson, Charlie Buchanan, Martin Phelps, Vern Wood, Edgar Orcutt, Lou Bolton, and John Tralnes.

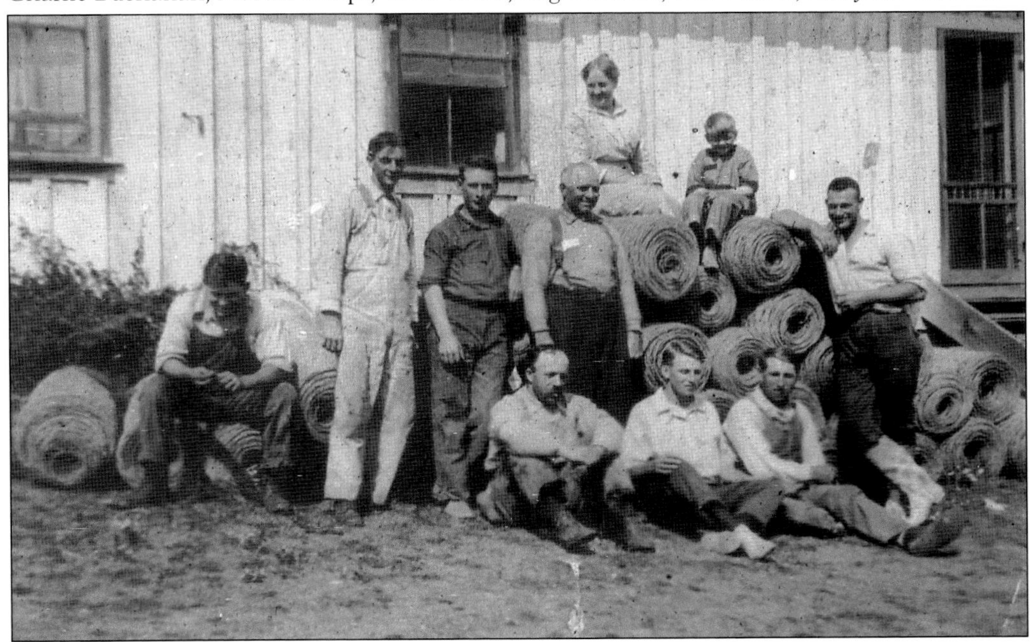

The fish camp crew at Barlow Bay from left to right are (first row, seated) Carl Mueller, Charlie Greenwood, and Niels Nielsen; (second row) Ray Burt, Roy Gawley, Elmer Vogt, Bill Wilson, unidentified cook, unidentified cook's child, and R. T. Biggs. Fishing provided year-round employment for many people. In the off-season, workers cut piles, tarred webs, hog-ringed wire, and built scows.

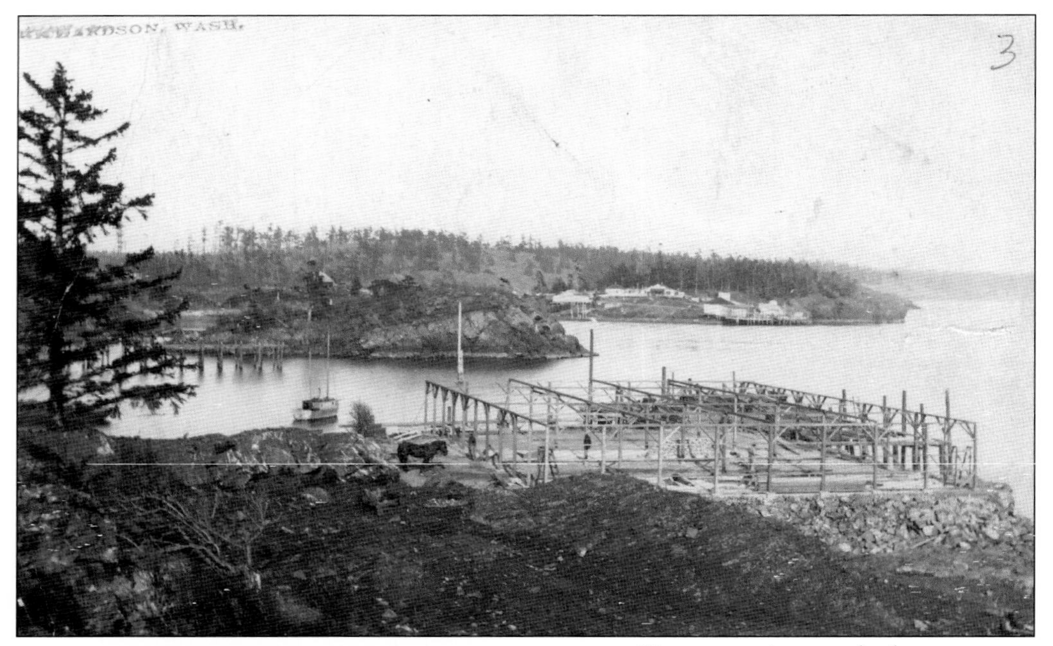

Two canneries were built at Richardson in 1913, the Hidden Inlet Cannery owned by Fred Comieu and the Hodgson-Graham Cannery, shown here under construction. Lack of a sufficient water supply made canning at Richardson difficult, despite six wells on the Hodgson and Graham properties. Barge loads of water were brought in from Blakely Island.

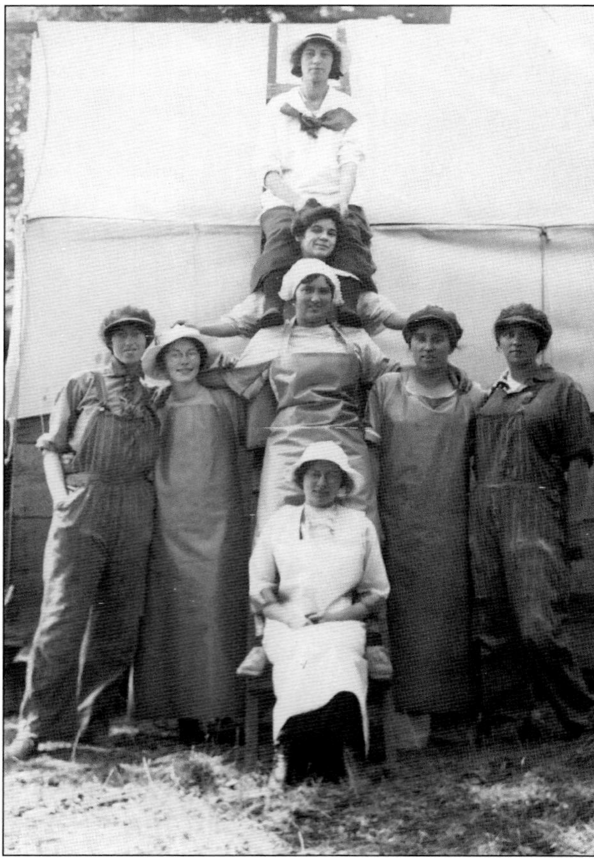

Canneries employed up to 400 workers at a time. Imported Chinese laborers handled the machinery. Women hand packed the salmon. Hodgson-Graham Cannery workers are pictured here in 1915. From bottom to top are Gladys Burt, Eva Thornton, Vesta Nichols, and Mabel Marchant. From left to right are Abbie Hammond, Ethel Bruns, Victoria Porter, and Gertrude Towell. The Chinese workers lived in a China house at Davis Head. The women stayed at the Wander Inn.

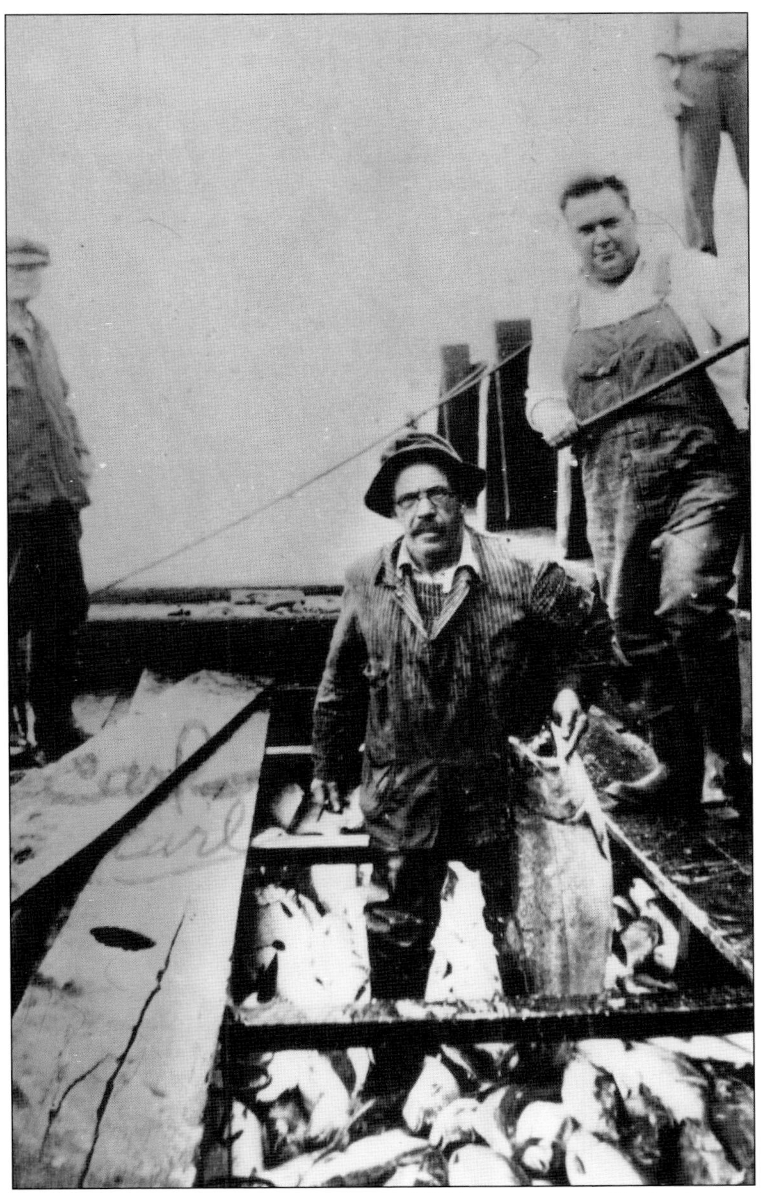

Carl Mueller holds a massive salmon, as Howard Wilson, in overalls, looks on. Mueller was orphaned as a child and traveled alone at age 12 from Berlin, Germany, to Wisconsin to live with his uncle. He taught himself to speak English by reading a newspaper and later worked in the lumber industry in Wisconsin. After Mueller married his wife, Edna, her uncle Pete Landon, an aging Civil War veteran, asked Maybelle Troxell to write a letter to Edna, imploring her to move to Lopez to care for him. The Muellers agreed to come and arrived on Lopez in 1907 with their one-year-old son Edward. The Troxell and Mueller families became close friends. Mueller managed the Rochdale Cooperative Store for a time, as well as the Hudson farm. Later John Troxell hired Mueller to become superintendent of the MacKaye Harbor fish trap operations for the Astoria Puget Sound Canning Company. Mueller oversaw the operation from 1920 to 1934. In later years, Carl and Edna were gillnetters together, basing their boat at MacKaye Harbor.

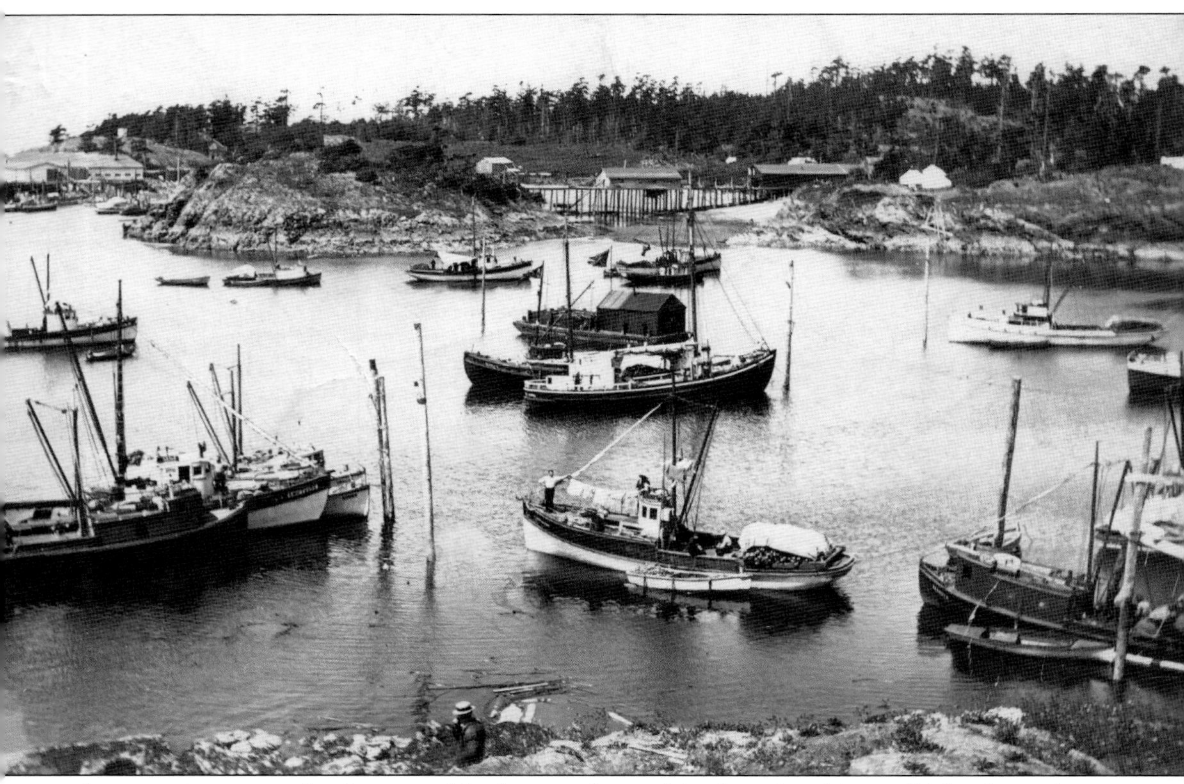

A perceptive postcard writer sent this photograph to a friend, noting this was Richardson when "the fish was king." The Hodgson-Graham Cannery juts out over the water on the left. The Hidden Inlet Cannery lies along the shore in the center. Canning peaked prior to World War I, with local fish traps in operation and 1,000 purse seiners fishing island waters. Over time, fishing began to reduce the salmon runs, and the notorious Hell's Gate Slide blocked the Fraser River in 1914. By 1916, N. P. Hodgson decided to sell the Richardson store and Hodgson-Graham Cannery to Ira Lundy. Shortly thereafter, an oil company supply boat exploded at the dock, destroying the wharf, warehouse, and a purse seiner and injuring its crew. In February 1922, the Hodgson-Graham Cannery burned down in a fierce fire, and the Hidden Inlet Cannery shut down afterward. Fish traps were outlawed by voter-approved initiative in 1934. Salmon canning became a mainland business, and Richardson's hotel, bakery, creamery, slaughterhouse, barbershop, dance hall, and pool hall faded away into history.

Seven

MAKING A LIVING

An old adage says islanders have to work two or three jobs to make a living. Although Lopez Island began primarily as a farming community, almost every farmer also was a fisherman. When the salmon run was over, fishermen went back to farming. The 1880 census bears this out, listing most of those who did not keep house or shop as a farmer, farmworker, fisherman, sailor, or vessel mate.

This chapter explores what other work Lopezians did to make a living. Some captained steamboats or ferries. Others delivered mail, invented things, or ran a blacksmith shop. People fixed things, logged trees, split wood for steamers, and manufactured potash in the kelp plant. Lopezians operated switchboards from their homes for the Farmers Cooperative Telephone Company. One operated a telegraph in the earliest days of island electronic communication.

The 1900 census shows that by the dawn of the 20th century, Lopezians' occupations diversified. Among them were a marine engineer, musician, teamster, shoemaker, stonemason, sawmill owner, laborer at Groll's Mill on Fisherman Bay, teacher, machinist, pile driver engineer, pile driver, painter, dressmaker, boat builder, cook, gardener, and even an actor and actress. This chapter tells the story of Lopezians at work.

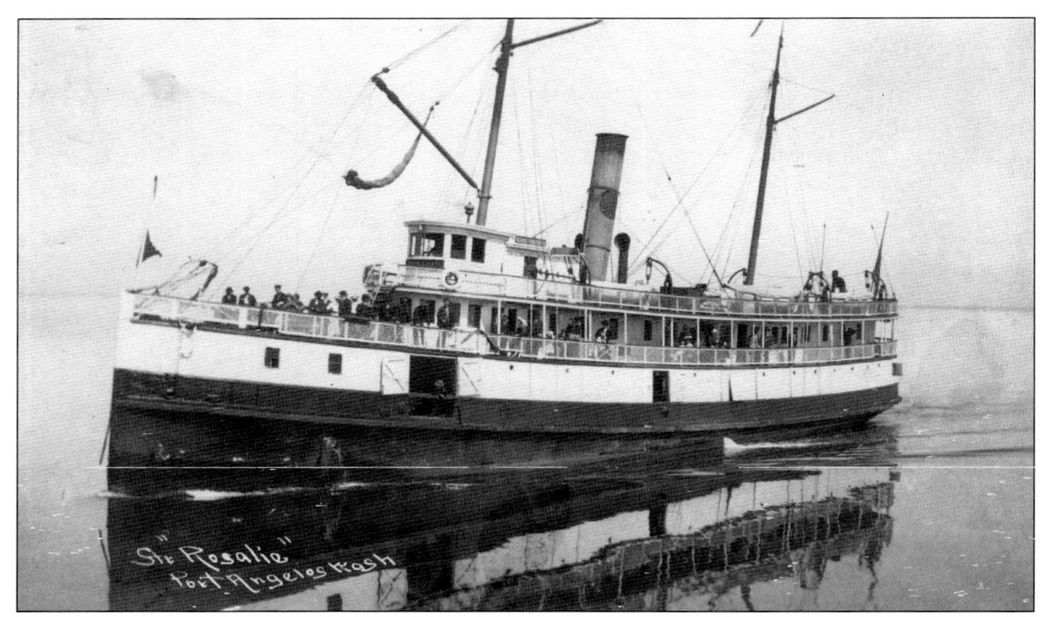

The steamboat *Rosalie* was built in 1893 in Alameda, California, and took prospectors and supplies to Alaska during the 1898 gold rush. In 1907, she began service in the San Juan Islands while captained by Louis Van Bogaert and Lopezian Sam Barlow, making stops in Port Townsend, Smith Island, Richardson, Argyle, San Juan and Orcas Islands, Anacortes, and Bellingham. *Rosalie* was destroyed by fire while at dock in Seattle in 1918.

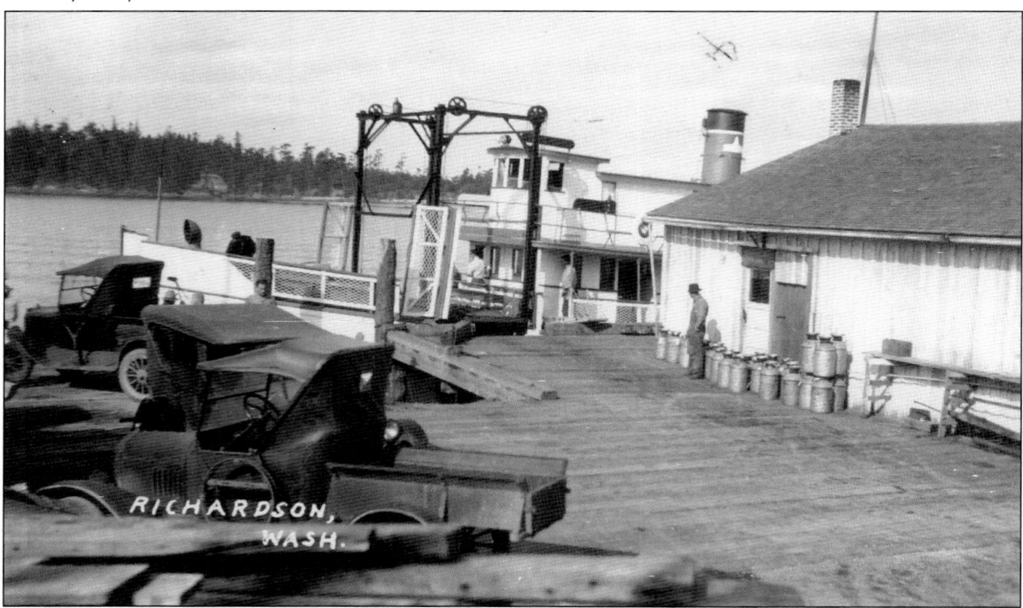

Following the 1916 oil supply boat explosion at Richardson, the Lundys built a new two-story wharf with a homemade elevator connecting the floors. Feed, seed, flour, and other staples were sold on the lower floor, where a mill ground grain. This photograph of the Richardson dock in the 1920s shows a boat equipped with the Barlow Steam Elevator, invented by Sam Barlow's brother Harry Barlow.

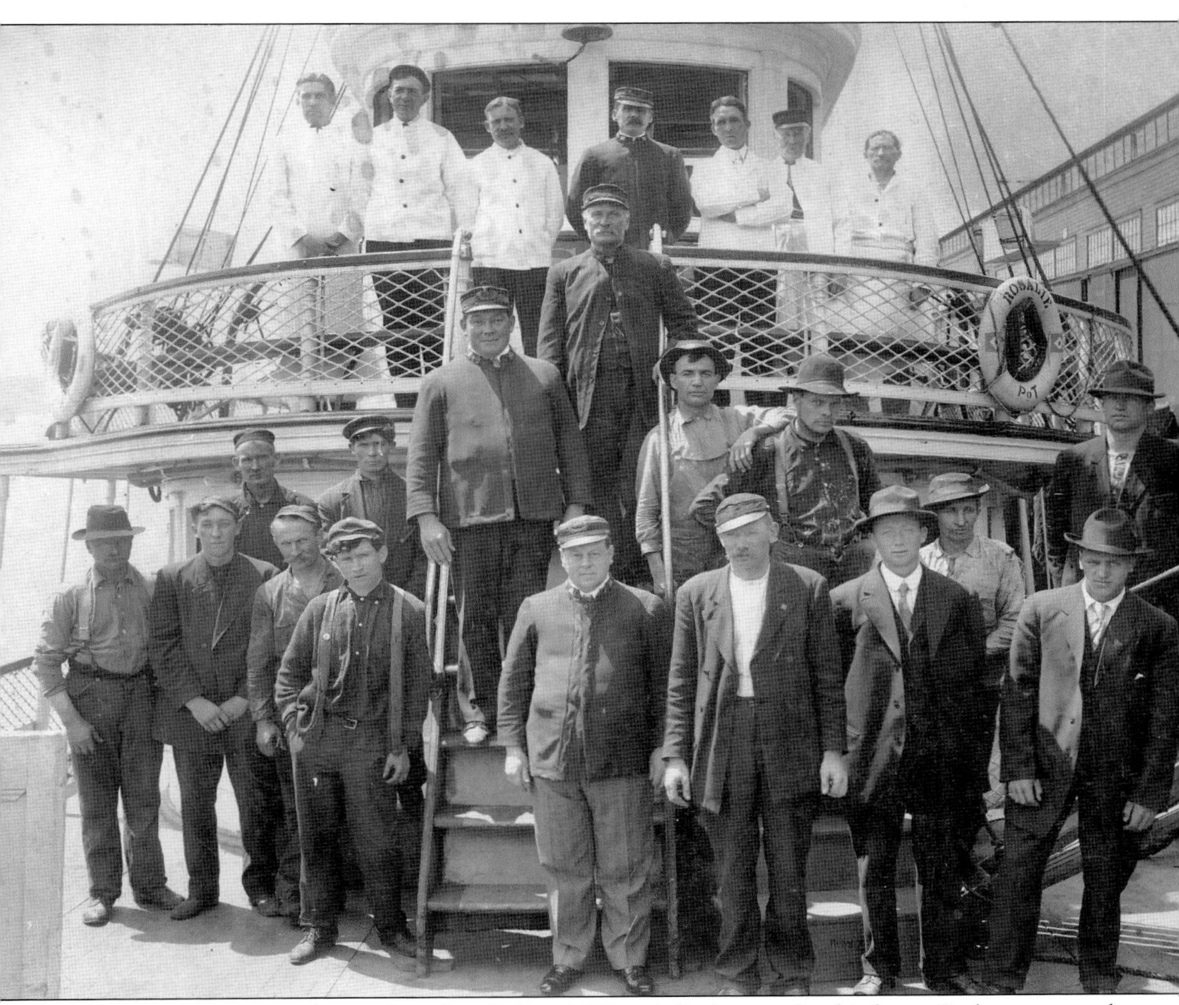

The crew of the *Rosalie* stands on her deck in 1915, with Barlow on the third step. Barlow possessed legendary navigational skills, relying on the smell of kelp, bark of an onshore dog, or bouncing echoes to assure his passengers' safe travel in dense fog. He made 20,000 trips without a single mishap and for 40 years after his death was honored annually in a ceremony at sea.

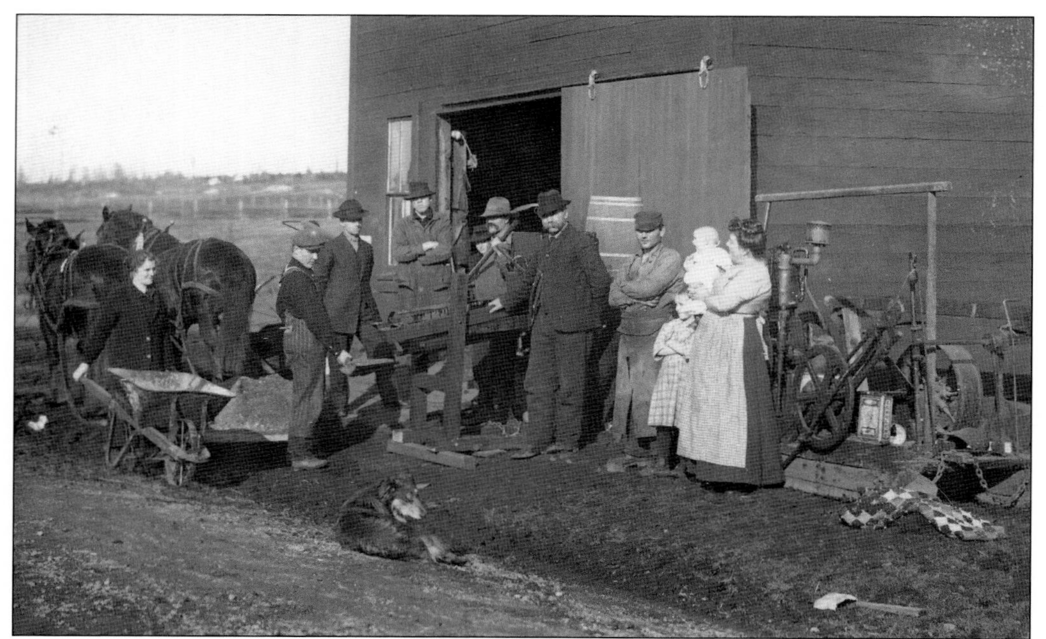

John and Lena Wilson stand on the right with their children Thelma, left, and possibly Vera at Wilson's blacksmith shop, located at the north end of Richardson Road. Descendent Frances Kring believed the Wilson's farmhouse was built about 1905 and that John and Lena moved to Friday Harbor in 1938, estimating Wilson ran the blacksmith shop at this location for 33 years. Mary Buchanan pushes the wheelbarrow, at left.

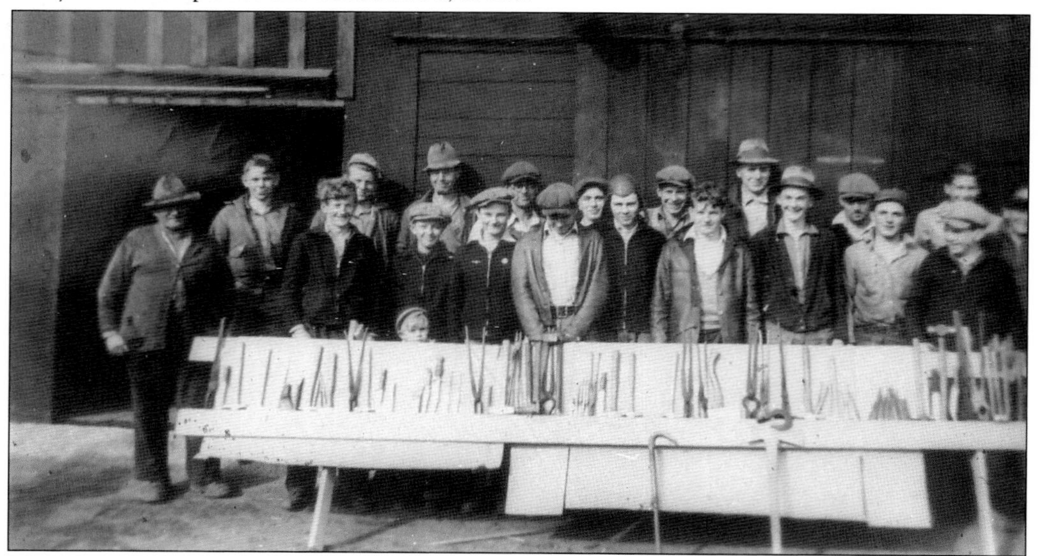

The Works Progress Administration (WPA) was the New Deal's largest agency, providing employment to millions during the Great Depression. Created by Pres. Franklin D. Roosevelt, the program allowed training for new skills. This photograph shows a WPA class at Wilson's blacksmith shop. Donald Fagerholm remembers his brother attended the class, where some students made hatchets and others made hunting knives. Almost every American community benefitted from the WPA.

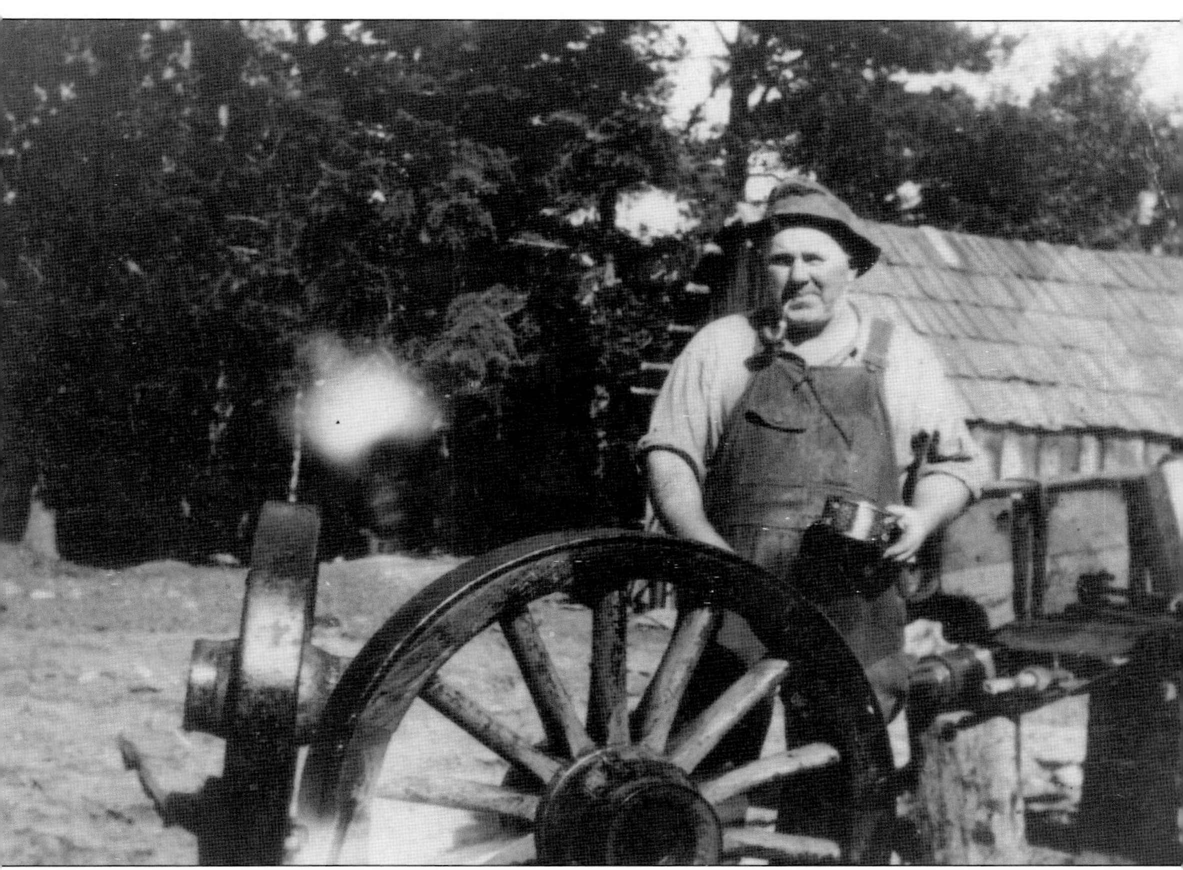

Seth Richey repairs wagon wheels in this 1923 photograph. Richey's neighbor, Lee Noderer, said about Richey, "A finer neighbor no one ever had." Noderer also said, "We were greenhorns up there. He helped us in many ways, many different times." Richey's pride and joy was the team of draft horses he used for logging. He would do anything for them as they would for him.

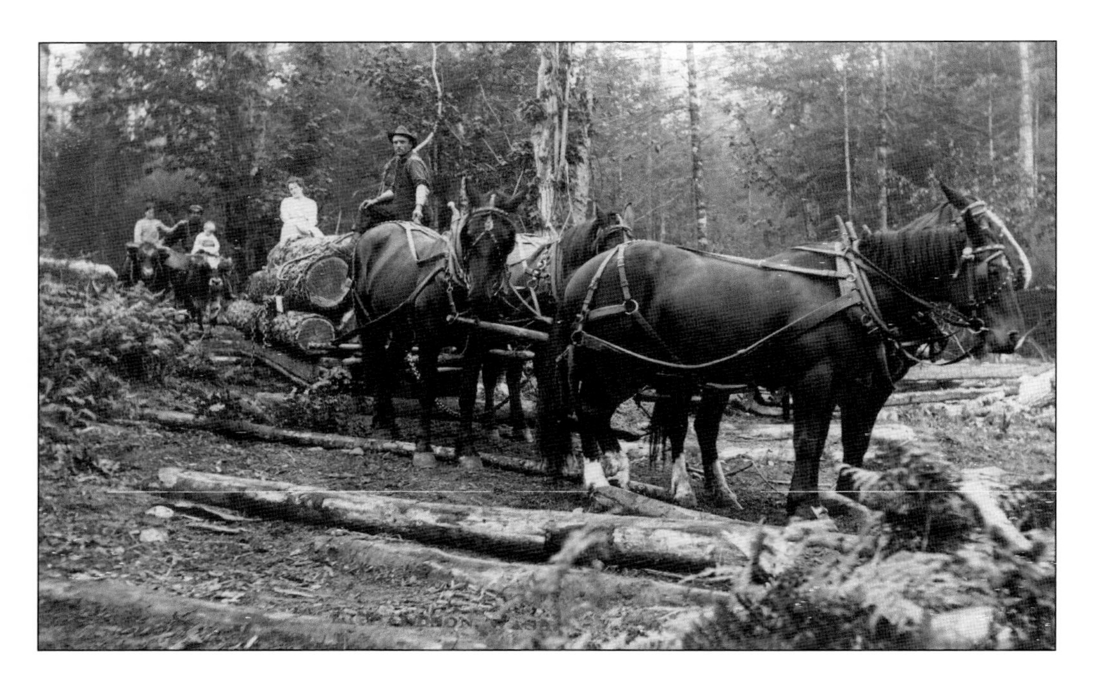

Above, Norman Wilson drives a team of horses, while a woman rides on the log and a man and child ride the oxen behind. Locally harvested fir and cedar trees were used to build houses and barns, and old growth trees were cut for cordwood and sold to fuel steamers, such as the *Rosalie* and *Lydia Thompson*. In the photograph below, Niels Nielsen stands on a stump with an unidentified man next to a huge pile of cordwood. Like many islanders, Nielsen did several things to make a living. He also fished traps locally and in Alaska.

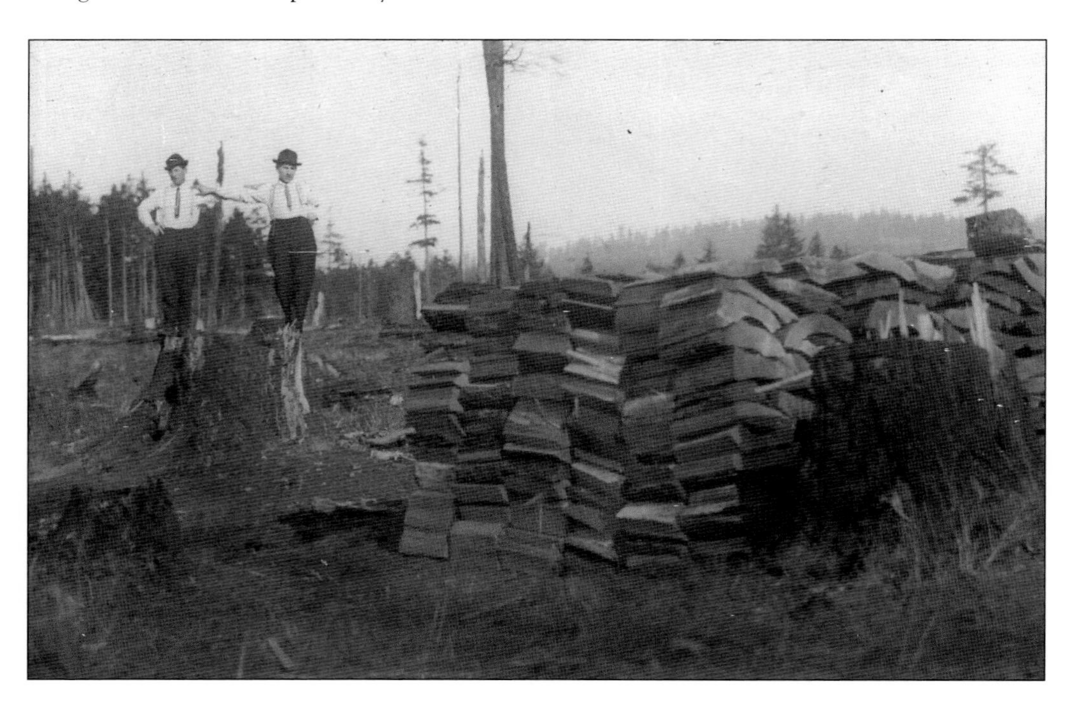

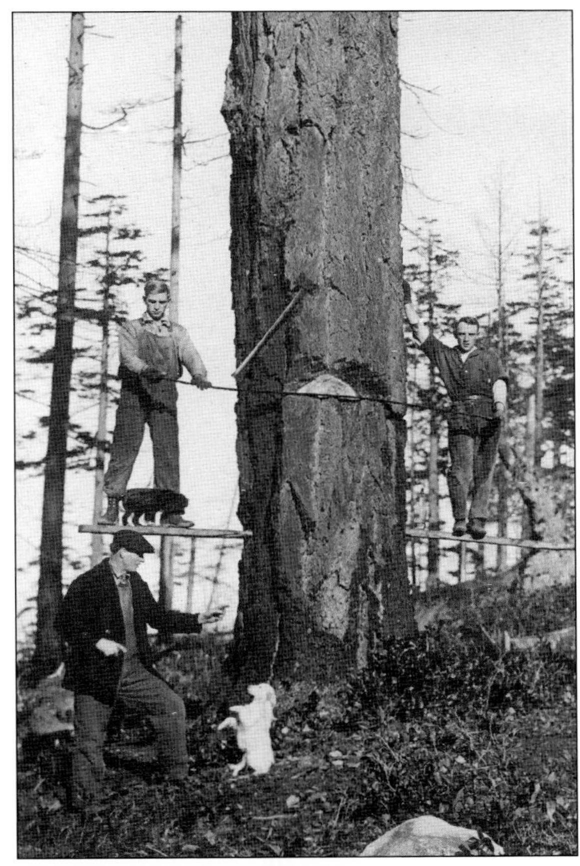

Irwin Blake, left, and Bob Wilson stand on a springboard holding their crosscut saw, with a small black puppy, in this humorous postcard. Mr. Inman points at a white dog sitting up in the foreground. Although Lopez had stands of old growth fir prior to settlement in the 1850s, an 1867 report to Congress said, "Lopez Island is . . . timbered but none of the timber here is large or dense enough to offer much of an obstacle to clearing . . . There are scarcely any trees of large size upon the island except in a few low and swampy places." The photograph below shows Bill Wilson and his oxen George and Max pulling a sizeable log out of the woods. Steve Orcutt stands at the oxen's head.

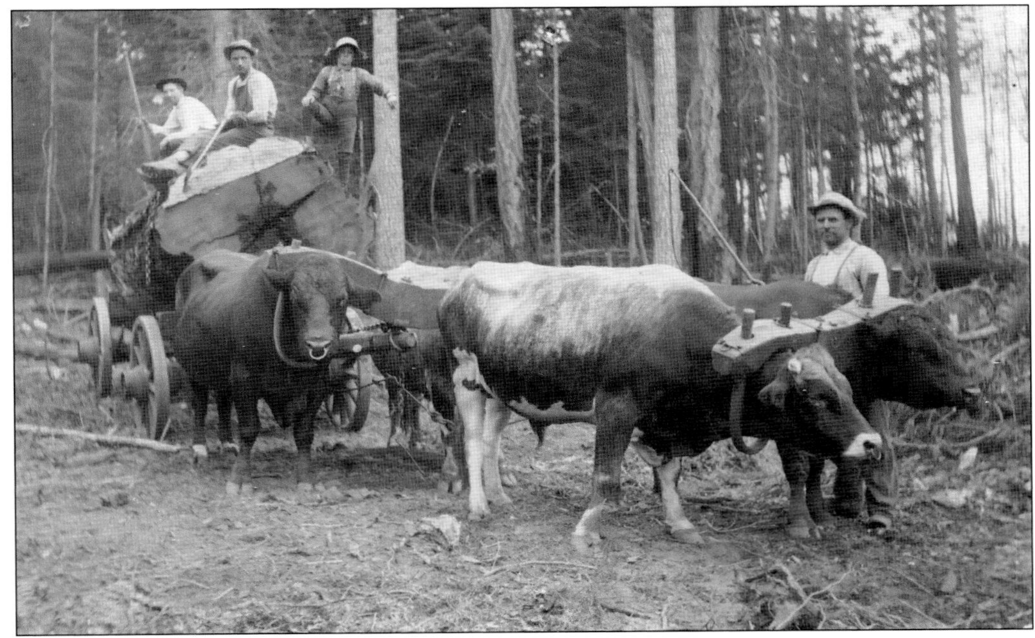

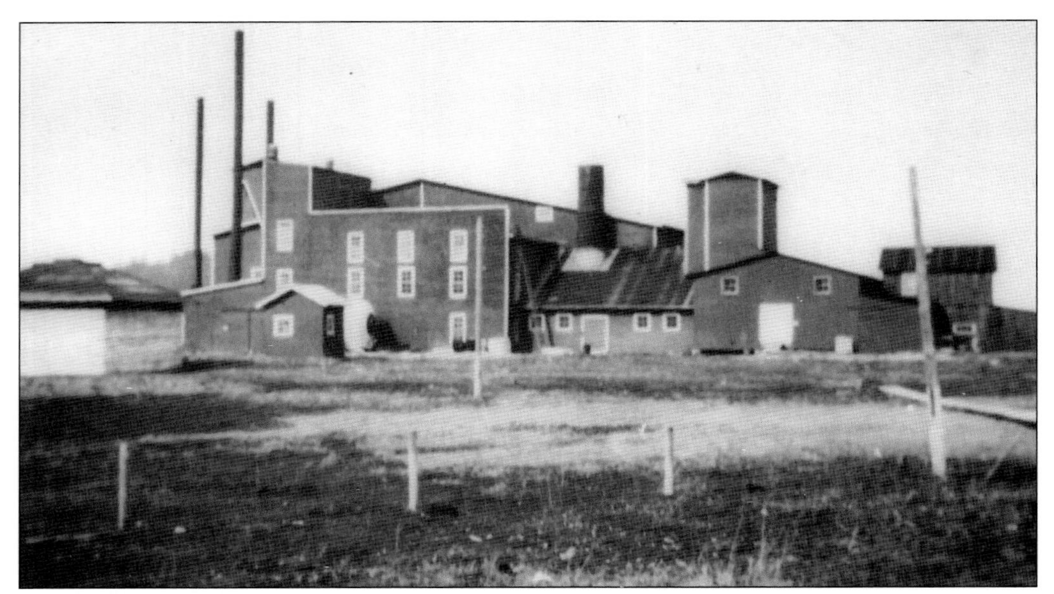

The Puget Sound Potash and Kelp Fertilizer Company was founded at Port Stanley about 1913 by Bill Devine and his partners. Three products were made from kelp: potash (for use in gunpowder for World War I), fertilizer, and iodine. Iodine production stopped when the man who knew the formula was killed on the job. After the war, demand for potash fell, the plant closed, and little trace of it remains.

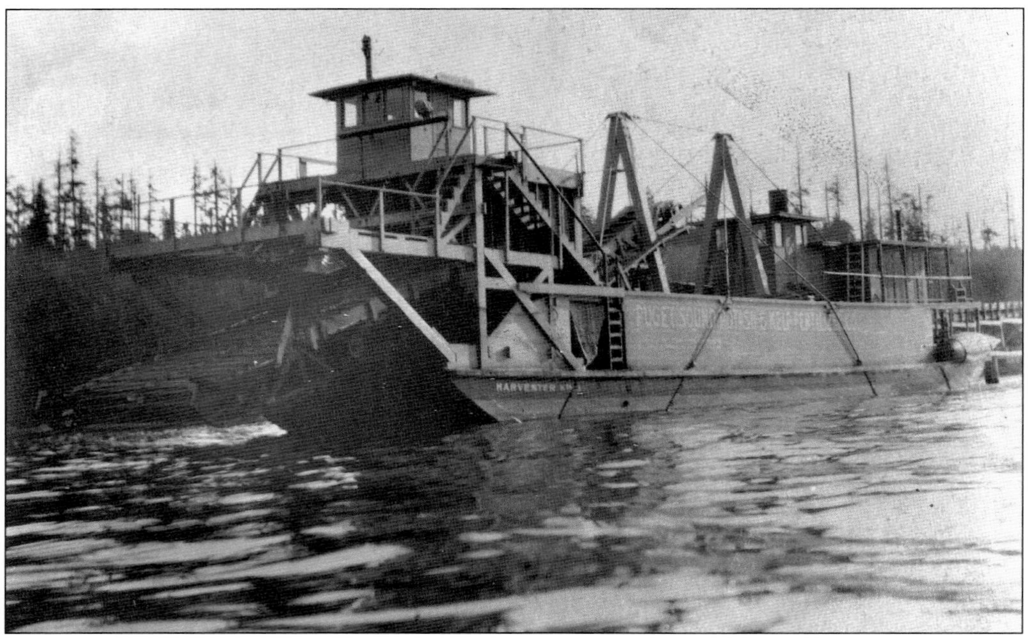

The steamer *Harvester King* was captained by Ray Spencer and harvested kelp from the waters surrounding Lopez for delivery to the kelp plant. After the plant closed, the *Harvester King* was reconfigured to become the first ferry to serve the San Juan Islands in 1922, running from Anacortes to Sidney, British Columbia. The run lasted only one season due to the ship's ill-suited design, which made for rough travel.

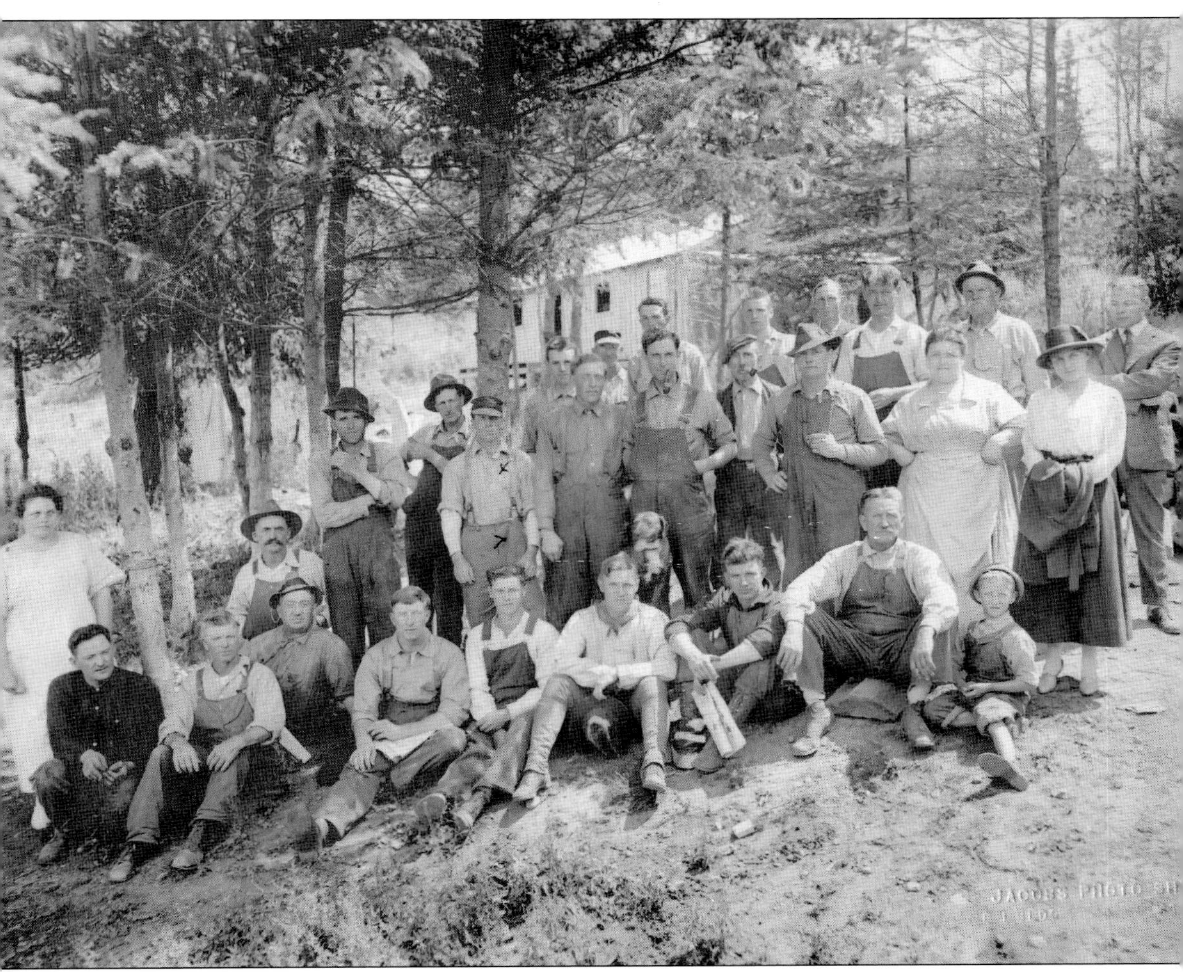

The kelp plant provided employment to many islanders in the early part of the 20th century. The process for converting kelp to potash was relatively new and highly successful, helping Port Stanley to grow. People moved there and built new houses. It cost about $40 a ton to make the potash, and it sold for $100 a ton. When the war ended, the price dropped to $20 a ton. Crew members, in no particular order, are Dad Kendell, Emory Rayman, Jess Coffelt, Bert Whalen, Zeph Stocker, Howard Bell, Bert Weeks, Harry LeMaister, Ed Kendell, Jack Roberts, J. R. Martin, Mrs. Petrie (the assistant cook), Mr. Noderer, Hewey Jensen, Mr. and Mrs. Gates, George Devine, Lincoln Weeks, Ed Hanson, Bob Shane, Mr. Kitridge, Jack Roberts, Theron Hower, Roy Spencer, and Jeff Stocker. The bunkhouse where some of them lived is in back.

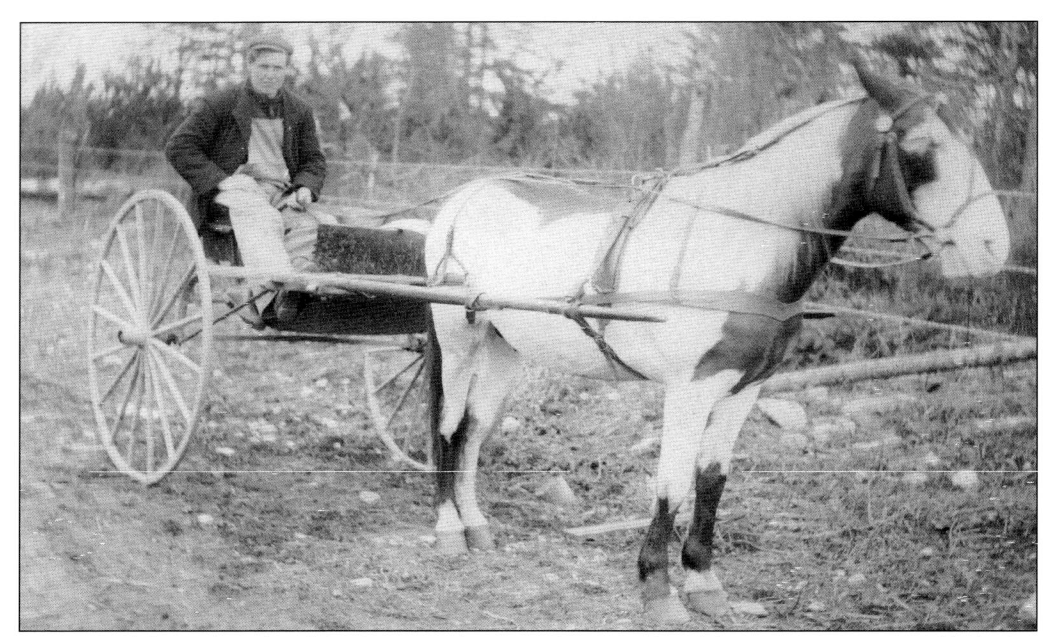

Guy Kent delivered mail with his horse and cart. Early post office delivery routes were established at Lopez Village, MacKaye Harbor, Richardson, Port Stanley, Mud Bay, and Islandale. The MacKaye Harbor, Edwards, and Islandale routes did not last long. One by one, routes consolidated into the village branch, and the last to close were Port Stanley in 1940 and Richardson in 1953.

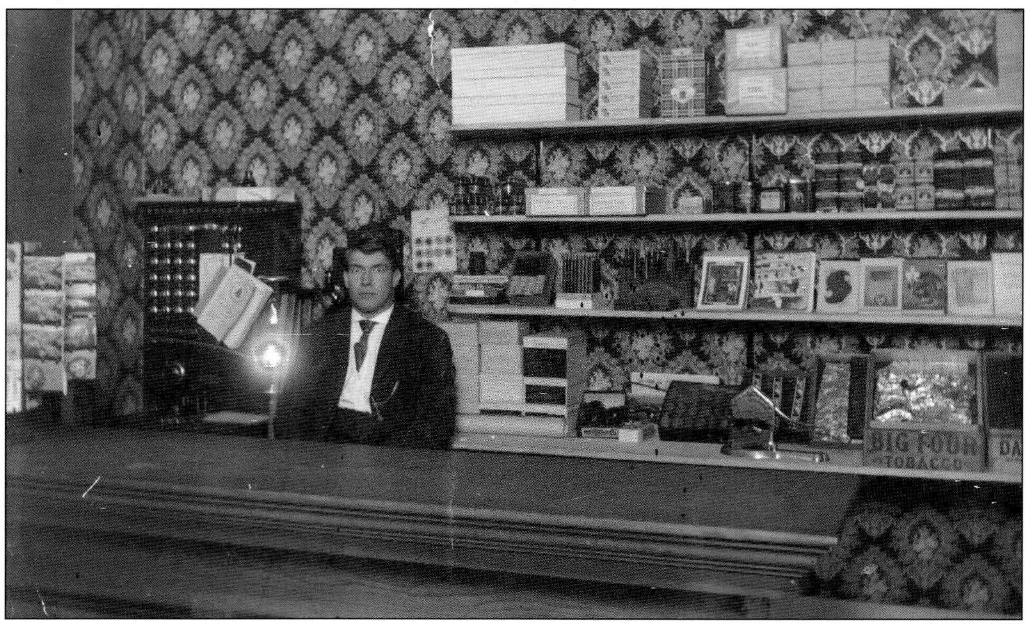

Harry McMillan sits with an amusing look on his face behind his store counter, where he sold candy, pop, tobacco, cards, pencils, and school supplies. McMillan lived there and also ran the long-distance telephone switchboard. The Pickering family moved to Lopez in 1922, and Dick Pickering Sr. reportedly repaired the underground cable to restore the island's long-distance service. He and his wife bought the telephone system.

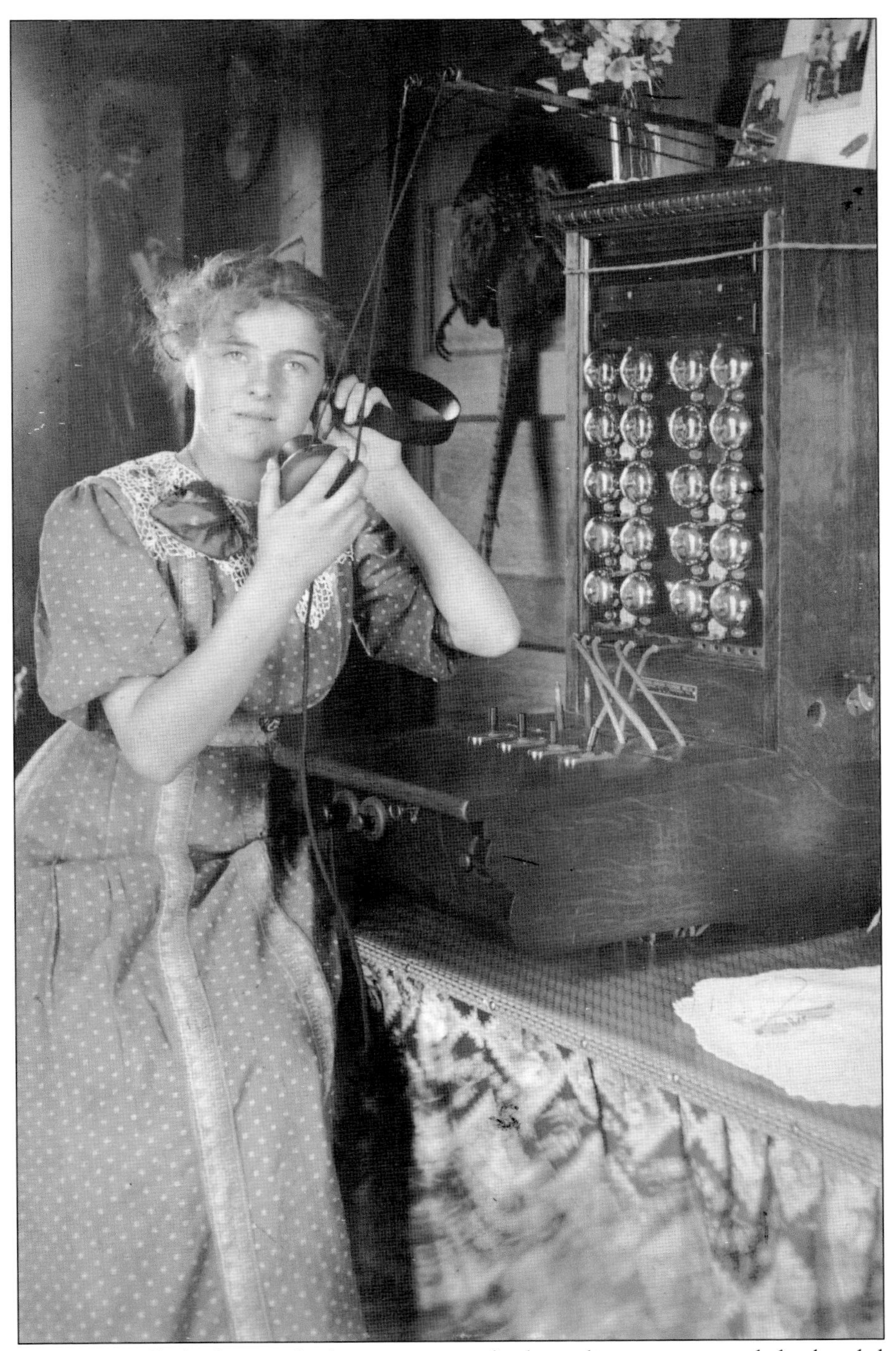

The island originally had two telephone systems, the long distance one and the local, known as the Farmers' Telephone System. Mary Buchanan Wilson stands at the system's switchboard, called "Central." Islanders shared party lines, and each family had a distinctive number of rings. People who had local and long-distance services were often called to relay messages to people who only had one. Farmers' Telephone System went out of business in 1923.

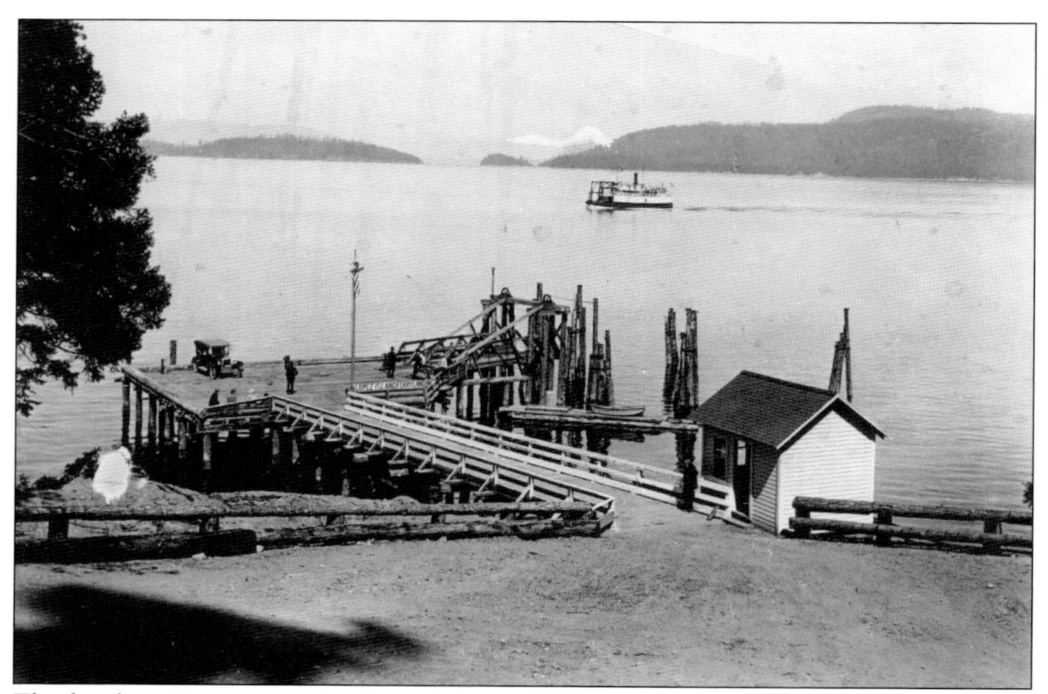

The ferryboat *Puget* approaches Lopez's first car ferry dock in the 1920s. The steamers *Bailey Gatzert* and *Whatcom* were converted to car ferries, and the *Harvester King* also carried cars. After the Golden Gate Bridge opened, the Black Ball Line brought boats up from San Francisco, and by 1940, Washington ferries made more than 300 daily trips. By 1951, Washington State bought out the line and created the ferry system.

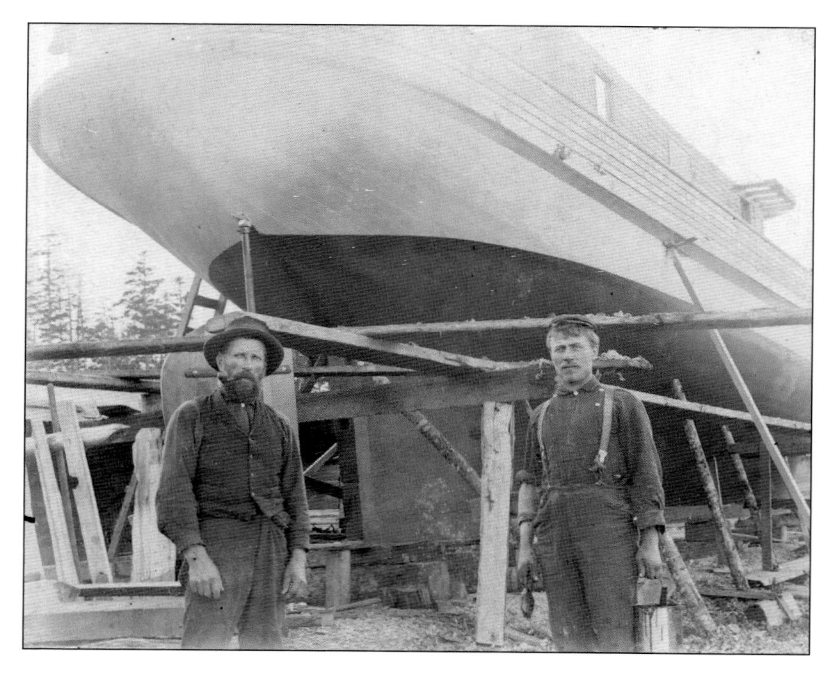

Peter Schruder and his son, Louie, with paint brush and paint can in hand, stand beneath the boat *Alpha* that they are building. Louie worked at the Norman shipyard and was a widower with two children to raise, Sigwald and Cora. Michael Norman ran the Norman shipyard, and he and his son Arthur also made their living building boats on the beach at Mud Bay.

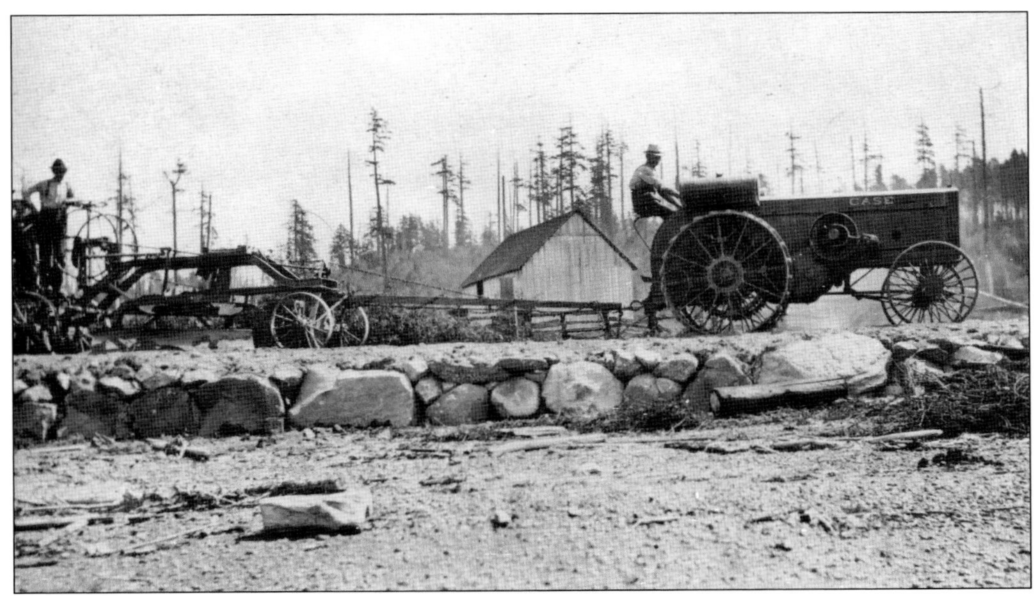

Ontie Bruns drives a Case tractor performing road work on Fisherman Bay Road about 1918. The Bruns farm lies behind him. Few island roads existed in the early days when people, livestock, and farm products were transported more easily by boat. Ferry Road was cleared by Albert Dill, Oscar Weeks, Jack Gallanger, Bertie Weeks, and Charlie Coffelt, among others.

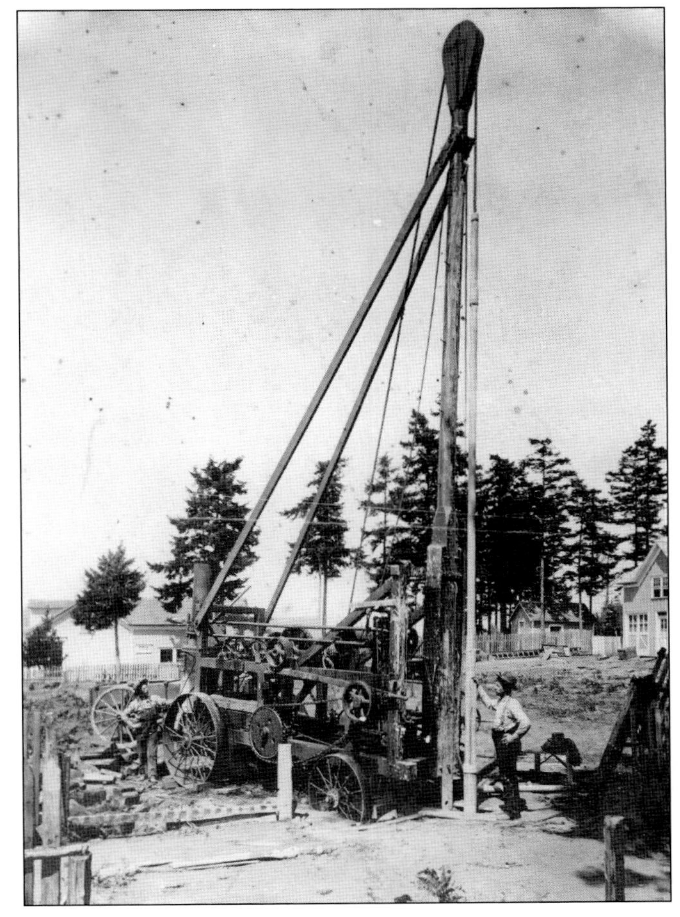

Two men stand near an old well drilling rig, with a gabled house and outbuildings in the background. George Walrod owned and operated this early well driller. Walrod married Mary Wilson, the daughter of Sam Wilson Sr. and Eliza Wilson, and they had a large family. The drill rig was kept in Friday Harbor most of the time and brought to Lopez when needed.

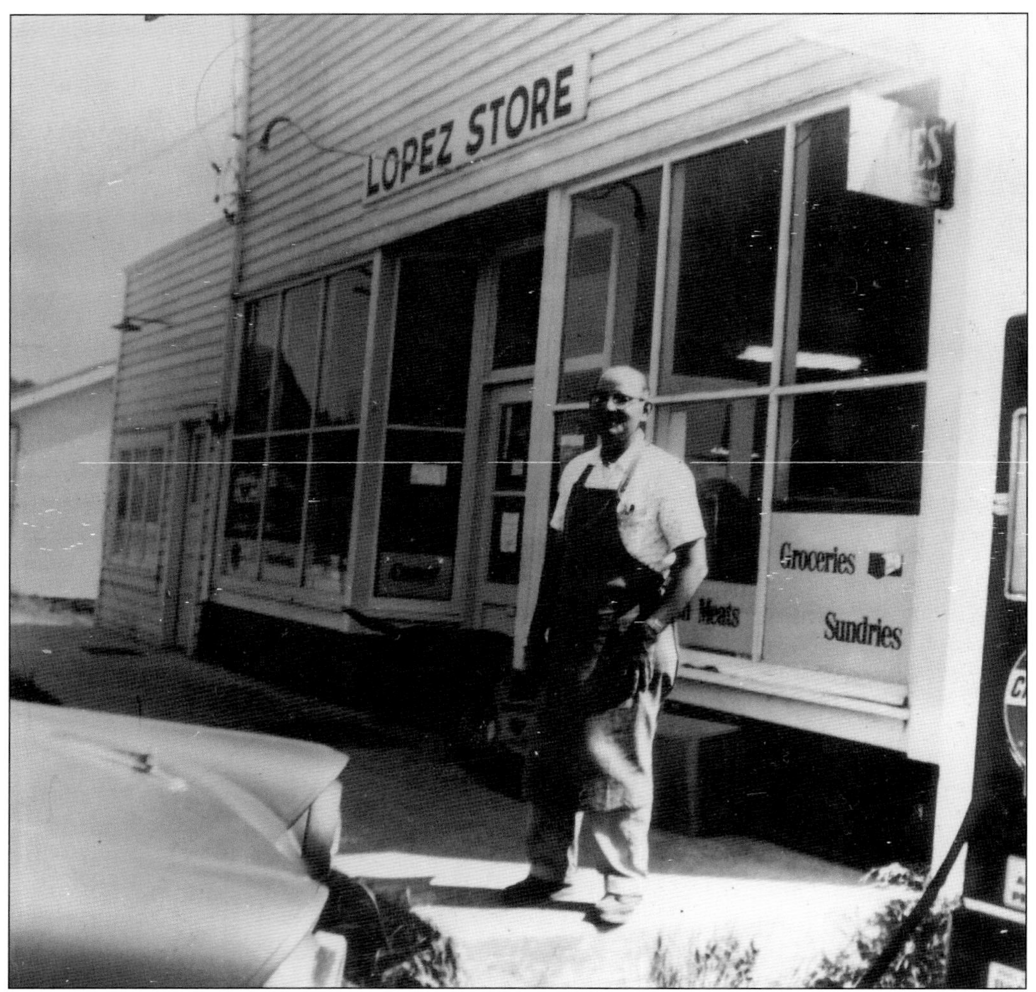

Bill Carpenter Sr. stands outside the old Lopez Store. With the exception of a brief time after World War II, when the village store was run by Wilson Horne as Trader Horne's, Leroy Jensen ran it from 1930 to 1959, calling it Lopez Purity Store. In 1959, Bill Carpenter Jr. was in the meat business in Seattle, and he and his wife, Bonnie, came to Lopez on vacation. When he ran out of gasoline on a Sunday, he went in search of Jensen to ask him to open up. Jensen was poised to become the Lopez postmaster, and after talking to Carpenter asked if he wanted to buy the store. Carpenter replied, no, but his parents would. Bill Sr., who had worked in the grocery business all of his life, moved to Lopez, and he and his wife ran the store until 1965, when Bill Jr. and Bonnie bought them out. As he got older, Bill Sr. continued to work in the store, spending most of his time talking to customers.

Eight

Then and Now

An old saying goes, "Use it up, wear it out, make it do or do without." The give and take at the Lopez transfer station today, affectionately known as "Neil's Mall," after Neil Hanson, who originated it, exemplifies islanders' belief in recycling useable things. Looking at the photographs in this chapter, one realizes Lopezians have long practiced this philosophy.

The little red schoolhouse still stands in Lopez village but now is the library. A team of horses moved a little house down from Lopez Hill to Center Road where it was transformed into a Dutch colonial. A dilapidated schoolhouse was restored for modern use. Buildings that appeared in earlier chapters, such as Woodmen Hall and Center School, which became the Grange Hall, also exemplify this community practicality.

Although the photographs in this chapter demonstrate that Lopezians understood the meaning of the adage, they also show something more. As generations blended together, the community's belief in preserving things of value was handed down from older family members to younger ones. Sometimes preservation was not possible, and Lopezians mourned the loss of an important icon. But despite such losses, the community pulled together to meet the next restoration challenge.

A U.S. Supreme Court justice once said, "We don't accomplish anything in this world alone . . . whatever happens is the result of the whole tapestry of one's life, and all the weavings of individual threads from one to another that creates something." Over the years, Lopezians' individual threads wove together a vibrant community that lives on as a legacy to its fortunate heirs.

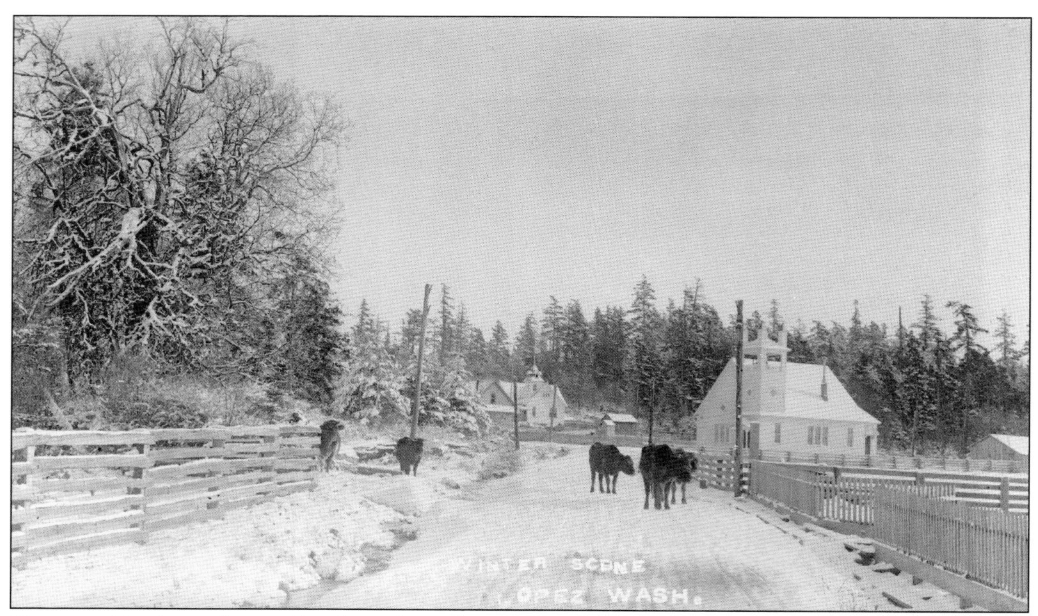

Cows amble down Lopez Road in the village winter scene above. The Lopez Congregational Church, completed in 1905, stands to the right with the little red schoolhouse behind in the distance. The modern photograph is taken from approximately the same location, but the church is hidden by tree branches and the school has been moved out of sight. In the old days, farms in Lopez Village with large orchards radiated out from Hutchinson's trading post. Picket fences surrounded houses, and new landowners carefully planted and tended flowers, shrubs, and trees they brought as saplings or seeds from previous homes. (Below, courtesy of Delores Foss.)

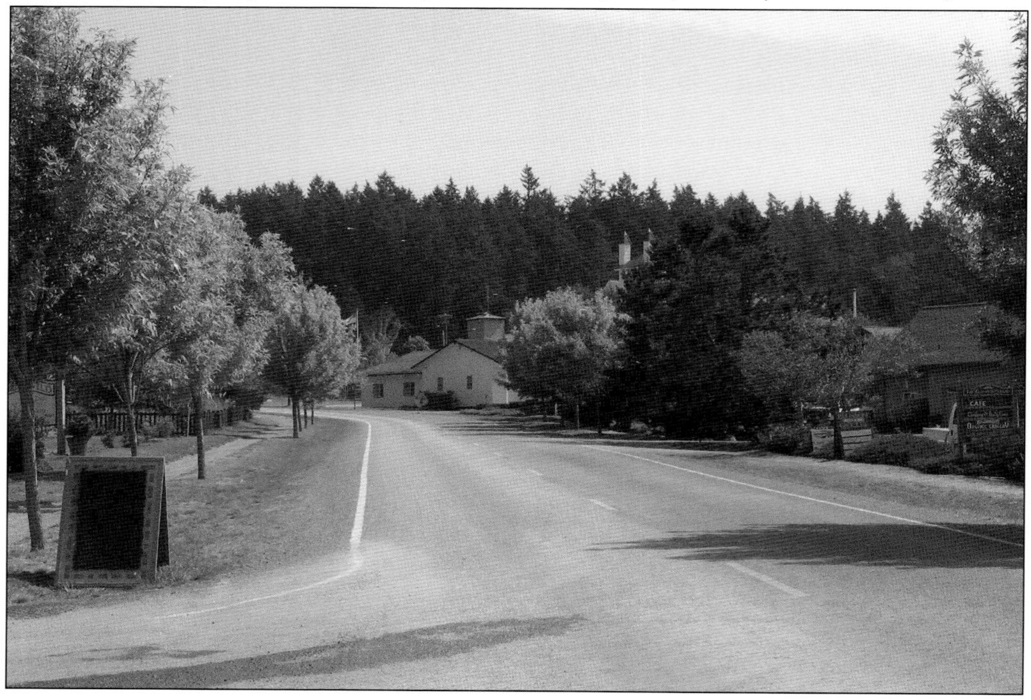

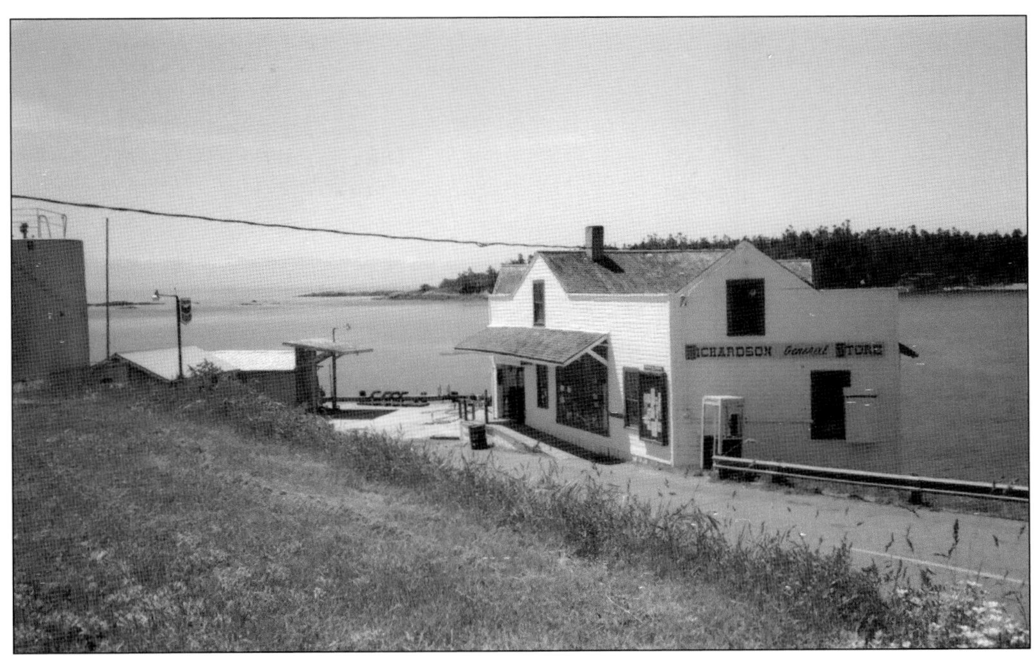

In early years, the Richardson store sat up the hill on dry land. In 1928, owner Ira Lundy built a new store on pilings overlooking the sound and the Olympic Mountains. The store became a beloved islander's retreat and carried most hardware, household, farm, and fishing necessities. Its worn wooden floorboards and Holly B's cinnamon buns drew many to the island's southern shores. In 1990, aging refrigeration compressors started a devastating fire, and firefighters were lucky to save the nearby fuel tanks. The store disappeared in flames and was not rebuilt, a loss still felt by many. (Courtesy of Delores Foss.)

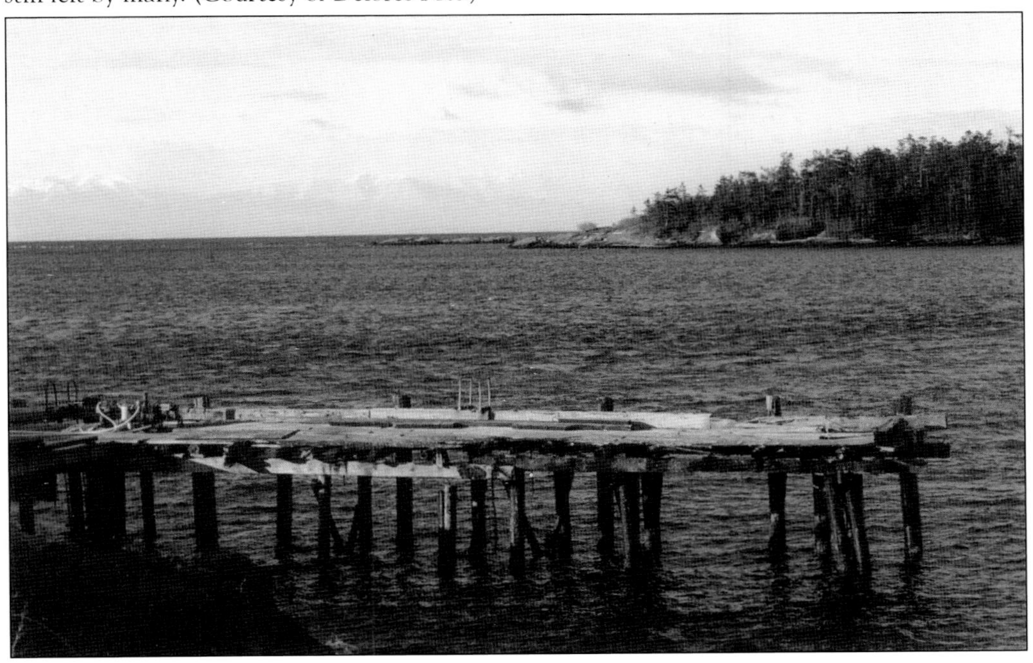

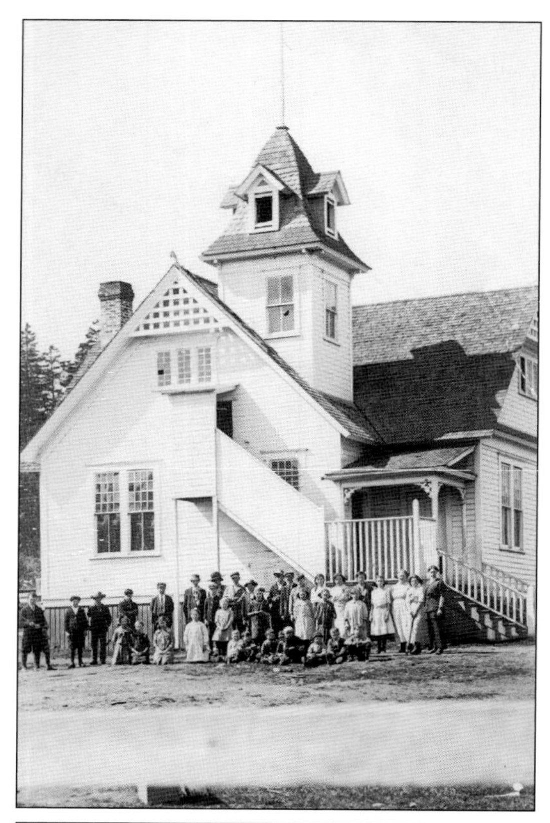

The village's little red schoolhouse served schoolchildren from the 1890s until its closure in 1941. It next housed a restaurant and later the Lopez Fire District. In the 1970s, the district constructed a new building and agreed to lease the old school to the Lopez Library League. Volunteers donated services, labor, furnishings, and thousands of books, and the library opened in 1977. In 1982, the district agreed to transfer ownership to the league if it moved the building. With indispensable volunteer help, the little red schoolhouse, now the Lopez Library, moved to the corner of Hummel Lake and Fisherman Bay Roads, where it stands today. (Below, courtesy of Delores Foss.)

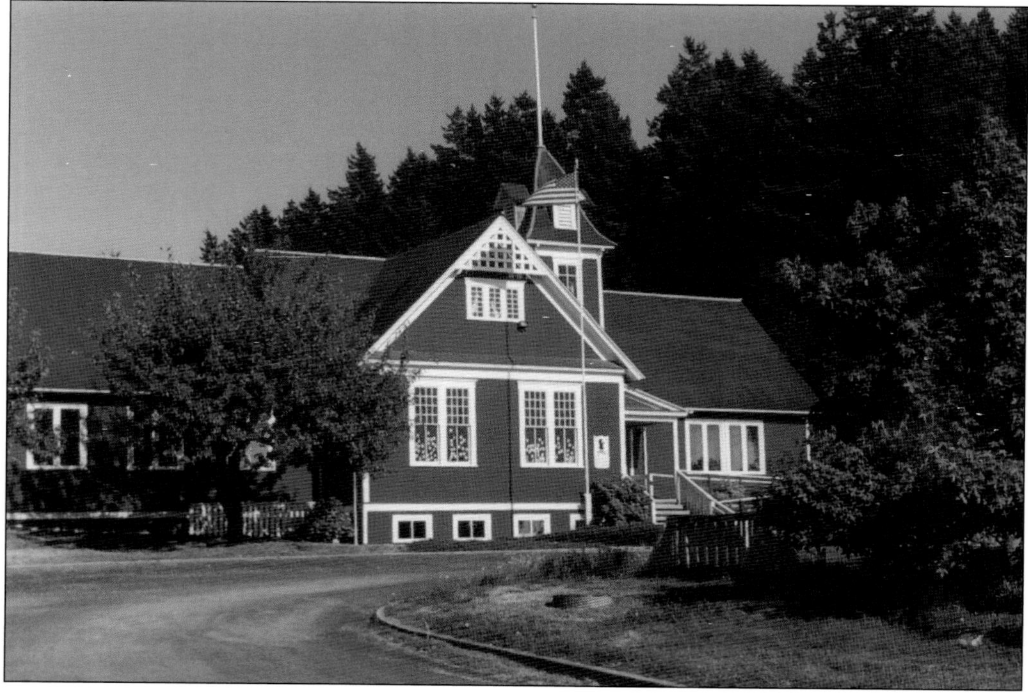

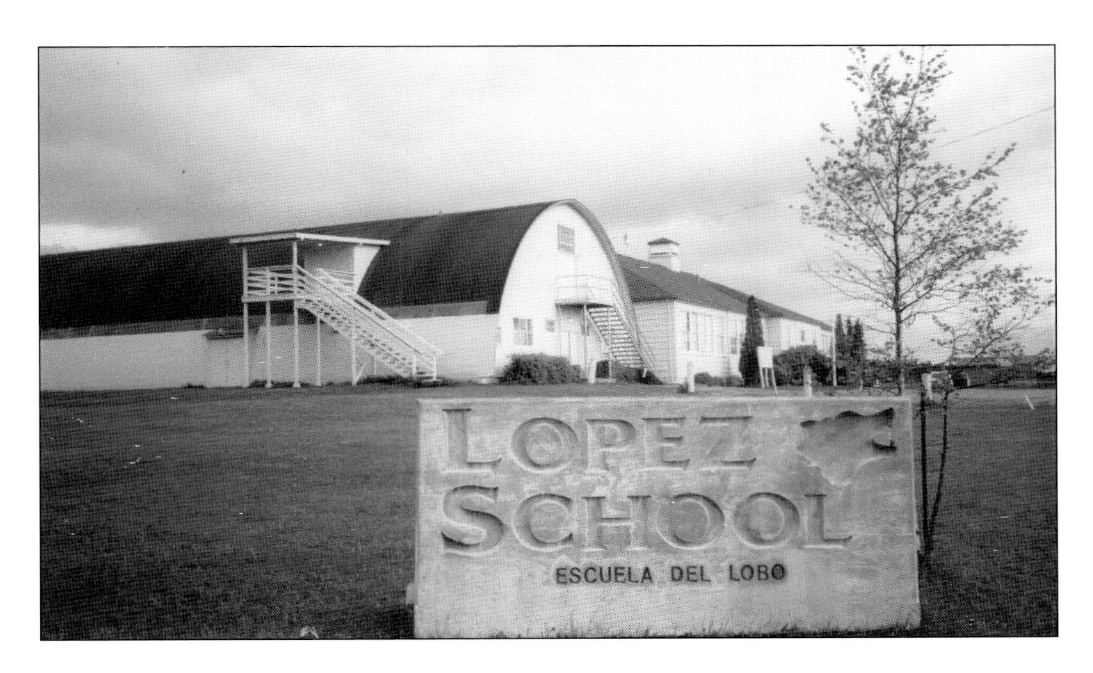

Following consolidation of four Lopez school districts into one by voter approval in 1936, islanders built a new school on Center Road, which opened in 1941. Students entered through wide front doors in the middle front of the building, and the Quonset hut seen above served many purposes. By the 1990s, the district recognized the need to upgrade the school's basic systems, to reconfigure classrooms and offices, and to build a suitable gymnasium. Classrooms were remodeled, and the school got a much needed face-lift. Today the Lopez School District excels at educating its students and prides itself on innovative, compassionate, and challenging programs. (Photographs courtesy of Delores Foss.)

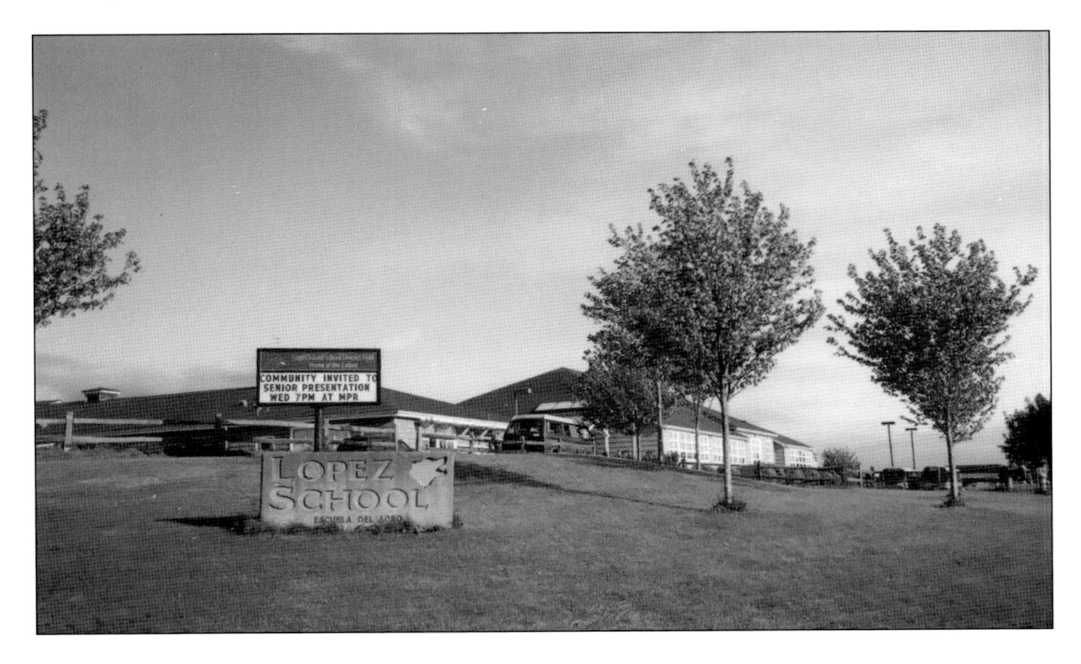

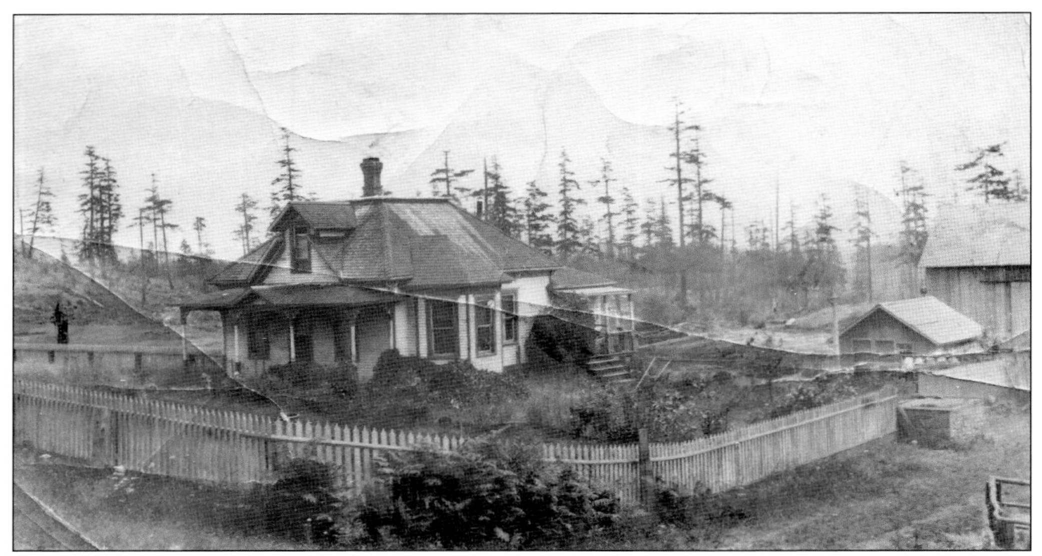

German immigrant Joseph Ender came to Lopez in 1890, settled on Lopez Hill, and in 1906 built the house his wife, Sarah, described as, "the little house upon the hill." Sarah yearned to socialize with passersby, so Ender moved the house with a team of horses down to Center Road and transformed it into a gambrel-roofed Dutch Colonial. By the 1940s, widower Ender agreed to sell the house to school superintendent Louis Washburn. Before leaving, Ender planted a large orchard along Lopez Hill Road that still stands today. When asked why he planted an orchard right before moving away, Ender replied, "Others will enjoy it." (Below, courtesy of Delores Foss.)

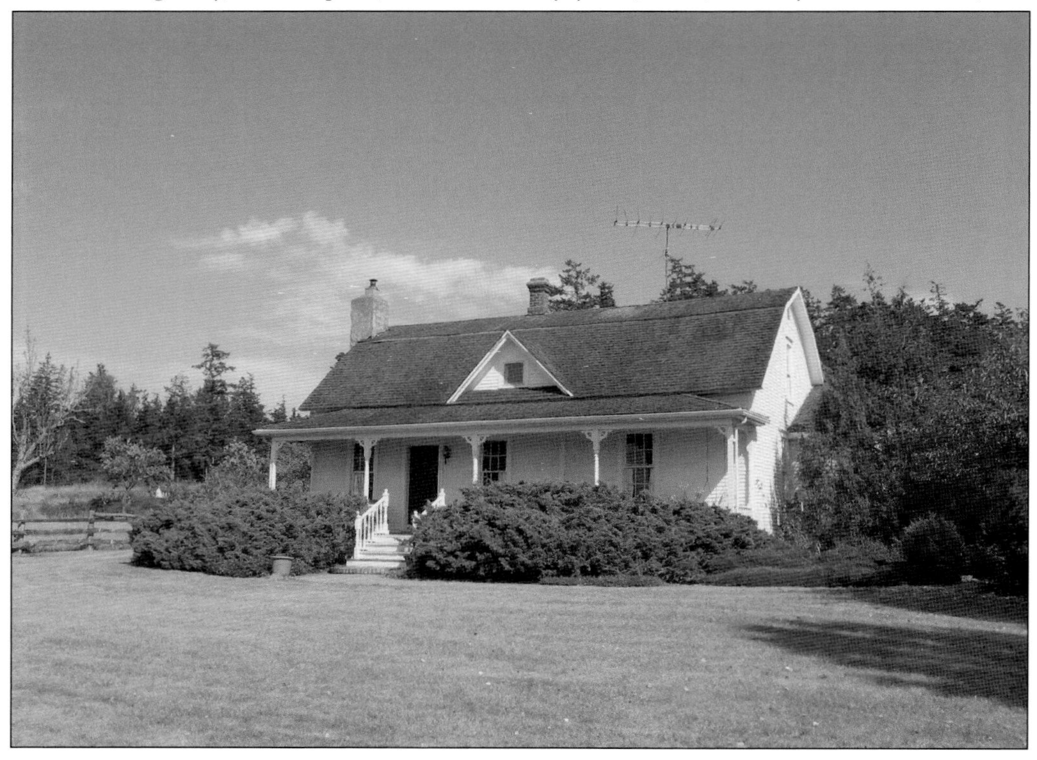

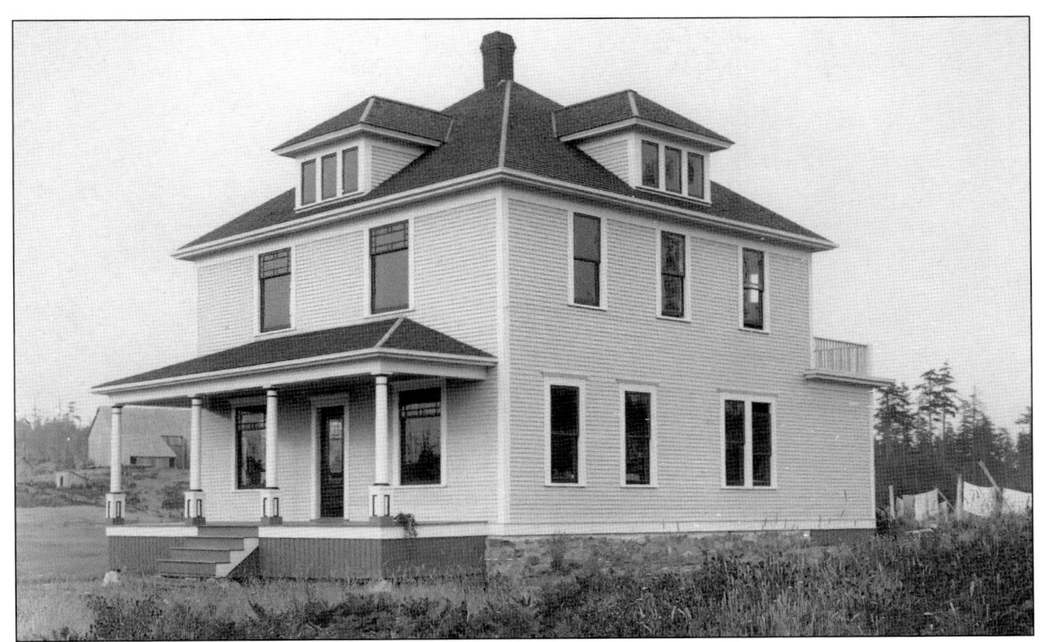

Thomas Graham Jr. and his wife, Hattie, raised 12 children in a small home on their property at the junction of Vista and Mud Bay Roads. Hattie died before this house was finished in 1912. Graham felled trees from their ranch, pulled the logs on skid roads to Hunter Bay, and then transported them to a Blakely Island sawmill to cut lumber for the house. A dairy rancher with a spread of 340 acres, Graham later leased the ranch for 30 years to his sons, Lyle and Elmer. Graham died in 1944 and over the years the house fell into disrepair. Legend says goats were once seen sticking their heads out of the second-story windows. Eventually, Nancy Lamoureaux purchased the home, restored it, and in 2005, it was accepted to be listed in the Washington Heritage Register.

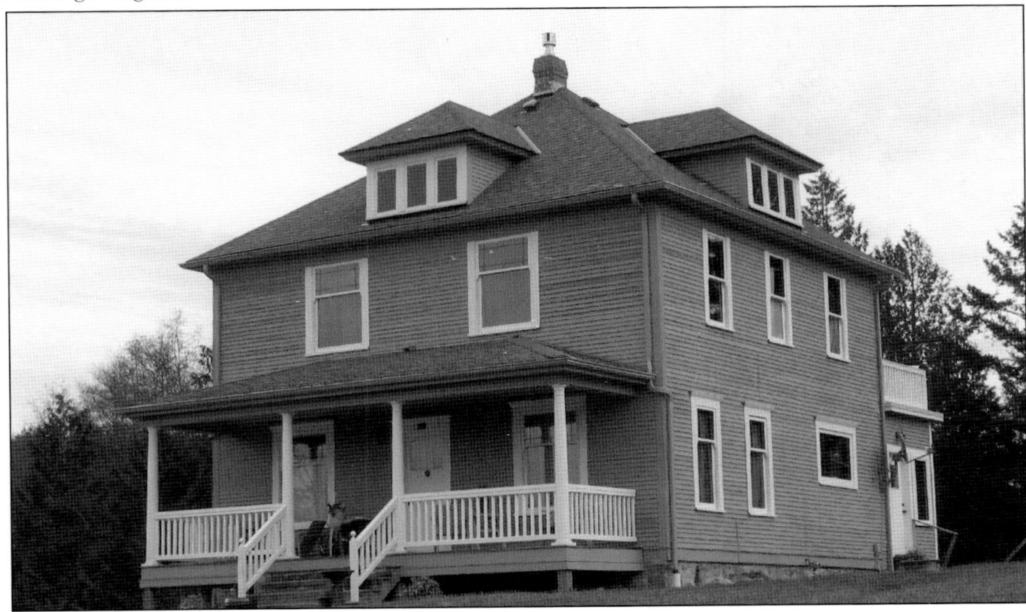

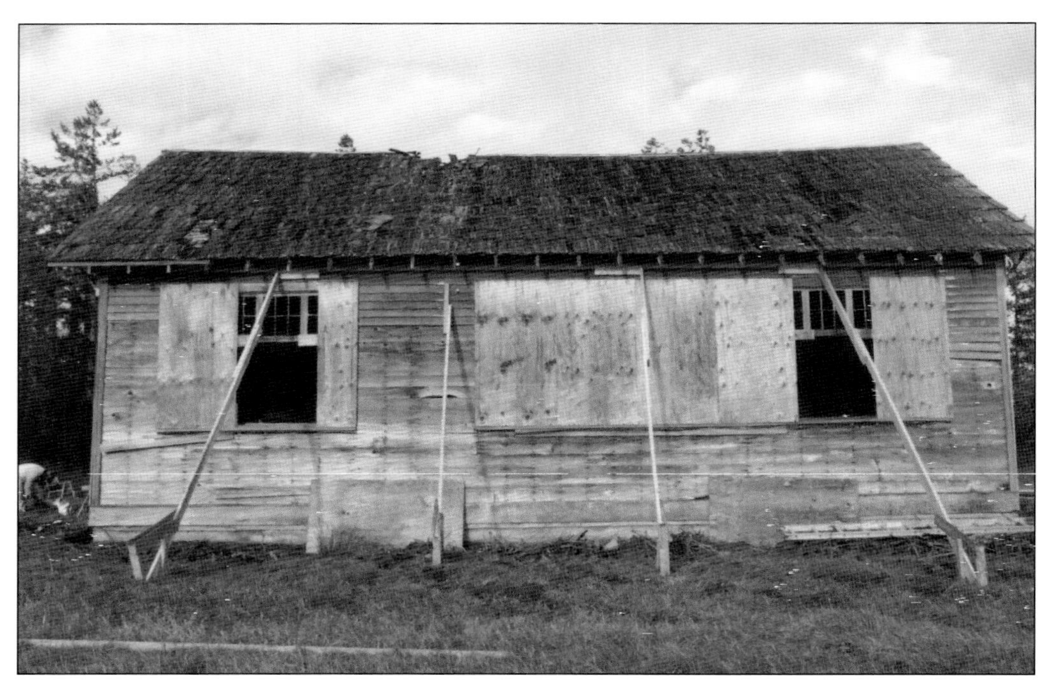

The third school at Port Stanley was in session from 1917 until the Lopez schools consolidated in 1941. It was later used as a meeting place, hardware store, and hay storage building until it fell into disrepair. Chris and Helena Jones donated the building to the Lopez Island Historical Society and Museum, and restoration began with much needed help from volunteers who contributed countless hours helping to shepherd the project through. The building restoration was finished in 2003, and the schoolhouse now hosts museum board meetings and is available for community and private events.

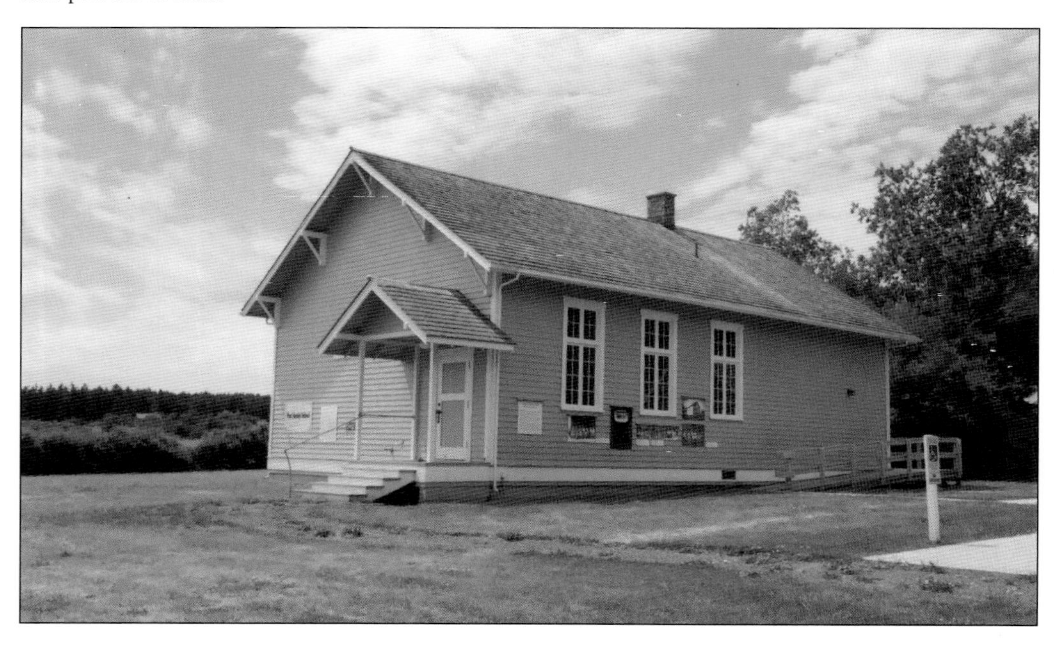

BIBLIOGRAPHY

Burn, June. *100 Days in the San Juans–A 1946 voyage through the San Juan Islands*. Friday Harbor, WA: Log House Printcrafters and Publishers, 1946.

Castile, George Pierre, ed. *The Indians of Puget Sound: The Notebooks of Myron Eells*. Seattle, WA: University of Washington Press, 1985.

Earle, Anna. *They Called Her Susie I've Called Her a Saint*. Nine Mile Falls, WA: self-published, 1996.

Lamb, Karen Jones. *Native American Wives of San Juan Settlers*. Decatur, WA: Bryn Tirion Publishing, 1994.

Graham, Donna. "The Consolidation of Four Lopez School Districts." Lopez, WA: *Islands' Weekly*, August 15, 1995.

Mason, Beryl Troxell. *John Franklin Troxell, Fish Trap Man, Puget Sound and San Juan Islands, Washington 1894–1934*. Oak Harbor, WA: Watmough Publishing, 1991.

McDonald, Lucile S. *Making History: The People Who Shaped the San Juans*. Friday Harbor, WA: Harbor Press, 1990.

———. *Lopez: Agricultural Island of the San Juan Archipelago*. Seattle, WA: *The Seattle Times*, 1958.

Morris, Gary, J. *History of Lopez Island*. http://freepages.history.rootsweb.ancestry.com/~lopezislandhistory/

Patton, Robert, J. *Inventory of Historic Properties*. Olympia, WA: Office of Archaeology and Historic Preservation, 1985.

Ramsey, Guy Reed. *Postmarked Washington, Island County, San Juan County*. Lopez, WA: Lopez Island Historical Society, 1976.

Richardson, David. *Magic Islands*. Eastsound, WA: Orcas Publishing Company, 1964.

San Juan Islander, The. *Illustrated Supplement to the San Juan Islander*: Friday Harbor, WA, 1901.